Quick Ethnography

For people who helped me think through the fundamentals of field research:
Joe Jorgensen, Verne Dorjahn, and Homer Barnett;

For people who helped me refine my thinking:
Leslie Zondervan-Droz, Danielle Wozniak, Russ Bernard, and James Boster;

But, mostly, for my key instructors

West Africans:
Se Wilson, Thomas Johnson, Johnson Doerue, Emmanuel Saingbe, and Victor Chumbe

West Indians:
Jan Ward, Cane Fire, Elma Robinson, and Hyacinth Bailey
and
Rose Jones,
the finest natural ethnographer I know.

Quick Ethnography

W. PENN HANDWERKER

PRESS

A Division of
ROWMAN & LITTLEFIELD PUBLISHERS, INC.
Lanham • Boulder • New York • Toronto • Plymouth, UK

AltaMira Press
A division of Rowman & Littlefield Publishers, Inc.
4501 Forbes Boulevard, Suite 200
Lanham, MD 20706

Estover Road
Plymouth PL6 7PY
United Kingdon

British Library Cataloguing in Publication Information Available

Library of Congress Cataloging-in-Publication Data

Handwerker, W. Penn.
    Quick ethnography / W. Penn Handwerker.
        p.   cm.
    Includes bibliographical references and index.
    ISBN 0-7591-0058-6 (cloth : alk. paper)—ISBN 0-7591-0059-4 (pbk. : alk. paper)
    1. Ethnology—Research.   2. Ethnology—Methodology.   I. Title.
GN345 .H39   2001
305.8′007′2—dc21   2001033583

Printed in the United States of America

Contents

Preface

I will show you how to collect systematic ethnographic data that can be subjected to systematic (numerical and statistical) analysis. Other books lay out many of the methods I talk about, but this book will walk you through actually using the methods to do ethnography very quickly.

Achieving the required subtlety means additions to our ethnographic tool kit that allow us to focus more closely on the domains of cognition, emotion, and behavior pertinent to individual lives and to establish which aspects of these domains one person shares with which specific others. This means questions bearing on the details of the social distribution of cognition, emotion, and behavior and about the patterns, networks, and character of social interaction through which culture evolves, locally, regionally, and globally. This requires attention to the design of ethnographic research and the application of methods that increase both research productivity and the precision of ethnographic descriptions and explanations.

Some of these methods entail specific forms of research management. Others follow from a more sophisticated understanding of culture. A theory of culture as cognitive elements and structure now dominates ethnographic research. Despite the difference between cognition and behavior, especially the troublesome and ambiguous relationship between the two, demonstrable patterns of behavior exist that correspond with specific cognitive domains. I define culture as a mental phenomenon. But, following Tylor, I recognize the existence of both mental and behavioral cultures. The methods I talk about in this book apply to cultures, however one wishes to define them. Explicit establishment of the construct validity of cultures—cognitive, behavioral, or both—allows us to clearly differentiate one culture from another and thus warrants generalizations about specific cultures. But it does so in a way that allows us to identify both intercultural and intracultural variability very precisely. This method helps us produce precise, as well as nuanced, interpretations of cultural variation.

This book thus consists of a relatively short, easy-to-read guide to the rapid collection of lots of high-quality ethnographic data. I write primarily for graduate student and professional social and behavioral scientists in both academic and applied settings. I ground a step-by-step layout with the theoretical foundations of ethnography. In the process, I introduce the new ways to collect and analyze cultural data, which allow greater precision and subtlety of ethnographic description and explanation.

I illustrate largely with my own experiences and data. As an anthropologist, I've enjoyed the freedom to engage in research on an extraordinarily wide range of topics. My studies of entrepreneurship, agriculture, and food distribution through marketplaces applied ethnography to topics also addressed by agricultural and development economists and geographers; I undertook some of this work for the United States Agency for International Development (USAID), through the Institute of Development Anthropology (IDA), and another portion for the United States Department of Agriculture (USDA). My study of culture and management and public sector corruption applied ethnography to topics also addressed by sociologists, political scientists, and development economists; this work, too, resulted in reports for USAID and IDA. My studies of parental involvement in their child's education and parental, teachers', and children's experiences of violence in schools and my thinking about problems in math education in bilingual classrooms applied ethnography to topics also addressed by educators; I undertook this work as part of my involvement with the University of Connecticut's doctoral program in bilingual/bicultural education. My studies of sexual and reproductive behavior, prostitution, sexually transmitted disease epidemiology, substance use and abuse, suicide and other forms of violent death, depression, and the sources, forms, and consequences of traumatic stress (emotional, physical, and sexual abuse) and social support applied ethnography to topics also addressed by nurses, physicians, and public health practitioners. Various parts of this work resulted in reports to Family Health International and the Ministry of Health, Government of Barbados, and a presentation on the long-term effects of hurtful words to a national conference of officials who oversee teacher education and certification.

Cohorts of former students prodded me to clarify my thinking and simplify my presentation. Russ Bernard produced singularly helpful suggestions for this final draft of something that evolved over the last decade from a short paper to the current book. During the evolution, editor Mitch Allen, who asked me to write this book, remained patient and enthusiastic. Several colleagues gave me an opportunity to address issues I would have missed otherwise: Rose Jones (mammography needs assessment), Robin Harwood and Mary Gannotti (child development), and Robin Harwood and Michele Shedlin (the contributions that migrants make to cultural evolution in host countries). Rose Jones and Robin Harwood also contributed significantly to the evolution of my thinking about the nature of culture. Bryan Byrne let me peek into the real world of business consulting and thus provoked rethinking of the fundamentals of needs assessment research. Jami Liebowitz provided a fine-tuned reading just before this manuscript left my hands for AltaMira. All added significantly to the quality of this book, and I am *very* grateful.

I

FOUNDATIONS

1

Introduction

WHY QUICK ETHNOGRAPHY (QE)?

This book explains how to collect high-quality ethnographic data quickly. In the process, this book addresses the needs of ethnographers grappling with a world in which a successful rap group comes out of Japan, you can watch the movie *Out of Africa* in an African bush village, and Russians play jazz, compose country music, and turn capitalist—as well as the ongoing dynamics of social interaction and cultural change in any contemporary community.

The challenges of understanding and working with cultural diversity in the twenty-first century require more subtle approaches to ethnography than we've applied in the past. This need for subtlety requires that we put aside a set of commonplace, albeit false assumptions—that only groups have a culture, that ethnography means "qualitative" research, and that social identities like Nuer, Navajo, and African American constitute cultural groups.

A need for speed complicates matters. Whether the issue is human rights, violence prevention, or effective community outreach for health promotion/disease prevention, practitioners of ethnography need results quickly. Ethnographers who contribute to product design teams need results *yesterday* but no later than three days, or three weeks, from the start date. Growing costs of field research mean a demand for greater research efficiency and productivity. Ethnographers working in education, public health, nursing, business, and development faced these demands initially. Today, however, even graduate student anthropologists appreciate the need for research efficiency and productivity.

Social and behavioral research characteristically takes the viewpoint of an observer looking in (at "subjects") from the outside. Ethnographers don't have subjects, however. By contrast, we ask people to help dispel our ignorance. We aim to see cultural phenomena from the viewpoint of the people who create and use them, looking out from the inside. To achieve this goal, ethnography requires distinctive methods. Historically, this meant long periods of fieldwork—a minimum of a year and preferably two or more.

Ethnographers who began to undertake applied, contract research that required a report in ninety days or less resorted to methods they called Quick & Dirty or, more formally, Rapid Assessment Procedures. Achieving the necessary subtlety, however, requires something beyond Rapid Assessment. It requires that we do ethnography more effectively. Speed comes from doing effective ethnography more efficiently.

QE BASICS

The methods I call Quick Ethnography (QE) consist of a package that integrates conventional means of collecting cultural data (like key informant, structured, and cultural mapping interviews), analyzing cultural data (like grounded theory forms of text analysis and conventional statistics), and project management (like Gantt and PERT charts) with more novel forms of data collection (like successive pile sorts) and analysis (like the application of multivariate statistical procedures to similarities among informants). The integration of these tools puts into practice the triangulation approach long advocated by Donald Campbell (e.g., Campbell and Fiske 1959, Campbell 1970). Each individual tool for collecting or analyzing cultural data achieves specific, complementary, and overlapping project goals; their integration yields findings with high reliability and construct validity.

This distinctive feature of QE comes from the use of a theory of culture to solve the core problems of ethnographic fieldwork. We need to answer four questions:

- What kinds of people, social relations, events, and processes comprise the study phenomenon?
- How do people experience specific social relations, events, and processes

to create, maintain, and change the meanings by which they currently interpret and respond to the world around them?

- Who agrees with whom about what and to what degree?
- What precursor life experiences explain who agrees with whom about what and to what degree?

QE procedures thus assume that things and ideas constitute qualitatively different phenomena. Our senses provide information about things, but we can only know things through the medium of ideas (Barnett 1953, Handwerker 1989b, Gray 1995, Gazzaniga 1998). Unlike naïve realism, QE procedures don't confuse ideas for things. Unlike subjectivism and its recent incarnation as postmodernism, QE procedures don't confuse things for ideas. QE procedures thus provide means for making observations and arriving at findings in ways that help us distinguish what's there from what we put there (Campbell 1970).

Increased effectiveness comes from additions to our ethnographic tool kit that allow us to focus more closely on the domains of cognition, emotion, and behavior pertinent to individual lives and to establish which aspects of these domains one person shares with which specific others. This means questions bearing on the details of the social distribution of cognition, emotion, and behavior and about the patterns, networks, and character of social interaction through which culture evolves, locally, regionally, and globally. Increased efficiency requires attention to the design of ethnographic research. This means the application of methods that both increase research productivity and the precision of ethnographic descriptions and explanations.

In short, lack of time doesn't have to mean poor quality if you use explicit methods to:

- create a clear vision of where you want to go (chapter 2),
- create a clear vision of how to get there (chapter 3),
- get there without getting lost (chapters 4–8), and
- use personal time to greatest advantage when in the field (chapter 9).

Some of these methods entail specific forms of research management. Others follow from culture theory. Explicit establishment of the construct validity of cultures, for example, allows us to clearly differentiate one culture from another and thus warrants generalizations about specific cultures. But it does so in a way that allows us to identify both intercultural and intracultural variability very precisely. This method thus helps us to produce precise as well as nuanced interpretations of cultural variation.

QE yields high-quality ethnographic data from 30-day projects carried out for the United States Agency for International Development (USAID) or the Navajo Tribal Association, even when you fill ten with official meetings. Academics who undertake basic research on a grant from the National Science Foundation might get a book's worth of data from a single summer's (ninety days') fieldwork (Handwerker 1989a). You can get more done in less time even when you enjoy the luxury of longer periods of fieldwork. QE *really* pays off when you're given three days to conduct an ethnography and produce a report (see chapter 10). This book is thus for people who want short periods of ethnographic research to yield a wealth of high-quality data.

FALSE ASSUMPTION #1: DON'T CONFUSE CULTURE WITH CULTURES

QE procedures operationalize a definition of culture, stated most simply as the knowledge people use to live their lives and the way in which they do so. This definition comes to us from Edward Burnett Tylor who, in *Primitive Society* (1871), first identified culture as that complex whole that we acquire by virtue of living our lives with other people. Ever since, we've wrestled with issues implicit in that definition. In what sense is culture a "whole" and for whom—individuals or groups or both? If groups, how can we know them, and what are their boundaries? To what extent and under what circumstances, for example, do social identity differences correspond with cultural differences? How, exactly, do we "acquire" culture by virtue of living our lives with other people? Usually, we've translated "acquire" as "learned," which raises the question of what, exactly, this means. Why do we learn the things we learn but not learn the things we could have but didn't? Does culture come to us from other people, or do we create culture in response to what we experience by virtue of living with others? Since learning "just happens," how and in what ways does learning take place volitionally?

After more than one hundred years, we can begin to answer some of these questions. The answers suggest that we re-frame questions about culture and change how we go about studying it. *Ethnography*, as I use the word, consists of the processes and products of research that document what people know, feel, and do in a way that situates those phenomena at specific times in the history of individual lives, including pertinent global events and processes. Historically, anthropologists distinguished *ethnography* from *ethnology*. The former referred to descriptive accounts of culture, the latter to comparative, explanatory analyses of culture. Historically, we also used assumptions, not evidence, to equate cultural boundaries with social identities like Nuer, Navajo, and African American; we dismissed, overlooked, or downplayed both cultural variation among people who use the same social identity and cultural consensus among people who use different social identities. Rather than look at cultural variability between reified and essentialized social groups, QE procedures direct your attention to cultural variability between individuals. This means extending ethnographic practice to correspond with a line of ethnological practice (see Bidney 1944, Barnett 1953, Wallace 1961, Murdock 1971, Geertz 1973, Pelto and Pelto 1975, Wolf 1982, Keesing 1994, Handwerker 1997). To do so, QE procedures make the reality of social groups, the existence of cultures, and the location of cultural boundaries, empirical issues that require explicit tests for construct validity.

Two observations warrant this shift. First, reification and its corollaries—treating culture as if it were a thing that could be owned and that could act—pose significant theoretical problems that too easily lead to real-world damage. For example, in the recent *Exxon Valdez* oil spill case in Alaska the assumption that the world consists of "a sum of self-contained societies and cultures" rather than "people of diverse origins and social makeup who take part in the construction of a common world" (Wolf 1982:385) warranted reifications on the part of both defendants and plaintiffs. Defendants alleged that native culture had been "smashed" centuries before the oil spill. Plaintiffs alleged that native culture was "damaged" by the spill. As Joseph Jorgensen points out, both constitute irresponsible and indefensible claims that obfuscate the issues and lead to court decisions grounded on fantasy. The oil spill did not "damage" native culture—it couldn't because culture is not a thing—but it significantly damaged natives, who experienced real losses of wild resources, real damage to the areas in which they gained their livelihood, real alterations to the manner in which they made a living, and real threats to the future generations of animals on which they based their subsistence. Similarly, native culture had not been "smashed" centuries earlier—it couldn't because culture is not a thing—and native and non-native inhabitants of the oil spill region responded to the spill in culturally characteristic ways that reflected the processes of social interaction that maintained cultural differences (boundaries) among people in the spill area (Jorgensen 1995:89).

Second, only individuals learn, and individuals embody and constitute the only source of cultural data. In the field, data collection reveals culture as potentially ephemeral ideas, feelings, and behavior unique in their details to each individual. To make the world we live in sensible, each of us assembles out of our individual experiences ways of thinking about what we have experienced. We still understand only vaguely how we accomplish this. We construct our understanding of the world without being conscious that we are doing so (Barnett 1953, Gazzaniga 1998, Bargh and Chartrand 1999). The construction process invariably infuses ostensibly intellectual products with often intense and complex emotional associations. The core products of this arational process consist of premises and definitions that individuals use to understand and respond to the world of experience. No two people can live precisely identical life histories. No one person can experience all things. The processes by which individuals perceive, store, and manipulate information and so create culture make it physically impossible for any two people to hold identical cultural configurations. These processes make it physically impossible for any one person to hold identical cultural configurations at two points in time. Effective and efficient ethnographic research thus hinges on a clear understanding of the implications of two observations:

- Cultural differences reflect variation in personal experiences.
- Culture evolves.

First, what we know and how we organize what we know into different cultural domains come from where we live and the web of social relations through which we have lived our lives. This means:

- Where we were born and raised;
- When we were born; and
- With whom we have interacted, in what ways, and what we experienced at specific places and times over the course of our life.

All clinicians share a common set of understandings that comes from their training in biomedicine, for example, but physicians work with a body of knowledge that distinguishes them from, say, nurse practitioners. Similarly, family practice physicians work with a body of knowledge distinct from that used by surgeons. Variation in life experiences leads people to see the world differently and to work with distinctive bodies of knowledge. Older people—whether physicians, plumbers, or anthropologists—share a distinctive vantage point owing only to age, and older anthropologists typically share a body of knowledge that distinguishes them from junior faculty or graduate students, just as older plumbers typically share a body of knowledge that distinguishes them from apprentices. The knowledge of men and women the same age—sociologists, developmental psychologists, or airline pilots—may differ solely because of gendered experiences. Men and women the same age may work with a common body of knowledge merely because they grew up in poverty or experienced the privileges bestowed by wealthy parents. Puerto Ricans, irrespective of age, gender, and class, may use a common body of knowledge because they share an ethnic heritage, which may differ significantly from a body of knowledge shared by Mexicans. Fathers—whether Puerto Rican or Mexican, Eskimo or Navaho, whether physicians or nurse practitioners, whether old or young, rich or poor—may share a body of knowledge simply because they share the experience of being fathers. Academics, whether they live in China, Russia, Nigeria, Mexico, or America, share a distinctive culture irrespective of other differences.

In short, except for the set of understandings and behavioral patterns that makes each of us unique, *no one possesses a single culture.* Everyone participates in many cultures. When you first meet someone, you can't tell very well by that person's age, gender, dress, or skin color which cultures you share and which you don't. Knowledge about the visual signals of pertinent cultural differences comes only from listening for the right cues. Thus, good ethnographers must interact intensively and create personal relationships with the people they want to understand. Spending time getting to know someone opens the only door available for you to learn what that person sees and what it means when he or she looks out at the world. Ethnography thus calls for the personal sensitivity and creativity to allow people to feel comfortable with you; it requires that you communicate clearly to people whom you ask for assistance that you are nonthreatening. Being a good listener helps. Sharing yourself helps even more.

Second, over the course of our lives and through various means—listening to news reports, reading, traveling, talking with friends or family members, taking courses or attending workshops, or engaging in explicit and rigorous research—we come to think differently about the components of a given cultural domain. We think of new ways to organize activities and new ways to think about the domain of knowledge itself. We tend to incorporate into our lives the new ways of thinking about the world that we infer yield better results. By interacting with other people—acting and responding to what we experience of other people's words and acts—we thus actively participate in an unceasing process that leads to the evolution of what we know and how we act. Because culture evolves, it makes a moving target. Ethnographers who have many years of experience working with a specific population may miss cues that signal important new cultural differences if they don't keep up with the cultural evolution that goes on around them all the time. Effective and efficient ethnographic research thus requires a conscious awareness of culture and means for identifying cultural differences.

In short, Tylor's definition of culture contains two largely overlooked and undervalued implications: (1) the culture that specific people use to live their lives constitutes an evolving configuration of cognition, emotion, and behavior unique to themselves, and (2) *a* culture consists of an evolving configuration of cognition, emotion, and behavior at the intersection of individually unique cultural sets. The central problem for ethnography thus consists of identifying and describing that intersection (or *those intersections*), and ethnography becomes ethnology when we examine the means by which cultures come into being and change over time (or not). This means a focus on who agrees with and acts like whom about what and to what degree and on how specific social relations and life experiences contribute to the construction and change of culture. We thus need to pay attention to details bearing on the social distribution of cognition, emotion, and behavior and ask pointed questions about the patterns, networks, and character of social interaction through which culture evolves, locally, regionally, and globally. QE principles thus tell you to focus your study on who agrees with and acts like whom about what and to what degree and on how specific social relations and life experiences contribute to the construction and change of culture.

FALSE ASSUMPTION #2: DON'T CONFUSE ETHNOGRAPHY WITH QUALITATIVE METHODS

All too often, discussions of methods frame the subject with the dualism "qualitative and quantitative" and equate ethnography with qualitative methods (e.g., Searight and Campbell 1992). Persisting dualisms like Qualitative and Quantitative, Interpretivist and Positivist, or Art and Science caricature good research, however. The best science comes from creative and skilled artists.

Why? Because the best science tries to answer specific questions, and the best answers come from people who use their imagination to frame those questions. These are also the people who select from the wide array of tools available the ones most well suited to the collection and analysis of data with which to answer the question at hand. Some questions require data measured qualitatively, which may best be analyzed by numerical analysis. Other questions require data measured quantitatively, which *always* require imaginative, qualitative interpretation. Qualitative interpretation *always* entails quantitative (more/less, higher/lower, or better/worse) claims. Superior ethnography, in short, ordinarily blends numbers, words, and pictures (Bernard 2001, Cleveland and McGill 1985, Efrom and Tibshirani 1991).

A caution, however: ethnographic numerical analysis requires what, for most people, constitutes a novel approach to quantitative analysis. Ethnography requires that we look at the interconnections between our informants. Standard forms of numerical analysis can't see these interconnections because they examine informant-by-variable matrices. Ethnographic analysis transposes matrices, turning them onto their sides, so we can see the connections, similarities, and differences among our informants.

To appreciate how silly it is to perpetuate a distinction between qualitative and quantitative, consider the basic activities entailed by ordinary ethnographic fieldwork. All ethnographic research begins by collecting data from one person. When we go to the next person, we always find something different, as well as something much the same. And so it goes. We keep track of similarities, note variability, and keep at it until we decide that we've exhaustively identified significant cultural variation or until we exhaust ourselves (which is often the same point). Then, we construct a story from the inferential generalizations we arrived at about the people we worked with, their lives, and the circumstances in which they have lived; about what those people now think, feel, and do; about who agreed with whom about what and to what extent; and, so, about who is similar to whom and to what extent and how they differ from others and to what extent. This considerably simplified account highlights six fieldwork activities:

1. We *measure variables.*
2. We identify *what is typical* in one sense or another.
3. We evaluate *variation from what is typical.*
4. We evaluate *similarities among variables* to try to identify the events and processes that go together and those that don't and
5. *similarities among informants* to try to identify who agrees with whom about what and to what extent.
6. We aspire to an understanding of what we see during fieldwork that goes beyond the few people we had a chance to learn from.

Some data with which to approach these tasks will come directly from individuals, collected through informal and semistructured interviews and observations. Other data may come from structured interviews or observations focused on specific issues or from national or regional surveys that integrate several data collection tasks into a single interview. Complementary data may come from focus group interviews and observations and from unpublished and published texts, including diaries, letters, historical documents, and government-assembled national or regional aggregated data sets.

Texts from informal and semistructured interviews give you insight into the assumptions that your informants use to understand and respond to the world of experience, the variables that make up that world, and how those variables are organized to form social and behavioral ecosystems. But all data contain errors. Unmeasured internal validity confounds saturate text data (see chapter 3), and you most efficiently collect text data in ways that rule out explicit comparisons. This leaves you guessing about what's really significant and provides no warrant for generalization. Structured interview data collected for numerical analysis allow you to measure and control for internal validity confounds, allow you to see nuances you'd otherwise miss, and provide a warrant for generalization. Which kind of data you should collect, in what quantity, and which textual, visual, or numerical tools you choose for analysis depends on what you want to know. Your answers will come from the application of explicit research designs and a judicious selection made from the wide variety of tools available for collecting and analyzing data.

Natural selection designed us to pay attention to variation. To make variation part of our consciousness and subject to investigation, we use assumptions about the nature of variation in the world of our experience and explicitly identify specific *variables*. As Wilkinson et al. (1999:3) point out, a variable "is a method for assigning to a set of observations a value from a set of possible outcomes." You can't identify variables without measuring them. Measurement refers to what you do when you make and record observations about what you experience in the field. *Measurement error* constitutes a principal source of invalid research findings. Intensive and prolonged interaction predicated on personal relationships with informants provides one check on this source of error. *Triangulation,* using a variety of data collection and analysis tools to address any one question or issue, helps even more (Campbell 1970, McNabb 1990b). Much ethnography entails altering the constructions you take into the field in ways that improve their correspondence with those used by the people in your field setting. In the process, expect to create new ways to think about the world that help you better understand what you experience in the field. Create an understanding of what you see during fieldwork that corresponds with what your informants tried to teach you and take that understanding a step further. This aim corresponds with the research design issue of *internal validity* (did I get it right?—see Campbell and Stanley 1966, Cook and Campbell 1979).

Measurement consists of a theoretical process that transforms sensory information into intelligible mental constructions. The assumptions you use to identify the set of possible outcomes from which you can assign specific values to a set of observations may yield qualitatively different assignments of meaning. For some purposes, the variable *kin* may be brother, sister, husband, or wife, for example. The variable *gender* may be woman, man, girl, or boy. For other purposes, variation may best be understood as incorporating a dimension of quantity. For example, daughter, sister, and son's wife may be components of the construct of *family*, but daughter may be *more* or *closer* family than sister, and both daughter and sister may be *more* or *closer* family than son's wife. These forms of measurement entail only relative rank, an *ordinal* form of measurement. The variable *family size* may be assigned values like small, medium, or large (*ordinal* values); or five, ten, and twenty (a *ratio* form of measurement characterized by a true zero; a true zero identifies the absence of what you measure, which allows any two values to be expressed as a meaningful ratio of the other).

When you carry out ordinary ethnography, you will want to know

- how *most* people conceptualize specific people, events, and processes (measured explicitly by a statistic called the *mode*),
- the age at which, *on average* (measured explicitly by a statistic called the *mean*), as well as how, children become adults and people first have sex, marry, give birth, and become grandparents.
- important and unimportant people, events, and processes; or when people who move into adulthood first have sex, marry, give birth, and become grandparents early or late. The warrant for judgments about relative placement consists of a middle point (measured explicitly by a statistic called the *median*) that distinguishes important from unimportant or early from late. The *median* is one of a set of statistics called *quantiles*, which measure relative placement in a distribution. The median, for example, is the 50th percentile. Other quantiles include the 10th percentile (which identifies the location below which lie the earliest or lowest set of cases), the 25th and the 75th percentiles (between which lie the middle 50 percent of the cases), and the 90th percentile (which identifies the location above which lie the latest or highest set of cases).

Use reference points like these to evaluate *variation from what is typical.* When you carry out ordinary ethnography, for example, you will want to know

- how commonly you find a particular way of conceptualizing specific people, events, and processes. You can explicitly measure how commonly something occurs as a simple count (*frequency*) of the number of people who take one point of view or another. The *modal frequency* is the point of view with the highest count. More usefully, we can express this number as a *proportion* (the modal frequency/the total count), a *percentage* (100* a proportion), or a *ratio* (e.g., number of people who express the most common point of view/the number of people who express any other point of view). You might be inclined to generalize a consensus if 80 percent of the people you talk with express the most common (*modal*) point of view, for example. You probably would infer much cultural diversity if you find many ways of thinking about an issue and only 20 percent express the most common (*modal*) view. In the former case, the modal view occurs (80 percent/20 percent) four times (400 percent) more often than any alternative; in the latter, it occurs (20 percent/80 percent) 25 percent less often than the alternatives. Great variation suggests the operation of many contingencies that influence how people conceptualize themselves and the world around them. Little variation suggests the operation of significant constraints.
- how much variation on average exists in the age at which children become adults and people first have sex, marry, give birth, and become grandparents (measured explicitly by a statistic called the *standard deviation*). Great variation suggests the operation of many contingencies that influence when, and perhaps how, life course events occur. Little variation suggests the operation of significant constraints bearing on life course events.
- the earliest point at which an event occurs in people's lives (the *minimum*), the latest point that event occurs (the *maximum*), the distance between these points (the *range*), and the relative frequency with which an event occurs between these points (a variable's *frequency distribution*). The distribution of events may be *skewed* over a given range of occurrence—most people marry first at relatively young ages, but some

first marry late in life, for example. In skewed distributions, cases at the extreme pull the median away from the mode in the direction of the skew and pull the mean even further away. A distribution may be *symmetrical*, or approximately so, as might be the case for the age at which children undergo one or another puberty rite. In symmetrical distributions, the mode, median, and mean all fall at the same point (or approximately so).

- events that occur unusually early or late (*outliers*) relative to others.

Similarity coefficients like *Pearson's r, Simple Matching coefficients*, or *Jaccard's coefficient*, each in different ways, explicitly measure the extent to which any two variables go together or not, or the extent to which any two informants agree with one another. Explicit measurements of relationships among even a few people, events, or processes produce hundreds, if not thousands, of details, which human minds appear particularly unsuited for comprehending. Numerical analysis tools like *factor analysis* (Rummel 1970, Harman 1976), *cluster analysis* (Sneath and Sokal 1973), *multidimensional scaling* (Kruskal and Wish 1978), and *correspondence analysis* (Greenacre 1984) reduce this complexity and transform these details into pictures, which human minds appear particularly well-suited for comprehending. Pictures of the distribution of a variable—*stem-and-leaf plots, box plots,* or *dot density plots,* for example—make it easy to evaluate salient characteristics of a single variable's distribution (Chambers, Cleveland, Kleiner, and Tukey 1983).

Think of data analysis as a process of discriminating sets of data with structure from sets of data with none. The more subtle the variation, the harder you will find it to distinguish structure from randomness. Explicit numerical analysis helps you see what you otherwise might miss.

For example, all data collection entails sampling—gathering information from only *some* of an indefinitely large number of people, places, and times. Gathering information from other people or the same people at different times (the next day) and places (next door) almost always yields different findings even when population characteristics (*parameters*) don't change. We can't tell from looking at differences—whether they appear in our fieldnotes or in survey results—whether they represent something real (people changed, people living in different neighborhoods think and act differently) or not (people haven't changed, and people living in different neighborhoods think and act pretty much the same). Measures of similarity might suggest that two variables go together or two informants do or say much the same thing. The application of *statistical tests* like *Chi-squared, t-tests,* and *F-ratios* provide additional information to help us evaluate variation because they yield probabilities that tell us how often specific differences or relationships occur merely by chance. Research design and sampling procedures (see chapter 3) address the issue of *external validity* (to whom, if anyone, can we generalize—see Campbell and Stanley 1966, Cook and Campbell 1979) and recognize that, having studied with only a handful of teachers, you generalize to a community of hundreds, perhaps hundreds of thousands of people you never met.

In ethnography, however, distinguish carefully between cultural phenomena and data on the life experiences that may have shaped culture. *Culture* consists of the systems of mental constructions people use to interpret and respond to themselves and the world around them. *Cultures* consist of systems of mental constructions and behavior isomorphic with those systems of meaning shared among sets of people. *Cultural* data thus consist of measurements of the systems of mental constructions people use to interpret themselves and the world around them and of the behavior isomorphic with those systems of meaning. *Life experience* data, by contrast, consist of measurements of characteristics (like age, gender, class, or ethnicity) and events or processes that mark the prior life experience of particular people (like how many years people spent in school, if they grew up in poor or wealthy households, or the degree to which they experienced one or another form of violence as a child). Cultural phenomena thus consist of multilayered meanings that we share variously with other people, having shared equivalent experiences or negotiated a common understanding in more direct social interaction. Each of us, consequently, belongs to or takes place in multiple cultures, at different levels.

The difference between cultural data and life experience data hinges on a difference in the point of view you bring to their analysis. You make substance abuse a dependent variable if you ask whether it reflects a history of child abuse. You make it an independent variable if you ask whether substance abuse influences the likelihood of violent death. By their focus on similarities among variables, questions like these transform measurements of substance abuse and child abuse into life experience data. By their focus on similarities among informants, questions like "Who uses what substances, how often, and in what way?" or "Who experienced what forms of childhood traumatic stress and how often?" transform measurements of substance abuse and child abuse into cultural data. The distinction possesses important methodological implications.

Once we define culture as the system of mental constructs that people use to interpret and respond to the world of experience, we imply that culture evolves through a process in which people actively create and change culture through social interaction. The methodological implication of this definition arose the first time an anthropologist used numerical methods and came to be called Galton's Problem. In the late 1800s, Tylor tried to explain the origins and distribution of kin avoidances (1889). One of the originators of classical statistical theory, Sir Francis Galton, asked Tylor how he knew his cases were independent, since the similarities he tried to explain by reference to individual needs and social functions might merely reflect social interaction—the similarities might have come about merely because the people lived near each other or because they shared common ancestors. Tylor had no answer.

The second time an anthropologist used numerical methods, Franz Boas addressed this problem with a cluster analysis of regional and historical social relationships bearing on the distribution of myths and stories found among tribes of the Northwest Coast of North America, the adjacent Plateau, and three widely scattered communities (1894). Boas found that neighboring communities shared more than distant communities (e.g., Northwest Coast tribes were more similar to each other than to tribes on the Plateau, but Northwest Coast and Plateau tribes shared more than either did with the interior Athapaskan, Ponca, and Micmac), and that people who may share a common ancestral community (who spoke languages from the same language family) shared more than people who spoke languages from different language families. Boas thus demonstrated case-dependence in cultural data collected in and taken to characterize different communities.

More recent research extends Boas's findings to cultural data collected from and taken to characterize different individuals. The socially constructed nature of cultural phenomena means that any one person who knows about a particular cultural phenomenon participates with other experts in its construction. In short, cultural phenomena inescapably embody what statisticians call spatial and temporal autocorrelation. What one cultural participant does or tells you will correspond closely to what any another cultural participant does or tells you. The errors you make in predicting what one cultural participant will do or say will correspond closely to the errors you make predicting what any other cultural participant will do or say.

Three methodological implications follow. First, this conclusion means that a random sample of people does not constitute a random sample of culture. The culture of an individual consists of configurations of cognition, emotion, and behavior that intersect in multiple ways the culture or other individuals. Hence, random samples of individuals will yield a random sample of the intersecting configurations of cognition, emotion, and behavior (i.e., the cultures) in a population. But random samples (defined by case-independence) of cultural phenomena (which necessarily contain case-dependence) cannot exist: they constitute mutually exclusive alternatives.

Second, it means that in seeking to understand people from the inside, looking out, ethnographic research aims to accurately characterize spatial and temporal autocorrelation, not correct for it (as we would attempt to do with life experience data). To accurately characterize spatial and temporal autocorrelation in cultural data, design sampling frames that encompass regionally and historically situated life experiences that may influence the patterns of social interaction through which people construct culture. In ethnography, you randomly select informants only when you want to estimate the frequency with which different cultures occur in a population. Ordinarily, random selection of informants constitutes a superfluous and wasteful activity for ethnographers. In ethnography, select informants for their cultural expertise. For many if not most purposes, everyone you meet will constitute a cultural expert.

Third, strictly speaking, hypothesis testing requires the use of bootstrap, jackknife, or permutation tests (e.g., Edginton 1980, Moony and Duval 1993) because cultural data violate the case-independence assumption necessary for the valid use of classical statistical tests. Case-dependence produces small standard errors that classical tests overestimate (see chapter 5). If you use classical statistical tests, rather than bootstrap, jack-knife, or permutation tests, you make it harder to detect subtle forms of structure in your data.

You may go further than mere description to try to determine why and how the patterns and variability you found might have come into being, why and how they persist over time, and why and under what circumstances they may change. Aim to explain variability in culture and behavior as a function of variability in experience, and search for concrete events and circumstances that shape those experiences. Remember that what people think and do must reflect not only their individual life history but broader regional and global histories of people, events, and social interaction into which they were born and in which they grew up. So try to identify events, circumstances, and processes that provide one set of choices to some people and a different set of choices to others. Ask individuals to identify life experiences that were significant to them and to help you understand why those experiences were significant. Pay particular attention to discrepancies between the two and how and under what circumstances individuals iron out the discrepancies. Keep in mind that core mental processes, which occur consciously only after the fact, may work primarily to rationalize what people actually do. Plan to explain why people believe, feel, and act the way they do by reference to information you collect on their prior experience, on their current experiences, on how those are perceived and conceptualized, and on the inferred processes by which individuals integrate these to produce knowledge and behavior.

Similarity coefficients and statistical tests applied to data such as these can tell us what goes with what and how strongly and thus provide a warrant for believing that a given relationship between a specific life experience and a specific cultural configuration is *real,* not merely a figment of our imagination (McEwan 1963). Unfortunately, analysis of the relationship between only two variables (*zero-order analysis*) tells us next to nothing. Adding another variable to the analysis may produce dramatic changes—a zero-order similarity coefficient may disappear, grow stronger, or change from positive to negative. Warrant for inferring that a relationship is *determinant,* as well as *real* (McEwan 1963), requires us to isolate a suspected relationship so we can tell whether or not it exists, and its strength, when we rule out the other internal validity possibilities.

Experimental designs were created to achieve precisely that goal. Although you will rarely find yourself in a position to employ experimental designs in ethnographic research, pay close attention to the logic of experimental design. Multiple regression techniques approximate the goals of experimental designs and thus permit explicit analyses that test for the variation in life experiences that accounts for intracultural and intercultural variation.

FALSE ASSUMPTION #3: DON'T CONFUSE CULTURES WITH SOCIAL IDENTITIES

Culture, to move beyond the metaphor of culture-as-knowledge, refers to the systems of mental constructions that people use to interpret and respond to the world of experience and to behavior isomorphic with those systems of meaning. More specifically, culture consists of three phenomena:

- Labels, names, which identify the existence of distinct configurations of phenomenal experience;
- Definitions, which, however ambiguous in specific cases, differentiate one thing from another; and
- Intellectual and emotional associations, which give mental constructions distinctive meaning.

For any given domain of meaning and behavior, variation in the data we collect in the field may reflect four conditions (also see Caulkins and Hyatt 1999):

- random variation around a single cognitive, emotional, or behavioral pattern that characterizes the domain or some aspect of it, which may be weak or strong;
- subpopulation differences in the strength of the pattern,
- two or more qualitatively different sets of meanings and behavior, which may differ little or constitute polar opposites; or
- no patterning in the domain or some aspect of it.

The first three conditions signal the presence of one or more *cultures,* specific configurations of cognition and emotion and isomorphic configurations of behavior generally shared among a set of people. The first condition indicates the absence of *cultural boundaries* (after Keesing 1994) within a given population and, thus, the existence of a single culture. The second condition identifies the existence of important forms of (intracultural) variation within that culture. The third condition identifies the existence of two or more cultures. The fourth condition signals the presence of individually unique configurations of cognition, emotion, and behavior.

Standard approaches to numerical analysis do not lend themselves to ethnography because they focus on variables, not informants (Handwerker and Wozniak 1997). Consensus analysis procedures (e.g., Romney, Weller, and Batchelder 1986), by contrast, directly address the analytical issues raised by the question of who agrees with and acts like whom about what and to what degree. Unfortunately, current software written to implement consensus analysis procedures facilitates analysis of only a single culture. More important, consensus analysis formally derives from a specific branch of learning theory and contains highly restrictive assumptions. One central assumption, not often met in field research, is that a specific body of knowledge exists, bearing on a specific cultural domain for which there exist cultural experts who know a lot and others who know less. Where such assumptions obtain (e.g., Weller and Mann 1997), consensus analysis answers the analytical question directly.

Under most field conditions and for most ethnographic goals, however, everyone constitutes a cultural expert in what she or he knows, feels, and does—like women who report on the meaning of stress and social support, men who report how they were treated by their parents, or men who tell about the substances they use and may abuse. This less restrictive assumption makes the question of who agrees with whom about what and to what degree bear directly on the empirical problem of identifying many possible cultures and the boundaries between one culture and another. It also makes the answer the simple outcome of standard construct validation procedures and akin to the procedures Boas (1894) used more than a century ago to evaluate the social distribution of knowledge across space and (implicitly) time. Formal consensus analysis procedures thus constitute a special case of the more general set of procedures available for establishing the construct validity of generalizations about cultures.

To assess internal validity, *construct validity* analysis allows explicit tests for the existence of specific cultures and, thus, valid generalization to populations defined by the studied life experiences. Weller (1987) has shown that Cronbach's alpha (the Spearman-Brown Prophesy Formula) can be applied to informants rather than items, which allows us to measure the reliability and validity of the cultural data we report. Ethnographic findings based on information from small numbers of informants (three to thirty-six, depending on the average level of agreement, from .5 to .9) exhibit exceptional reliability (.90–.99) and validity (.95 – ~1).

Ethnography thus differs from other modes of social and behavioral analysis in its focus on similarities and differences among informants rather than among variables. QE procedures direct you to

- identify, describe, and name cultures by reference to their distinctive configurations of cognition, emotion, and behavior, and
- look for explanations for distinctive cultural configurations in the historical regional, as well as global, processes that shape the experiences of individuals and lead them to create, maintain, and change the cultures in which they participate.

QE procedures thus follow from Wolf's central assertion that "the world of humankind constitutes a manifold, a totality of interconnected processes, and inquiries that disassemble this totality into bits and then fail to reassemble it falsify reality" (1982:3) and from his argument that "By turning names into things we create false models of reality. By endowing nations, societies, or cultures with the qualities of internally homogeneous and externally distinctive and bounded objects, we create a model of the world as a global pool hall in which the entities spin off each other like so many hard and round billiard balls" (1982:6). But QE procedures tell you to take a step further. Cease perpetuating by assumption rather than evidence what constitutes the "bits" into which this totality of interconnected processes can best be understood.

Our historical data come to us in labeled bits we call societies or cultural groups. But Wolf (1982), among many others, shows how the constituency of such groups, their labels, even their existence change by means of the interconnected historical processes through which people seek access to resources. On the Pepper Coast of West Africa, men who differentiated themselves as father and son became undifferentiated members of a regionally localized patrilineal *dako* that competed with its neighbors for control over land, rights over women and children, and trade; men of competing *dako* became undifferentiated "Kru" when they sought work on ships plying the commercial shipping lanes off the West African coast (McEvoy 1977). A few "Kru," along with "Yoruba" and despite marked differences in language, customs, and physical attributes, became undifferentiated "slaves" who worked plantations in the West Indies and the southern United States. Those who found a way to own their own plantations and slaves came to be called "Gens du Colours" in Haiti and equivalent names elsewhere, although their descendants, as well as those of their slaves who now live in the United States, became undifferentiated "African Americans." Surely, each such constituted group created a distinctive culture. Just as surely, each member of each group participated in many other cultures, most of which received no names because it wasn't relevant to the political problem of resource access to give them names.

And just as surely, we cannot know precisely what cognitive, emotional, and behavioral configurations made up those cultures until we make the reality of social groups, the existence of cultures, and the location of cultural boundaries empirical issues that require explicit tests for construct validity. Indeed, until we identify cultures by reference to specific configurations of cognition, emotion, and behavior, we shall forever find ethnographically incomprehensible a world in which a successful rap group comes out of Japan, you can watch the movie *Out of Africa* on a VCR run by a kerosene generator in an African bush village three hours' walk off the road, and Russians play jazz, compose country music, and turn capitalist—or the ongoing dynamics of social interaction and cultural change in any contemporary community. Indeed, as I write this, I listen to an NPR report about type-casting and stereotypes in the entertainment industry. A Japanese American explains how he walked out of a casting session for a Japanese mobster after having been told repeatedly that his accent was wrong for the part, until he selected one that represented a stereotypical Cantonese Chinese. A Latina scriptwriter explains her successful writing career by reference to her non-Hispanic professional name. An African American actor and director explains how bias enters into the choices made by most of the people who control the industry because they have little or no historical experience with real people who have brown skin tones and minority ethnic labels. The construct of "cultural group" fits these observations no better than equivalent observations made centuries earlier on the culturally diverse populations that came to be merged into British, German, Italian, French, or Russian identities (e.g., Wolf 1982:379). And to the extent that we perpetuate by assumption the construct of "cultural group" bequeathed to us by structural-functionalist ancestors, we beg what may constitute the most important questions ethnographers can address in the early twenty-first century: "What groups, by what criteria, where are their boundaries, and how can we know any of this?"

In defining culture as that complex whole that we acquire by virtue of living with other people, Tylor raised the question of the sense in which, and for whom, we might consider culture a "whole." The challenges of understanding and working with cultural diversity in the twenty-first century require us to raise and answer questions like this with considerably more subtlety than we've applied in the past. Culture always constitutes a complex whole for individuals. But each individual exists as a multicultural being. Achieving the subtlety of perspective necessary for identifying and understanding contemporary cultural diversity means specific attention to the domains of cognition, emotion, and behavior pertinent to individual lives and establishing which aspects of these domains one person shares with which specific others. This means questions bearing on the details of the social distribution of cognition, emotion, and behavior and about the patterns, networks, and character of social interaction through which culture evolves, locally, regionally, and globally. This requires attention to the design of ethnographic research.

QE procedures thus embody an extension of ethnographic practice in ways that correspond with a line of ethnological practice (Boas-Kroeber-Driver; e.g., Jorgensen 1974), which allows you to identify cultures independently of social identity labels. Explicit establishment of the construct validity of cultures allows you to clearly differentiate one culture from another and thus warrants generalizations about specific cultures. But it does so in a way that allows you to identify both intercultural and intracultural variability very precisely. This method thus helps you produce precise as well as nuanced interpretations of cultural variation. By helping you see cultural phenomena you'd otherwise miss, this approach will help you more precisely construct what Keesing (1994) called a "political-economy of knowledge."

THIS BOOK

I divide the remaining chapters into two sets. Chapters 2–8 cover steps to take *before* you get to the field. Chapters 9 and 10 cover steps to take once you're there. The size of the former relative to the latter warns you that what you do before you get to the field will dictate your success once you arrive.

Chapter 2 focuses on QE's Field Preparation Rule No. 1, "All ways to think about the world of experience contain errors, but you have to start somewhere." To create a clear vision of where you want to go, think about your research topic as a variable. Identify no more than five *focus variables* that embody the essentials of your research goals. Identify your field tasks by building on your focus variables. Imagine what each focus variable may consist of. Ask yourself why each dimension of each focus variable may exhibit one value rather than another. Keep asking "Why?" Link one variable to another (or others) until you're exhausted. Don't worry about being wrong. You will be. Correct your mistakes in the field, where you'll have access to corrective information. Do research to create a *better* way to think about the world.

Chapters 3–8 focus on QE's Field Preparation Rule No. 2, "Murphy's Law understates the facts; it *will* go wrong even when it can't." Management has to begin before you get to the field if you want to improve fieldwork productivity. Confusion inheres in doing good fieldwork. It requires you to select and complete an extraordinary number of tasks—and to coordinate each task with all the others. One set of inefficiencies in ordinary ethnography comes from the lack of a clear vision of where you are going. Focus variables provide you that vision.

A second set of inefficiencies comes from the lack of a clear vision of how you might best get there. To create a clear vision of how to get to where you need to go, identify the ends you need to reach to complete your project. Then select the appropriate research tools for each end.

Integrating the two creates a research design that addresses the two questions at the heart of all research:

- Did I get it right? (internal validity)
- To whom, if anyone, can I generalize? (external validity)

A third set of inefficiencies comes from getting lost along the way. *Iterative* data collection distinguishes good ethnography from bad. Design each observation and question to test at least one part of your theoretical understanding. Note errors. Ask for clarification. Rethink the theory. Link microlevel observations and interviews with historical records and macrolevel trends that only time-series data can reveal. Try again. As you do so, your fieldwork tasks will acquire complex linkages. Minimize your chances of getting lost by using detailed Gantt charts and PERT (Program Evaluation Review Technique) charts to coordinate the necessary iterations efficiently.

Plan to accomplish three management goals: (1) build a foundation, on which you can (2) build your data base, analysis of which and further data collection will allow you to (3) fine-tune your findings. The Gantt charts in figure 1.1 outline the basic components of a 12-week (90-day, summer) and a 4-week (30-day, contract) research project. The actual time involved in meeting these goals will vary with your project's duration, of course. Management goal overlap will not. Begin building your data base about midway through the tasks involved in building the foundation for your project. Begin to fine-tune your findings about midway through the tasks involved in building your data base.

Chapter 3 focuses on basic management issues. To create a clear vision of how you might best get where your focus variables tell you to go, identify the ends you need to reach to complete your project. Then, select the appropriate research tools for each end. Your job is to accurately identify, describe, and characterize:

- variables (*X*s and *Y*s, the labels that identify the components of cultures, the criteria that distinguish one from another, and the intellectual and emotional associations that give specific components their meaning) and

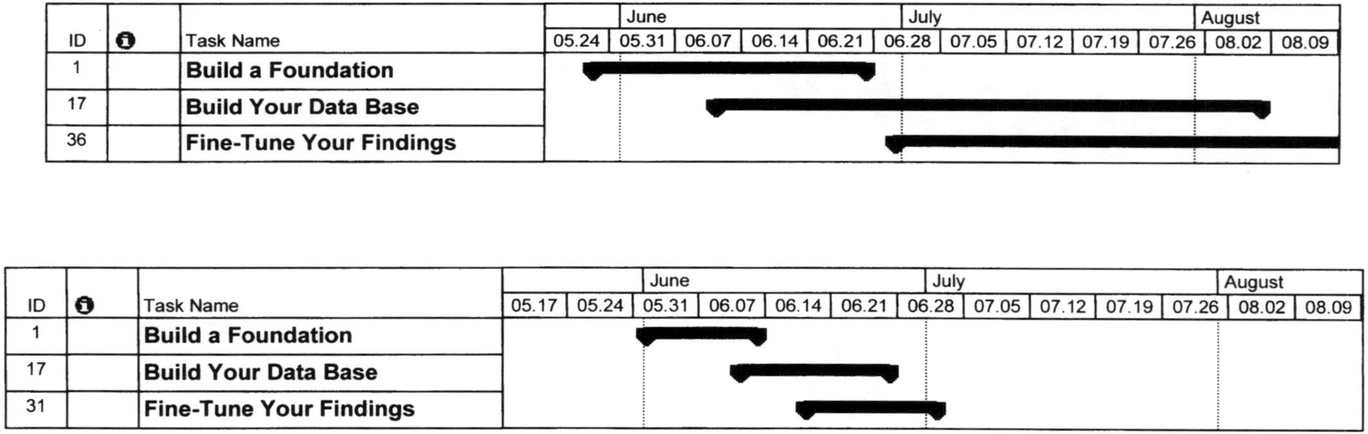

ID	⚙	Task Name	June 05.24	05.31	06.07	06.14	06.21	July 06.28	07.05	07.12	07.19	07.26	August 08.02	08.09
1		**Build a Foundation**												
17		**Build Your Data Base**												
36		**Fine-Tune Your Findings**												

ID	⚙	Task Name	05.17	June 05.24	05.31	06.07	06.14	06.21	July 06.28	07.05	07.12	07.19	07.26	August 08.02	08.09
1		**Build a Foundation**													
17		**Build Your Data Base**													
31		**Fine-Tune Your Findings**													

FIGURE 1.1
Gantt Charts for 90-Day and 30-Day Projects

- relationships between and among variables (the intersections among individually unique cultural sets and the life experiences that create, maintain, and change them).

Make your first priority the collection of text data from informal and semistructured observations and interviews of cultural experts. Then introduce rigor so you can identify and control the various forms of internal validity confounds embedded in your fieldnotes and can see nuanced intercultural and intracultural variation. Select a random sample of informants if you need to estimate the prevalence of cultural phenomena. If you design your research to test specific hypotheses about intracultural or intercultural variation, conduct a power analysis of your key test hypotheses and use appropriately large samples of variables measured reliably. Otherwise, employ nested sampling frames for intentionally selected comparisons. Use findings from your analysis of text to formulate structured interviews to nail down key comparisons. Use these comparisons to establish the construct validity of key multidimensional variables, like the culture or cultures you study. Then examine and try to explain intracultural and intercultural variation. Employ a Posttest Only Control Group experimental design with explicitly measured internal validity confounds (see Campbell and Stanley 1963).

Chapters 4–8 discuss your basic fieldwork tasks, organizing them by reference to the three phases of your research project. Chapter 4 discusses the first phase of your project. Build the foundation for a 90-day project by completing three major tasks within your first three weeks in the field: (1) beginning tasks, (2) aggregated data collection, and (3) research team assembly. Some of your beginning tasks entail official meetings, but turn all beginning tasks into data collection opportunities. Focus on informal interviews. Use them to introduce yourself and your project, to explore the assumptions that your informants use to understand and respond to the world of experience, the components of that world, and how those components are organized to form social and behavioral ecosystems, as well as to begin the process of confirming your findings. Collect aggregated data. Create timelines. Use Lexis Diagrams, along with historical scatterplots and icon analyses, to integrate key historical events and trends with your fieldnotes. Use your selection of a research site and a research team to make a transition into the second phase of your project. Use semi-structured interviews carried out one-on-one and in focus groups to find the limits of cultural variation. Use them, too, to fill out your understanding of the variables that compose cultures—how informants construct things like "families," "gender," and "age"; how they identify these things and discriminate one kind of thing from another; and how they identify, discriminate, and experience things like "power," "competition," and "cooperation." Incorporate focus group interviews into the training of your team of research assistants.

Chapter 5 discusses how to use structured interviews to build your data

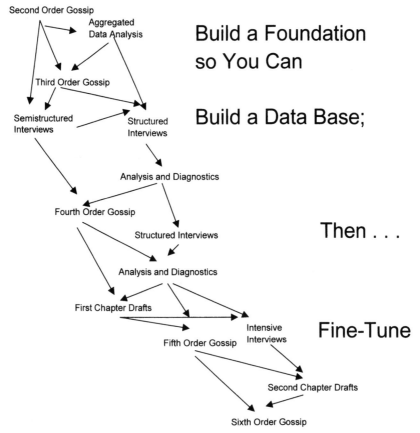

FIGURE 1.2
Selected Project Iterations

base. Use structured interviews to collect the data necessary for making explicit comparisons among informants and, so, to address the analytical tasks of identifying cultures, cultural variation, and cultural change, controlling for measured internal validity confounds. Keep your structured interviews short and sweet and ask questions for which you already have preliminary answers from informal and semistructured interviews. Use questions that ask for binary responses to identify the properties of people and the world you investigate. Use rating scales to assess relative importance and pile sorts to assess relative similarity. Use Likert Scales for multidimensional variables. Use scales developed in earlier studies to contribute to a comparative data base, but alter established scales so that they make sense to your informants. Don't hesitate to create your own scale to suit your specific research goals. Assess the construct validity and reliability of all scales you use. Collect time-series (historical) data. Draw on aggregated data collected by governmental and nongovernmental organizations. If necessary, incorporate design features into your survey to create your own time-series data.

Chapter 6 outlines the basic comparisons you should plan to make early on, to complete building your data base, and illustrates many of the explicit forms of analysis mentioned earlier in this chapter. Employ norming and standardizing operations to facilitate comparison, and use pictures to assess the distribution of your variables. Look for relationships between variables and informants. In the process, beware of the effects of random error. Test hypotheses, and use the regularity of sampling distributions to assess plausible effects of random error. Employ bootstrap, jackknife, or permutation tests to take advantage of the low levels of random error built into cultural data.

Chapters 7 and 8 discuss the final phase of your project: fine-tuning your findings. Chapter 7 focuses on the core goal of documenting the construct validity of the culture or cultures in your data. *Cultures* consist of configurations of cognition and emotion and an isomorphic configuration of behavior shared by a specific set of people. *A* culture thus constitutes a multidimensional variable, much like variables such as "violence" and "affection." You cannot see variables like these and cannot measure them directly. Validate that construct by demonstrating that specific people do share that configuration of cognition, emotion, and/or behavior. You can easily answer questions like "Do Iñupiat Eskimo give answers or act in ways that differ from West Indians?" but, as Keesing (1994) pointed out, the answers beg the question of the location of cultural boundaries. Questions like these impose cultural differences by assumption rather than evidence. To avoid this error and to pinpoint cultural boundaries, if they exist, use principal components to establish the construct validity of the culture or cultures in your data. Findings from such an analysis will tell you whether or not, or the extent to which, cultural boundaries correspond with social labels like Eskimo or West Indian, men or women, or old and young.

Chapter 8 focuses on tools that allow you to explore and explain intracultural and intercultural variation. Similarity coefficients and statistical tests can tell us what goes with what and how strongly and thus provide a warrant for believing that a given relationship between a specific life experience and a specific cultural configuration is *real*, not merely a figment of our imagination. But analysis of the relationship between only two variables (*zero-order analysis*) tells you next to nothing. Adding another variable to the analysis may produce dramatic changes—a zero-order similarity coefficient may disappear, grow stronger, or change from positive to negative. Warrant for inferring that a relationship is *determinant* as well as *real* requires you to isolate a suspected relationship so that we can tell whether or not it exists, as well as its strength, when you rule out the other internal validity possibilities. Multiple regression models implement quasi-experimental time series designs or cross-sectional designs equivalent to the Post-Test Only Control Group experimental design that test for the variation in life experiences that account for intracultural and intercultural variation, controlling for internal validity confounds. Use multiple regression models to focus your thinking about the sources of intracultural and intercultural variation and cultural change. Use Ordinary Least Squares (OLS) regression to explore the sources of intracultural variation. Use logistic regression to explore the sources of intercultural variation and cultural change. Be prepared to find cultures you didn't anticipate.

If you know little or nothing about numerical analysis, read chapters 6, 7, and 8 very, very slowly. Remember that numbers contain a tremendous amount of information. If you don't take your time, you'll become overwhelmed by the information. To avoid a panic reaction, dissect the chapter into tiny bits. Study the interplay between textual explanation and graphics. Create a mind game with yourself to come up with your own examples for each data analysis question and the statistic that can answer that question. Consult a basic textbook (e.g., Bernard 2000) to see more examples.

Chapter 9 focuses on QE's Fieldwork Rule No. 1, "Start collecting data the moment you arrive in the field, don't stop until you leave, and don't waste time studying variables not built from your focus variables." Even then, you can't do it by yourself. You can't even do it well. Use your time in the field to greatest advantage by building a research *team*.

Chapter 10 focuses on QE's Fieldwork Rule No. 2, "Develop a high tolerance for ambiguity." Fieldwork realities usually mean the collapse of the research plans you made before you arrived. Use theory and methods imaginatively to survive. Build a project that improves on the one that collapsed—even if you have to complete it in three days.

Acquire and master appropriate software to do all this quickly and efficiently:

- project management software (e.g., Microsoft's Project 2000);
- text analysis software (e.g., Atlas-ti);
- general purpose statistical analysis software (e.g., SYSTAT);
- special purpose statistical analysis software, including
    - LogExact software, if you anticipate working with tiny samples and/or want to produce exact probabilities for logistic regression models;
- power analysis software (e.g., SamplePower, from SPSS), if your general purpose statistical package doesn't come with the capability;
- Anthropac (from Analytic Technologies; http://www.analytictech.com/), if you want to conduct classic consensus analyses, Quadratic Assignment Procedures (QAP), permutation tests or to create and analyze random-ized structured interviews (e.g., triads, ratings, or paired comparisons) and are willing to tolerate a DOS program; and
- UCINET (from Analytic Technologies; http://www.analytictech.com/), for much of what Anthropac delivers but in a Windows version, plus social network analysis; and
- spreadsheet software (e.g., Lotus 123), to produce simulation models

based on OLS multiple regression solutions (SYSTAT's built-in logistic regression module produces its own simulation models of logistic regression solutions).

To keep up with new, related methods, subscribe to the journal *Field Methods,* published by Sage Publications.

II

BEFORE YOU GO

Identify the Question

QE's Field Preparation Rule No. 1 states:

> All ways to think about the world of experience contain errors, but you have to start *somewhere*.

Clearly designed and tightly focused projects yield coherent, publishable ethnographies and ethnographic reports. Clearly designed and tightly focused projects come from tightly focused research questions. Indeed, the word *research* refers to processes you engage in to answer questions. Tightly focused questions come most easily from theory that clearly identifies the variables that comprise and (potentially) influence the phenomenon you want to study. In the absence of good theory, precise identification of what's not understood generates the necessary questions.

In either case, consider a thorough literature review essential. Read everything pertinent to your interests published in the last decade, and consult key earlier studies. Supplement this review with talks with colleagues. Assume that the theoretical understanding you create, even if it consists merely of a research question, contains fundamental errors. Remember that to create new knowledge, you have to subject yourself to new experiences. Do research to create a *better* way to think about the world.

STUDY TOPICS YOU FEEL PASSIONATE ABOUT

You will begin research from one of two starting points: (1) a personal passion, and (2) an explicit research question handed you by someone else. You may love the hustle and bustle, the sounds, smells, and colors of *marketplaces* and want to learn more about how they work, for example. Alternatively, *environmental issues* may claim your attention, the construction and implications of *identities* may intrigue you, or *health;* or *human rights.*

However general your passion, you can't do research until you narrowly specify the research problem. Select a specific instance of the general, like *marketplaces in Monrovia, Liberia,* or *farmer's markets in eastern Connecticut.* If environmental issues claim your attention, study something like *pesticide use.* If your passions run to questions bearing on the construction and implications of identity, perhaps you should study *prostitution.* If health, study *stress.* If human rights, study *violence.*

In academic work, research most commonly comes from a personal passion, but major advisers may assign a research question to one of their graduate students, and students may prod a professor to look at a topic he or she otherwise might never have thought of—like the group of working women in an ethnographic methods course I taught for Public Health students who asked to study stress among working women (Handwerker 1999b). Applied work always entails research on a problem or question of concern to the contracting individual or organization, not necessarily one you would have selected for its intrinsic interest. When you prepare for research on such a topic, find ways to relate it to your passions. What may appear initially as the most banal issue may yield insight into significant theoretical problems. What started as a Social Institutional Profile of the Liberian agricultural sector, for example, turned into a study of corruption (Handwerker 1987) and an opportunity to make coherent a theory bearing on topics as diverse as the origins and evolution of culture (Handwerker 1989a), entrepreneurship (Handwerker 1990), and fertility transition (Handwerker 1989b). Edward Green (1999) turned his extensive contract experience into an opportunity to make explicit a line of medical theorizing widespread in Africa that had gone unrecognized by biomedically trained health planners and providers. In the process, he suggested an important way to reframe issues in medical anthropology. His reframing of issues integrated rather than maintained the separation of biological and ecological studies from cultural and ethnomedical studies.

In contract work, you will not often have the opportunity to design the whole project. Indeed, occasionally you may encounter a situation in which all design, data collection, and data analysis tasks have already been spelled out. You can't carry out ethnography in cases like this, and QE procedures hardly apply, although Rapid Assessment Procedures might (e.g., Beebe 2001).

More often, however, contracting organizations will expect you to bring to bear on their problem or question the expertise for which they hired you. Use QE procedures to formulate their problem or research question sensibly. Social impact assessment, marketing research, technology development research, and most other forms of contract research readily lend themselves to ethnography (e.g., van Willigen 1993). Increasingly, educators, nurses, and public health researchers turn to ethnography to answer questions and illuminate issues that conventional research tools miss. Most commonly, applied research calls for an evaluation research design. I shall illustrate the application of QE procedures to two different forms of such designs: needs assessment (including a special form of needs-assessment research common in business consulting, product design) and outcomes evaluation.

ORGANIZE YOUR STUDY AROUND NO MORE THAN FIVE FOCUS VARIABLES

To transform a passion into a doable research project, create a focused research question. Don't approach this task by writing out a list of all the questions you can think of. Such lists go on forever. Even if you could construct an exhaustive list of questions, your final list identifies a long list of questions. It fails to identify what you *must* know before you can go further—a specific *starting point*.

To find this starting point, think about your passion as either a variable or as one value of a variable. Dredge your memory and write down everything you can think of that bears on your area. Read more. Better, read widely on topics ostensibly *unrelated* to your interest area. Talk with colleagues, including, where appropriate, policy-makers, program officers, and people subject to specific policies and programs. Use your imagination to pull together bits and pieces from diverse sources of information to create different ways of thinking about your subject and its relationship with other phenomena. Create a way to think about your interest area that encompasses no more than about five *focus variables.* Information constraints in our short-term memory mean that adding more just creates confusion.

Marketplaces provide a simple example in which focus variables identify the principal components of the study topic. Marketplaces can be thought of as one component of an "economy." Economies, in turn, may be thought to consist of interrelated systems of production, distribution, and consumption; these, in turn, may be thought of as one component of the global (or regional) ecosystem (or ecosystems). Thus, to answer the question how marketplaces work, you have to identify the components of the economic system and look at their interrelationships. A generic set of components includes (1) producers (probably small farming units), (2) consumers (probably household units), (3) market sellers who buy from producers and sell to consumers, and (4) "markets"—places and relations of exchange between buyers and sellers. Hence, a research question: What social relationships characterize the operation of specific marketplaces?

If you're interested in another question related to marketplaces, ask that one. But ask one and *only* one research question. Adding more leads you astray. The single question posed here requires answers to, and so generates, a very large set of questions to ask once you arrive in the field. To cite a simple example: Given that marketplace "retailers" sell to consumers, for example, how do they vary in terms of the stock they offer for sale, their sources of supply, how they attract customers and how they seek to maintain or enlarge their clientele, their sales volume, and where and when they conduct business?

The following four vignettes illustrate different ways to transform a passion into the kernel of a research project:

1. The first illustrates research appropriate for someone interested in *the environment* and shows how to draw on conventional models to create a focused research question.
2. The second illustrates research appropriate for someone interested in *identity* issues and shows you how a conceptual model developed for one subject matter may help you understand another.
3. The third illustrates research appropriate for someone interested in

health and shows you how to generate a focused research question by applying findings from one field to the subject matter of another.

4. The fourth illustrates research appropriate for someone interested in *human rights* and shows you how to approach subject matter that remains so poorly identified that even the most fundamental questions remain unanswered.

Vignette 1: Pesticide Use

Conventional models provide a ready source of focused research questions (i.e., one with a small number of focus variables: profit, pesticide use, crops, cropping practices, and edaphic and biotic context). For example, *pesticide use* may be thought of as one input used by a production unit. Production can be thought of as a process that transforms inputs (land, labor, capital) into outputs (e.g., food). You might suspect that whether or not farmers use pesticides might be a function of their relative profit. What is the impact on the profitability of specific crops produced in specific regions and microenvironments with specific cropping practices (e.g., crop rotations, tillage) of pesticide use of various kinds? The conventional framework tells you that you might think about pesticides as one form of capital used in a production system run for the purpose of profit. If this is so, pesticide use might reflect its impact on profit. Of course, people do things for many reasons. Even if they believe pesticide use creates greater or more assured profits, they may be mistaken. Hence, the research question: What is the impact on the profitability of specific crops produced in specific regions and microenvironments with specific cropping practices of pesticide use of various kinds?

Vignette 2: Prostitution

Alternatively, explore the possibility that a conceptual model developed for one subject matter (e.g., *entrepreneurship*) may help you understand another *(prostitution)*—a possibility one of my students recently pursued in doctoral research carried out in Barbados (Paul 1997). Prostitutes may work full time or part time; individually or as part of a group that may be organized in many different ways; with or without protection; at a variety of locations, including the street, clubs, hotels, and their homes; and at varying points of time over their lives. Any one or a combination of these qualities might provide a starting point for an investigation. The most general observation, however, is that prostitutes make a living by selling sexual services. In fact, many prostitutes appear to run one-person firms, like retailers in marketplaces. Hence, a research question: Are (at least some) prostitutes also entrepreneurs?

Given that entrepreneurship consists of activities that initiate change in production or distribution (e.g., Kilby 1971), you can decide this issue by focusing on three questions. First, what different kinds of prostitute businesses exist, and how do you enter each kind (what are the capital requirements, if any)? Second, how are they run (where do they operate, for what hours, what services are offered, to clients of different kinds, attracted by what means, at which rates? What firms of what kind supply what sorts of inputs—information, services—to prostitute businesses)? Third, how do these businesses expand, contract, or disappear (how and under what circumstances can you expand profits? When do you leave the business or cut back? When and under what circumstances do you change how you run your business?)? Prostitutes who initiate changes in how they run their business constitute entrepreneurs; those who don't, aren't. Prostitution taken to be a form of entrepreneurship thus tells you to focus on (1) how prostitutes initiate firms, (2) how they run them, (3) how and under what conditions prostitute firms change (expand, contract, or cease business); (4) the identities they construct and how those identities influence each other and shape social relationships of different kinds; and (5) how their working identity (as an "entrepreneur"?) may influence how they run their businesses.

Vignette 3: Stress

Ask how findings from one field might apply to the subject matter of another. An e-mail now circulating the Internet begins:

BEING NDN IS . . .

Being Indian Is—missing work at least 2 days a month because so many of your friends and relatives are dying.

Native Americans exhibit the poorest health indices of any socially labeled population in the United States. These indices range from infant mortality, accidental death, suicide, bacterial meningitis, substance abuse, and sexually transmitted disease rates anywhere from twice as high as the national average to nearly twenty times the national average (e.g., McNabb 1990a, Young 1994). To understand why and what might be done about it, you might link this observation with three others: (1) A large body of literature now shows that the risk of death falls for people with high social support and that stress contributes, directly or indirectly, to morbidity and to death from *all* major causes of death, (2) the ritual and ceremonial that served to create socially integrated Native American communities largely ceased in the early twentieth century but (3) has, in some areas and among some people, experienced a significant resurgence. Is the health of Native Americans, like the health of other populations studied, a function of stress and social support? If so, stress coming from poverty and relative deprivation (e.g., Dressler 1997, Dressler et al. 1996, 1998, 2000) and demeaning daily social interaction with non-Indians (e.g., Handwerker 1999a, b) may account for differential morbidity and mortality indices; social support provided by participation in a common body of ritual may be a means to achieve improved mortality and morbidity.

Historically, Native American populations engaged in a variety of rituals and ceremonial gatherings that had as their purpose the re-establishment of health and balance in the human and natural worlds. These rituals constituted the focus of key ceremonial gatherings that served to integrate participants in defined communities of varying geographical scope. In many communities, these ceremonials largely ceased by the early 1900s. They did not reappear among local Native American communities until the 1970s. The last thirty years, by contrast with the previous eighty, have witnessed a marked resurgence of interest and participation in Native American ceremonial by native and non-native alike. These historical events have created a natural experiment in human health. *Cases* now exist of people who, for up to thirty years, may have experienced improved health from the social integration provided by their participation in community ritual. *Controls* also exist of people who may have experienced poor health because they did not. Hence, the project components: (1) morbidity and mortality indices, (2) ceremonial and ritual, (3) participants, (4) nonparticipants, and (5) stressors and social supports.

Vignette 4: Violence

There remains the case of subject matter so poorly identified that even the most fundamental questions remain unanswered. If you hope to begin to answer them, plan to survey and integrate theory and findings from highly diverse fields. Let's begin with some of the basic human rights issues. In a powerful *Anthropology Newsletter* commentary, Gene Hammel asks, "By what principle short of imperialism do we insist on the application of civil or human rights in societies that have not come to these ideas through their own histories?" (1994:48). As I wrote earlier (1997:799),

> Hammel intentionally asks the wrong question. To highlight his argument, he chose a provocative formulation which rests on a series of commonplace assumptions . . . [which necessarily lead to the conclusion that] Cultural differences at one point in time merely constitute standards and meanings situated at specific places and times by different historical flows of events and concrete social interactions, which, because of differences in history and context, must be what is "best" for each. Hammel thus asks a rhetorical question. By ingenuously ignoring "internal" power differences and unquestioningly equating "different" with "best" we rule out the possibility of universal human rights. Consequently, we don't ask the pertinent question: even if people do not call them by our words, do universal human rights exist?

Human rights thus may come from hardwiring that yields distinctively human animals who respond in regular ways to experiences with specific properties. Violence may constitute such a phenomenon, and *freedom from violence* may constitute a fundamental and universal human right. Given the intellectualized muddle that currently exists, however, the study of problem areas like violence requires us to dissect it into tiny units for effective research. Key questions include:

- What is the meaning of "violence," to whom and why, and how is that meaning created?
- What assumptions made by whom underlie current understandings of "violence"?
- How do those assumptions shape current policy and program formula-

tion and implementation—and their reception by people who have experienced "violence"?

- How do people subject to specific ("violent"?) acts incorporate that experience conceptually, emotionally, and neurologically, and under what circumstances (social identity, historical period, geographical location) does that vary?

- How does variability in the incorporation of those experiences influence how people define who they are, the range of alternatives from which they can make choices, and the criteria by which they choose among alternatives?

To take one example, violence against women is frighteningly prevalent by any definition (Heise 1995). Women and children who appear in emergency care centers with broken bones, cigarette burns, black eyes, gunshot wounds, or punctured lungs constitute a major health issue, with implications that extend far beyond the immediacy of the pain of particular injuries and deaths. Battered women also experience elevated risks of arthritis, hypertension, and heart disease (Council on Scientific Affairs, AMA 1992). Violence directed at women constitutes an excellent predictor of physical, emotional, and sexual violence directed at their children (Bowker, Arbitell and McFerron 1988, Handwerker 1993b, 1996a). Violence experienced in childhood and adolescence seems to create in adulthood an extraordinarily diverse syndrome that encompasses virtually all current behavioral health problems: depression, post-traumatic stress syndrome, borderline personality disorder, substance abuse, delinquency, suicide, partnership and parenting problems, and a pattern of sexuality marked by adolescent pregnancy and various forms of high risk behavior associated with sexually transmitted diseases and their sequelae, including HIV/AIDS—and, thus, the birth of infants with fetal alcohol syndrome, drug dependency, and HIV-positive diagnoses. The *least* important sequelae of violence against women and children are that its direct and indirect costs contribute inordinately to the size of our national health care and criminal justice system budgets and, by the constraints they impose on economic productivity, reduce national economic growth capacity.

Researchers in the social and behavioral sciences, medicine, and public health have barely begun the process of delineating the nature of violent events and processes. What constitutes "violence," "abuse," and "neglect" appears notoriously subject to cultural variation. A person who fits one cultural definition of "batterer" may legitimately deny it outright, using another cultural definition. A person who fits one cultural definition of "victim" may legitimately deny it outright, using another cultural definition of "victim." Conflicting cultural definitions of violence, abuse, and neglect lead, too often, to interventions that do harm. Defining violence by reference to the experience of people subject to violence (Handwerker 1997) and to functional outcomes (e.g., Handwerker 1993a, 1999a, b) constitutes one alternative. But much work remains to determine what definitions and which functional outcome measures work best.

An established body of evidence is consistent with the view that violence is embodied in *social circumstances* presumed to induce threat, stress, or frustration (e.g., Bersani and Chen 1988, Gelles 1987, Goode 1971, Straus and Gelles 1990). But many of the findings from conventional violence research come from poorly designed projects and may merely recast and rationalize long-standing Western folklore. To wit: the image of unemployed or underemployed men who, finding their dreams elusive and frequently even unable to support their families, drown themselves in alcohol and vent their frustrations on wives and children. Victims often repeat this tale, but people are notoriously good at telling what looks like what and notoriously bad at telling what goes with what, as Shweder (1977) and many others have pointed out. Social-circumstance explanations remain theoretically unjustified because they rest on the frustration-aggression hypothesis, which assumes rather than demonstrates or deduces a linkage between frustration and aggression. Social-circumstance explanations remain empirically unjustified because they rest on studies that fail to control for the pertinent variables.

By contrast, a mounting body of evidence is consistent with the view that violence (and, by implication, affection) is embodied in *individuals*—in many women's experience, that there are two kinds of men, "good" ones and "bad" ones. In this "rotten man" hypothesis, the expression of violence reflects one or another form of hardwiring (e.g., Malamuth et al. 1991, Malamuth 1993). Accumulated neurological studies suggest that violent events and processes may be mediated or expressed through variation in neurotransmitter levels that regulate fear, anger, depression, and their behavioral expression (e.g., Essman and Essman 1985, Valzelli, Bernasconi, and Dalessandro 1983); that a point mutation that alters pertinent neurotransmitter levels distinguishes individuals with a history of violence within at least one family line (Brunner, et al. 1993); and that neurological damage may elicit violence (Elliott 1988). Human mental and physical activity necessarily reflect the chemical activity and balance in our brains and these necessarily reflect our species' evolutionary history.

These and related findings do *not* warrant inferring either that "rotten men" have bad genes and good men have good genes or that violence is embodied in our cells. These bad metaphors rest on the patently false claim that genes and the proteins they manufacture function independently of their environment. Phenotypic expression varies with specific historical and social contexts (e.g., Broderick and Bridger 1984; Mawson and Jacobs 1978; Maier, Seligman, and Solomon 1969) and cannot be understood independently of those contexts. If "rotten men" exist (see Handwerker 1998), they must come ultimately from properties of our central nervous system that produced responses to those words and acts that contributed to our ancestors' survival and reproductive success.

The hardwired properties of our central nervous system that produce these responses remain at issue. Universal or potentially universal meanings assigned to historically and regionally specific forms of stressors and social supports, however, point to the existence of an evolved mechanism for responding to specific ecosystem properties, as envisioned in the pioneering work on stress carried out by Cannon (1929, 1942) and Selye (1956). One might infer that today's world, filled with chronic stressors (many as holdovers from childhood experiences), makes the stress response maladaptive, since it makes you sick if it doesn't kill you.

However, reproduction usually ends long before stress-related death. Evolved mechanisms come into being because they contribute to an organism's ability to avoid predation and exploitation, to eat, and to reproduce. It makes no sense to characterize something as maladaptive unless it contributes to relative reproductive failure, either directly or through impaired abilities to avoid predation and exploitation or to obtain access to resources.

Evolved mechanisms contribute to an organism's ability to avoid predation and exploitation, to eat, and to reproduce when they respond sensitively to ecosystem changes. Stress thus should not consist of a homeostatic response to environmental demands—or our interpretation of environmental stimuli—that tax or exceed the adaptive capacity of an organism (e.g., Cohen, Kessler, and Gordon 1997). Stress should signal both danger and opportunity and should induce specific choices that reflect different allostatic set points. The studies cited earlier point to the possibility that childhood experiences alter the set point of the stress mechanism, perhaps permanently, to induce specific, lifelong changes in brain structure and function (e.g., Mlot 1998, Pynoos et al. 1997, Teicher et al. 1997). People who experience traumatic childhood ecosystems, for example, should learn to be highly sensitive to power relationships, respond quickly and strongly when others attempt to inflict further violence on them, and search hard for ways to avoid dependency on others and thus minimize the chances of further exploitation.

The fact that violence can only be *expressed* as a social act within specific social relationships helps us understand why violence and violent events do not readily lend themselves to classification as a "disease." Social interaction generates the culturally variable meanings, symbols, and mental constructs people use to think about and make sense of themselves and the world around them. The meaning and, thus, both the sources and implications of "violence" and "abuse" emerge from concrete social interaction in specific historical and social contexts.

If, as in many women's experience, men tend to exhibit two constellations of properties ("rotten" and, if not "good," at least "other"), most plausibly they emerge from boys who experienced two kinds of gender and intergenerational relationships that we can fairly characterize as exploitative and nonexploitative. Unless pertinent environmental features remain constant over the course of development, we should expect evolutionary processes to produce developmental processes that are contingent on events in an organism's life history. A person's ability to survive, reproduce, and raise young to adulthood must be a function of his or her ability to secure access to the resources that make those events possible. Power relationships dictate resource accessibility and reliability. We should not be surprised that exploitative and empowering childhood environments teach the children raised in them very different ways to express and respond to power relationships. Rotten men may turn out to be those who, sensitized in childhood to the nuances of power, its expression, and the optimal behavioral responses to power relations, merely respond quickly to power inequities they experience as adults and do everything they can to avoid being exploited themselves (see Handwerker 1993a).

In shifting our focus from violent people to the ecosystem that may both produce them and elicit the expression of violence, we shift our research focus from individuals to specific individuals in specific social relationships or, perhaps, the social relationships themselves. This shift calls for a rethinking of what we have come to think of as a "cycle of violence," in which violence in one person is passed on to his or her child(ren) (see Widom 1989a, b; Widom and Kuhns 1996). Children subject to violence who grow up to subject others (and themselves) to violence may be embodied in a set of social *relationships* that can span generations. Change in the social relationships that generate violence should "break" the "cycle of violence." Barbados and Antigua constitute a case in point. Dramatic increases in the proportion of women who could make a good living (i.e., access resources) independently of men followed structural change in the Barbadian and Antiguan economies. In a single generation in both countries, the proportion of women who experienced spousal relationships marked by violence fell by 40 percent. Interventions aimed at reducing the incidence of domestic violence that aim to give women choices pertinent to the time and place in which they live, and so equalize gender power relations, should prove the most successful. This might also reduce the number of rotten men in the next generation.

More generally, selection cannot create a mechanism that changes behavior in advantageous ways in highly stressful childhood ecosystems that lead to marked disadvantages in minimally stressful adult ecosystems. What we now characterize as stress-induced morbidity thus may consist of adaptive responses to ecosystems in which children find themselves subject to predation and denial of access to resources. If so, those responses should contribute to a person's ability to avoid predation and exploitation, to eat, and to reproduce, roughly in that order of importance. *Predation* and *denial of access to resources* correspond with what we usually call social *exploitation*. Our species' stress response may generate behavioral responses to the threat or reality of social predation and denial of resource access.

Most traumatic stress experienced by children may not occur within family units but in daily social interaction with others, particularly across social identity lines like ethnicity. Common "causes of death" today include drug overdoses, HIV/AIDS, cirrhosis of the liver, cervical cancer, lung cancer, suicide, and heart disease. But the real killer may be hurtful words turned into chronic stressors, when a child hears them regularly or all the time in comments made by people with power or by people who belong to powerful groups—parents talking to their children; teachers talking to students; white-skinned kids talking to black-, brown-, and red-skinned kids; star athletes talking to nerds. During a child's school years, hurtful words may lead to depression and, so, to poor school performance, aggressive behavior, and alienation from peers—and thus may lead to dramatic and tragic endings, like the massacre and suicides that took place in Littleton, Colorado. During school and afterward, long-term sequelae may make it nearly impossible to create fulfilling social relationships. Tobacco, alcohol, and illicit drugs often substitute. Girls and boys move from one sexual partner to another and acquire and pass along sexually transmitted diseases. Girls get pregnant and bear children long before they can function effectively as parents. Substance-abusing girls, who may simultaneously be HIV-positive, give birth to children with their own drug dependencies, HIV-positive diagnoses, and neurological damage. Once they become parents, ongoing depression impairs their ability to pay appropriate attention to their children or to remain calm when dealing with the stresses that parenting inevitably brings. Their fear of closeness and dependence on another makes it nearly impossible to maintain two-parent families. Those who don't die early of overt suicide, drug overdoses, or the violence that surrounds the use of illicit drugs tend to experience a variety of physical impairments, including chronic and incapacitating pain, fatigue, and headaches. And they die early of cancer and cardiovascular disease. A study of great theoretical significance would test the hypothesis that among children who grow up in exploitative environments, children who develop an increased sensitivity to power relationships, who respond quickly and strongly to threats, and who search actively for ways to avoid dependency on others exhibit lower childhood morbidity and mortality than do children who may appear "resilient" and who exhibit characteristics of children who did not grow up in exploitative environments.

HOW TO WORK WITH AN EXPLICIT RESEARCH QUESTION

Explicit research questions usually boil down to one of the following: "What should we be doing?" or "Is what we're doing working and, if so, how well?" Answer the first question with a needs assessment. Answer the second with an outcomes evaluation. Both research questions call for the same handling and study organization as a research question that evolves from a personal passion: *stick with five focus variables!*

NEEDS-ASSESSMENT RESEARCH

Needs-assessment research calls for you to critically analyze an existing policy, program, or product and the set of assumptions that rationalizes it. Organize needs-assessment research around two focus variables:

1. the set of assumptions from which the policy, program, or product follows as a logical consequence.
2. the answers to two questions:
   - What evidence warrants each assumption?
   - What evidence points to missing assumptions?

If you change any one assumption, you create new implications and thus a new policy, program, or product. The implications of your findings may point to ways to fine-tune an existing policy, program, or product with small design changes. They may point to the need for a new policy, program, or product or fundamental design changes in existing ones. Make your recommendations the logical consequences of a new set of assumptions. Construct this new set by deleting existing-but-unwarranted assumptions and adding missing assumptions that are warranted by evidence.

Vignette 5: An Aging Population

Address the two focus variables in a needs assessment for an aging population with information on five variables: (1) activities of living, (2) func-

tional skills and disabilities, (3) personal resources, (4) community services and resources, and (5) knowledge and use of community services
and resources. Frame research on variable 4 to provide information on
the set of assumptions from which existing services and resources follow
as a logical consequence. Research findings on variables 1, 2, 3, and 5 provide evidence bearing on the assumptions that rationalize existing services
and resources and may point to assumptions that do not now guide the
provision of community services and resources. Once you identify living
activities, which may vary dramatically regionally and with age and other
social identities, you can identify the functional skills necessary to carry
out those activities, as well as how you might best measure functional
skills and disabilities. This information provides a foundation for knowing
which personal resources might bear on living activities and functional
skill limitations and which community services and resources fit with
these needs (and that now don't exist).

Vignette 6: A Mammography Clinic

Address the two focus variables in a needs assessment for a mammography clinic with information on five variables: (1) clinic facilities, services,
and procedures; (2) the meaning of breast cancer to patients; (3) patient
concerns and preferences; (4) patient constraints and complaints; and (5)
provider understanding of the patient variables 2, 3, and 4. Clinic facilities,
services, and procedures and providers' understanding of the patients they
serve constitute the primary environmental variables at the clinic that
shape patient experiences. Information on variables 1 and 5 thus provide
information on the set of assumptions from which existing services and
resources follow as a logical consequence. For example, clinics may be
designed around, and providers may act on, the assumption that patients
harbor great concerns over issues like experiencing pain or the exposure
and handling of their breasts during mammography procedures, as well
as fear of the procedure, exposure to radiation, or a possible finding of
breast cancer. Similarly, providers of clinic facilities, services, and procedures may implicitly assume that patients have no preferences regarding
the gender of their radiologist or when they can schedule a mammogram
and do not think about the competence of clinic providers. Information
on variables 2, 3, and 4 provides evidence bearing on the assumptions that

rationalize existing clinic facilities, services, and procedures and may point to missing assumptions. Patients may harbor no particular concern over issues like experiencing pain, the exposure and handling of their breasts during mammography procedures, fear of the procedure, or exposure to radiation. By contrast, patients may have distinct gender preferences for their radiologist, may feel great concern over the quality of health services, and may have a mammogram irregularly because of constraints stemming from family and work responsibilities and the available transportation. Improved service delivery may call for changes in clinic procedures. The most important may constitute training for providers in some basic ethnographic interviewing skills, to help them better listen to patient concerns, preferences, and constraints.

Vignette 7: Product Design

Product design constitutes an increasingly common application of ethnography in both for-profit and nonprofit business consulting (see Squires and Byrne 2001). Research teams carry out product design to discover new markets and opportunities for new products or services, to identify the criteria for product design, and to evaluate existing products and services. Design teams aim to reduce risk and increase return. Their existence thus constitutes implicit recognition that culture evolves. The shared ways to think about and act in domains like "eating breakfast," "using computers," or "fishing" that define specific cultures also define the characteristics of specific "markets" and the boundaries between one market and another. As these cultures evolve, markets change or disappear and new markets come into being (e.g., Wolf 1982).

As an ethnographer, you're likely to find yourself part of a product design team when the business chooses to experiment with the approach, when market conditions change, or when an existing product design fares relatively poorly in the market. Because you will participate in a business culture, you'll couch your discussions and reports by reference to *products, markets, business opportunities,* and *consumers.* Language like this may not suggest needs assessment to an ethnographer who works primarily in an academic setting. Product design research constitutes the most explicit form of ethnographic needs-assessment research, nonetheless. What makes product design a special case is its quick pace and result-oriented focus. Your schedule can be as short as three days, although you may be blessed with three weeks. I illustrate a three-day QE project in chapter 10.

Your primary contribution will consist of three to five recommendations concerning new markets and new products, criteria for product design, or evaluations of existing products. You *won't* produce a written ethnography. You *must* develop expertise in communicating to people who belong to distinct cultures—of marketing, engineering, and management, for example (Walls 2001). You will communicate your findings in discussions with team members, power-point presentations, and compact final reports that contain bullet-points, graphs, pictures, stories, quotes, and sketches of potential products. Your final report will consist of a short (ideally, only 3–4 pages, but no more than 20 pages) written summary that outlines the original business challenge, the assumptions on which it was formulated, the intended market, and the ethnographic research you conducted. The three to five recommendations, like Executive Summaries in technical reports written for governmental organizations, appear first in the report, since few people (if any) will read beyond them.

To arrive at these recommendations, organize product design research around the standard two focus variables: the set of assumptions from which the product follows as a logical consequence and the answers to two questions: (1) what evidence warrants each assumption? and (2) what evidence points to missing assumptions? The answers make arriving at three to five recommendations relatively simple. If you change any assumption or add a new one, you create new implications. You thus create a new market or a new or redesigned product and thus a new business opportunity. Make your recommendations the logical consequences of a new set of assumptions. Construct this new set by deleting existing-but-unwarranted assumptions and by adding missing assumptions that are warranted by evidence.

For-profit businesses contract for most product design research. One implication is that I can't illustrate this form of ethnographic research with real examples, since so much of this work entails the collection and analysis of proprietary data (although, see Squires and Byrne 2001). However, nonprofit businesses and some public agencies contract for closely related needs-assessment work. A State Department of Fish and Game, for example, may want to generate more tourist spending from fishermen and their families and may want to know how it might change the manner in which it manages fisheries resources to attract those dollars. We'll return to this issue in chapter 10.

OUTCOMES-EVALUATION RESEARCH

Outcomes-evaluation research tests the efficacy of interventions designed to induce specific forms of cultural change and thus comes with a built-in research question: Did the intervention work and, if so, how well? If it did, people who entered the intervention with one culture left with another. Example interventions include bicycle safety programs designed to increase the chances that a child will use a helmet while riding, training of health-care providers designed to improve their ability to carry out accurate physical examinations, and training of prospective college students in what it means to be a college student. Interventions assume the existence of, and teach, correct answers—riding with, not without, helmets; the correct way to conduct physical examinations; the components of college student identity necessary for a successful college career. Evaluation research assesses the degree to which trainees exhibit correct answers. Judgments about the efficacy of interventions like this one thus require information on whether or not, or the degree to which, people who started with one culture ended with another.

Vignette 8: Student Identity

For example, people who attend college bring with them an identity as *student* and elaborate that identity with experiences accumulated over their college career. The components of student identity may include *developing a sense of responsibility* and *getting to class on time* to *attending sports events* and *drinking on the weekend*. Faculty and college administrators would like to think that student identity also included components like *contemplating* and *discussing important ideas*.

Many universities have instituted programs to teach prospective students what it means to be a student before they begin their first semester. Such interventions often specifically target people admitted to the university with low SAT scores, with the aim of increasing the chances that such people would enjoy a successful college career rather than drop out before graduation. Trainees might take basic courses during the summer prior to their first semester and receive intensive counseling. One goal of the intervention might be to encourage specific forms of cultural change in the concept of student identity necessary for a successful college career, which include *contemplating* and *discussing important ideas.*

Outcomes research thus readily lends itself to a Post-Test Only Control Group experimental design (Campbell and Stanley 1966). People subject to intervention activities constitute cases; people not subject to intervention activities constitute controls. The evaluation research hypothesis resolves to this—Cases exhibit greater cultural similarities with the correct answers than do controls. Hence, the core project questions: (1) What are the correct answers? and (2) does the culture of cases show greater correspondence with the correct answers than the culture of controls? Randomization of intervention participants eliminates most potential ambiguities. In the absence of randomization, use multivariate regression models that explicitly control for internal validity confounds (see chapters 3 and 8).

Vignette 9: Math Education in Bilingual Classrooms

Hispanic students, an increasing proportion of whom speak Spanish as their first language, constitute the largest minority group in U.S. public schools. These students exhibit both poor test scores (particularly in mathematics) and frighteningly high dropout rates, the highest in the nation. To encourage more effective learning and lower dropout rates, the National Council for Teachers of Mathematics (NCTM) directs attention to the culture of classrooms and calls for increased communication among teachers, students, and parents; better preparation of students for academic discourse and class participation; and connections between mathematics and other disciplines, including the teaching of ESL (1989). It also calls for teachers to be aware of linguistic and cultural diversity among students and to incorporate this diversity into lesson delivery (see also Secada 1992). Both the NCTM and the Professional Standards for Teaching Mathematics (1991) point out the mutually enhancing effects of language and mathematics. A growing body of literature suggests that the use of oral and written language to formulate, solve, and explain mathematics concepts and problems encourages mathematics competence by requiring students to actively engage in and take ownership of mathematics problem-solving skills (e.g., Wright and Wright 1986, Ford 1990, Winograd

1990, Archambeault 1991, Rose 1992, Bebout 1993, Phillips and Crespo 1995, Burns 1995).

Cummins (1981) argues, with some justification, (e.g., Hakuta 1987 and Lessow-Hurley 1990), that mathematics, like other problem-solving skills, exists independently of language and can be transferred to and expressed readily through any language. He suggests further that the ability to master complex cognitive skills is a function of the amount of contextual information in the learning environment. Children engaged in learning cognitively demanding mathematics skills do so best in an information-rich environment. Information-rich environments contain a wide range of cues that earlier life experiences made meaningful, embodied in oral and written language skills, which make possible effective engagement with new concepts. Information-poor environments, by contrast, present students with little comprehensible input and evoke negative affective filters that further impede effective learning (Krashen 1985, 1994). Mathematics classrooms structured for children whose first language is English (monolingual students) present cognitively demanding skills in an information-rich environment that draws upon students' earlier experiences as understood, worked through, and explained in their first language. In the same classrooms, students learning English as a second language (bilingual students) find themselves attempting to learn cognitively demanding skills in an information-poor environment. The settings and problems remain foreign to their lived experiences, which remain embedded in their first language, and incipient English-language skills provide inadequate means for effectively engaging new concepts (Cummins 1994).

A proposed intervention thus might seek to: (1) document standard teaching procedures, protocols, lesson delivery, and student–teacher interaction patterns, with particular attention to the relationship between classroom information content and the lived experiences of monolingual students contrasted with the lived experiences of bilingual students; and (2) work with teachers to create the ethnographic skills necessary for implementing an ongoing, evidence-based pedagogy that both (i) enriches classroom information content for bilingual students by integrating their lived experiences into teaching procedures, protocols, lesson delivery, and student–teacher interaction and (ii) facilitates the movement of mathematics problem-solving skills into English. The outcomes evaluation for this intervention tests the hypothesis that bilingual students who experience enriched informational environments exhibit higher levels of mathematical and English language competence than do bilingual students who experience standard informational environments. Like the previous example, a test of the efficacy of the intervention readily lends itself to a Post-Test Only Control Group experimental design. People subject to intervention activities constitute cases; people not subject to intervention activities constitute controls. Your research hypothesis is this—Cases exhibit greater cultural similarities with the correct answers than do controls. Hence, the core project questions: (1) What are the correct answers? and (2) does the culture of cases show greater correspondence with the correct answers than the culture of controls? Randomization of intervention participants eliminates most potential ambiguities. In the absence of randomization, use multivariate regression models that explicitly control for internal validity confounds (see chapters 3 and 8).

BUILD FROM YOUR FOCUS VARIABLES

The preceding examples illustrate QE's requirement that you conceptualize research interests in terms of a small number of focus variables. To reiterate: find your focus variables by thinking about your interest area as a variable or a value of a variable. If you intend to conduct an exploratory study, ask yourself about the principal components of your subject matter. If you intend to examine a specific hypothesis, choose one dependent variable and up to four independent variables.

Once you identify your research question and its focus variables, *don't plan or do anything unless it leads to the collection of information on that set of focus variables.*

Much remains to be done, of course. Each focus variable exhibits many dimensions. You can arrive at an answer to your research question only by identifying the dimensions of each focus variable and other variables that might explain these dimensions. This process will generate the specific variables you will look at and the questions you will ask in the field. Handle each of those with the same procedure.

For example, given that "capital" consists of resources (like knowledge, goods, or services) that can be used to produce resources (like more knowledge, goods, or services), what constitutes a "capital requirement" for a prostitute business: prior sexual experience? (of what kind?) knowledge of pricing, sales, advertising, personal relations, or business locations? specialized clothing? condoms? makeup? What impact do capital inputs of one kind or another have on profits?

Similarly, if "power" refers to the ability to influence what others do and think even without their consent (following Weber), and "power" exists operationally as a relationship in which one party must access resources through another, what influences the relative power of men and women: relative physical size? education? job opportunities? a combination of education and job opportunities? the number and age of male children? one or another childhood experience?

What does "social integration" mean? frequency of contact with other people? intensity of contact? density of social networks? Is the concept "social integration" meaningful to the people in your fieldsite? Indeed, to what extent can people be conscious of the degree of their "social integration?" Is this relevant? What does their consciousness contain? If "social integration" reduces the risk of morbidity and mortality in significant ways, how much of this effect comes through change in the body's stress response, independently of practical assistance channeled through social networks? Maybe, as evolutionary theory suggests, social integration consists of events and ways of interacting that promote our ability to eat, avoid exploitation, and reproduce. By implication, stressors may turn out to be those events and ways of interacting that threaten our ability to eat, avoid exploitation, and reproduce. Do the events and forms of social interaction that people identify as stressors correspond to threats to their ability to eat, avoid exploitation, and/or reproduce, and the events and forms of social interaction that people identify as social support correspond to assistance in being able to eat, avoid exploitation, and/or reproduce? To what extent does the relative importance of stressors and forms of social support correspond to a person's ability to eat, avoid exploitation, and/or reproduce?

In needs-assessment research, you may find that a large proportion of people with mood disorder symptoms reports no prior treatment. Findings like this suggest that people who suffer much emotional pain do not recognize a legitimate illness for which treatment exists. High levels of untreated mood disorders also suggest that these remain undiagnosed by

health-care providers, who may focus too narrowly on overt, physical disorders. The most immediate mental health needs thus may be for outpa-
tient informational and clinical services that address mood disorders and
advanced training in mental health for primary health-care providers.
Organize this subsidiary needs-assessment component for community
services and resources into the following variables: (1) screening procedures and criteria used by clinicians, (2) mood disorder cases identified
by these procedures and criteria, (3) screening procedures and criteria
embedded in an instrument with excellent reliability and both construct
and criterion validity, and (4) mood disorder cases identified by these procedures and criteria.

DON'T LOSE SIGHT OF THE FOREST

Building from your focus variables thus will generate specific field research
tasks—a list of variables and questions, the answers to which will lead you
to conclusions about your study question. Anticipate that doing ethnography will immerse you in the grind of day-to-day living. It is easy to get
lost. You may wish to frame your research solely in terms of the people
you observe and talk with in the field. You need not frame your research
so restrictively. You'll probably miss much if you do. Many conditions
influence what people do and think. Some are built into us at conception.
Some are childhood experiences. Some emerge as people work their way
through life. All of these may reflect the interaction of genome and experience. The most important experiences may be those that people do not
perceive clearly. They may be events or processes that people never experience consciously.

   You will be trying to understand people who live their lives just like
you. They will tell you stories about their lives that they constructed
through the same processes that you use to construct understandings—
your culture—of and for your experience. Informant analyses and
descriptions, as well as elicited "reasons," intentions, or motivations, thus
may mislead far more than they provide insight (Brown 1963, Hammel
1990, Gazzaniga 1998). People lie. People forget. People do things for
many reasons. People aren't aware of all or even most of the influences on
what they do. People may be completely *unaware* of the most important
influences on what they do, particularly when those influences are histori-

cal, macrolevel phenomena that can't be perceived clearly in the minutiae of day-to-day living. People misjudge the relative importance of their reasons, intentions, or motivations. People rationalize what they do. Informant analyses and descriptions and elicited "reasons," intentions, or motivations constitute empirical claims with the same logical status as all hypotheses. All arise from people's imagination. All may be figments of someone's imagination with no empirical validity. Good data collection procedures, as well as convincing explanations, recognize the multidimensional origins of human behavior and culture. When you identify the variables and questions to focus on in the field, choose ones that imply recognition that behavior and culture reflect specific individual life histories embedded in broader regional and global histories of events and processes. Aim to explain variability in culture and behavior as a function of variability in experience, and search for events and circumstances that shape those experiences.

For example, the impact of any one experience (its explanatory power) may vary according to the time during a life trajectory when it was experienced, as well as with characteristics of the experience (e.g., duration, intensity). Similarly, different realms of experience mean that choices available to one generation or one part of a population may differ significantly from the choices available to another. Aim to identify events, circumstances, and processes that provide one set of choices to some people and a different set of choices to others. Look at how people identify better ways to act and think. What criteria do they use to discriminate options from non-options, and among different options?

One way to approach this task is to just ask "Why?"—and don't stop until you've exhausted yourself. The question "Why did you do that?" elicits "reasons," "intentions," and "motivations," data that allow you to identify the meaning of specific events, activities, and processes. The question "Why does someone do that for those reasons?" pushes you to identify circumstances that make sense of the meanings you found. The question "Why those circumstances?" pushes you to look for specific historical conditions that generate specific belief and behavioral patterns. The question "Why respond to those circumstances in that way?" pushes you to look for specific processes that may generate pan-human responses to circumstances of specific kinds. To wit: the following vignette.

Vignette 10: Just Ask Why?

A man may explain that he beats a woman because she made him angry. The man may have experienced anger, but what circumstances influenced him to blame her for his feelings—how his father treated his mother, how his mother treated him, or merely that he is bigger than she?

Perhaps he felt angry because he saw the woman talking with another man. What is it about "talking with another man" that might elicit anger? Why wouldn't "talking with another man" lead all three to have fun together? "Talking with another man" might elicit anger if men mistrusted women. Do men mistrust women because women act deceptively? Maybe men mistrust women because men act deceptively?

What constitutes "deception": attempting to hide or successfully hiding non-monogamous sexual behavior when both men and women say they want "faithful" partners? How do people (of different ages and genders) identify it: a woman who discovers she has gonorrhea? A man who discovers that his partner enjoys many different sexual positions, which he believes only prostitutes and promiscuous women should know? Who says that "deceptive" behavior is not deception at all, and under what circumstances: a woman dependent on a man who discovers a genital infection and calls it "coolant" so she can explain it by reference to having eaten cold rice?

Feeling anger predicts violent action poorly. Is this person prone to violence when he is angry and, if so, what distinguishes men prone to violence from men not prone to violence? Maybe "anger" merely rationalizes violence that arises from another source. Under what circumstances can "anger" or any other reason, motivation, or intention rationalize violence? Under what circumstances is violence not tolerated, for any reason, motivation, or intention?

Men prone to violence do not always act violently when they are angry. Did he "lose control" because he was drunk? Maybe he drinks and acts violently because of conditions related to how he was raised or neurological damage induced by a history of amphetamine abuse. Maybe he drinks, uses other illicit drugs, and beats women because he experiences no ill consequences when he does so.

He might experience no ill consequences merely because he has nothing to lose—no lost educational opportunity, no damaged career, and a woman who never leaves because she has no place to go and no one else to help.

Women who have no place to go may be isolated because their current experience replicated that of their mother, so it never occurred to them that life could be any different. They might be isolated because they never went past primary school or, if they did, could never get a good job. They might work for low wages as domestic help primarily because men get the good jobs, and men get those jobs because the people who run firms and create jobs give them only to other men, primarily to their closest friends and relatives.

The people who run firms and create jobs may give those jobs to their male friends and relatives because the regional economy functions as an oligopoly and the absence of competition means that job performance doesn't mean much. Why the region's economy functions this way at a particular time remains to be explained, of course. It may be sufficient to note that such practices create sharp gender inequalities. Inequalities of any kind may elicit violence because, as Lord Acton suggested, it is merely one of many tools the powerful can use to optimize resource access. Equality may elicit considerate behavior between people because resource access optimization demands it—equality between people forces them to treat each other well to achieve desired goals.

CONTEXTUALIZE WITH REGIONAL AND GLOBAL HISTORIES AND EVER-MORE-ENCOMPASSING GENERALIZATIONS

The preceding example shows that you automatically create an inexhaustible (and exhausting) line of questions when you think about research topics as sets of variables and explanations as relationships between one variable and another (or others). Behavior linked to a specific cultural construct thus may be viewed as a function of life history variables embedded in a historical flow of social interaction—embedded in turn in variables that define the global historical trajectory of our species as a whole. Specific social relationships, behavior, beliefs, and feelings may reflect constraints imposed on us by virtue of being living beings (see Barkow, Cosmides, and Tooby 1992).

Don't be content with data collection that only yields analyses that describe what people do and explain why by reference to inferred meanings and decisions. Search for variables that might explain the meanings and decisions you find. When you speak to farmers who use pesticides, they may explain that they can't stop because they'd lose their farms. Ask why that might be so. Consider the possibility that they are wrong. Farmers might in fact lose their farms if they stopped using pesticides but for many reasons unrelated to the cost-effectiveness of pesticide use. The farmer may not know how to grow crops any other way, or either may not know where to find or may not be able to get access to the necessary information. He or she may be so burdened by short-term debt that changing the mix of inputs may entail unacceptable levels of risk. The levels of risk may be unacceptable because "profit" calculation, which includes depreciation of equipment like tractors and barns, excludes the costs of groundwater pollution and depletion, soil loss due to erosion, and public health and research costs created by pesticide toxicity to living things other than crop "pests" and evolutionary processes that create pesticide-resistant pest strains. Reach for the larger temporal and macrolevel issues with questions like: Why might profit calculation exclude such costs?

Similarly, prostitutes may tell you they work in the business to make money. Prostitutes face considerable risks. Do they minimize their risks (if so, how)? Why do they take them? How does their income compare with that of people working at other jobs? What alternative job possibilities do prostitutes have to choose from—do they have any at all? Maybe they have few realistic options because they don't possess characteristics that grant access to resources in other ways—they may have no education but function as part of an economy that generally requires a high level of education for access to jobs that pay well, or they may have lost their families due to war, famine, or disease but function as part of an economy that grants access to other ways of making a living through family and kinship relations.

Search for additional temporal and macrolevel variables with questions like "What creates the demand for the services prostitutes sell?"—the sexual relationships and behavior that characterize noncommercial gender relations? How and under what circumstances does this demand vary over time and space? Similarly, if you want to evaluate a history of sexually transmitted diseases, don't just ask people if they ever had VD (Handwerker and Jones 1992). If you don't ask about specific disease labels (e.g., chlamydia), you may have people wrongly report they never had VD when they know they had chlamydia but don't think about it as a sexually transmitted disease. If you don't include labels that form part of indigenous knowledge (on St. Lucia, these would include leak and coolant; see Jones 1994), you contribute to an equivalent source of error. If you don't ask about characteristic symptoms (genital sores, vaginal or penile discharge), you will miss cases of people who had a sexually transmitted disease but never recognized it.

To understand more fully the differences between people who actively participate in the resurgence of Native American ceremonial and ritual and those who don't, ask questions bearing on the relationship between religion and identity. Religion is intensely personal, but religion also creates dramatic social movements. All religions provide their followers with guidelines for behavior; they may provide a formal structure that both identifies and integrates the members of a community. The social impact of a religion may stem from the distinctive cultural or ethnic identity it provides its membership. Christianity, along with the Ghost Dance among American Indians and Rastafarianism in Jamaica, arose with the aim of transforming the world. Many contemporary Christian sects, the Native American Church, and the world religion Buddhism aim at a more immediate objective—to create a total transformation of an individual, to help that person find a state of internal grace. Fundamentalist Islam, like early Christianity, the Ghost Dance, and early Rastafarianism, aims at world transformation. The antecedents of personal identities lie in earlier life history events. What early life history events might induce someone to seek one identity or another, to affiliate with fundamentalist Islam, the Ghost Dance, or Rastafarianism rather than the Native American Church, or Seventh Day Adventism, or to take part in a renewal of Native American ceremonial? To understand more fully the health effects of participation in Native American ceremonial and ritual, ask questions bearing on the relationship between religion and ritual, the signals that participation sends to other participants, and the hardwired emotional responses such signals may elicit (e.g., Sosis 1999).

Finally, and despite their importance, don't rest contented with historical explanations and don't confuse them with evidence. Historical explanations claim that an event at time t_0 leads to another event (or future events) at time $t_{1..k}$. For example, after World War II, Russians and Americans moved into the Arctic in increasingly greater numbers and assumed control over resources formerly used by natives; at the same time, the frequency of traumatic stress to native children from non-natives rose; later, native men began to die violently in greater and greater numbers, and native women began to experience elevated rates of depression. Evidence for these individual events or trends comes in the form of observations consistent with the individual statements.

But note that my arrangement of these events and trends in a temporal order doesn't constitute evidence that one led to the other. You can describe the events, but you can't evaluate the supposed relationship between events because each constitutes a unique phenomenon. To test something, you have to formulate an explanation as a generalization, which makes reference to classes of events and things. Evidence that one led to the other must come from theory and tested generalizations.

For example, you might make the general claim that people with power tend to inflict violence on people without power and observe that the Russians and Americans who moved into the Arctic constitute a specific regional and historical example of people who assumed power over others who were Arctic natives. If the general claim has merit, we should find evidence of increasing levels of violence directed at Arctic natives by Russian and American immigrants. One form of such ethnic violence consists merely of "hurtful words" directed at native children by non-natives. If, in addition, traumatic stress in childhood in the form of hurtful words increases the risk in later life of violent death and depression, we should find that people who experienced ethnic violence in childhood exhibit an elevated risk of violent death and depression later in life. We can test empirical generalizations like these. The following chapter provides an overview of how. The chapters that follow explain how to conduct research that integrates explicit tests of theory with ethnographic data on history and region.

USE ETHNOGRAPHY TO CORRECT YOUR MISTAKES

QE's Field Preparation Rule No. 1—All ways to think about the world of experience contain errors, but you have to start *somewhere*—follows from the definition of culture as the knowledge people use to live their lives and the way in which they do so. We individually create knowledge in our minds out of our past experience, we use knowledge to interpret sensory

input from the world of experience, and we use a variety of mental processes to alter both knowledge and behavior in ways that reflect variation
in sensory input. Because we find ourselves engaged in an unceasing process of interpreting sensory input and altering both knowledge and behavior in ways that reflect change in sensory input, culture changes as we
grow older and as we experience differences in the range and kinds of our
social interaction. These differences vary with internal processes of development and maturation, the time in human history when people live, the
region(s) in which life stories take place, and the details of the gender,
intergenerational, and intragroup relationships in which they take part.

Some things we do reflect the evolution of specific neural architectures
that respond in characteristic ways to cues embedded in the material properties of sensory input (Tooby and Cosmides 1992). But we respond to
these cues without being aware that we do so (Gazzaniga 1998, Bargh and
Chartrand 1999). To *understand* what and how we act and think, we have
to use our imaginations, and much of what people do also reflects the
evolution of intelligence. By "intelligence"—what Gazzaniga calls the
Interpreter—I refer to those mental processes that generate, by inference
(i.e., guessing), mental constructions—consciousness—as a means for
understanding the world of experience (e.g., Sternberg 1985, Handwerker
1989b).

Hence, our evolved central nervous system presents us with a central
dilemma: All human knowledge rests ultimately on labels to which we
assign specific definitions, but (1) we create definitions out of our past
experience, which, being limited and formed of memories and perceptions
that do not perfectly mirror the physical properties of things, may merely
constitute figments of our imagination; and (2) definitions can be proven
neither true nor false (definitions are true only by definition), only evaluated as more-or-less useful. Making those evaluations raises the question
of why we should think that a particular way of thinking about the world
of experience is not merely a figment of our imagination, that a label
defined in a particular way, that means used to distinguish one phenomenon from another (i.e., measurement), and that claimed relationships
between one phenomenon and any other(s) correspond with the world of
experience in some meaningful way.

In short, one essential quality of being human is that we cannot escape subjectivity. Research, like all other social activity, entails the construction of culture. At their simplest, explanations are labeled, defined concepts or sets of related concepts that answer questions about what you observe. Explanations thus constitute imaginary models about the things and processes that exist in the world of experience. The assumptions on which you base your understanding of the world, like mine, contain biases that mirror everything you have experienced and everything you have not experienced over the course of your life. Hence, your mental constructions, like mine, and like those of everyone you meet while you conduct research, consist, at least partly and perhaps largely, of *fantasy,* figments of your imagination. As Campbell (1970) pointed out, research thus consists of a search for ways to distinguish mental constructions that consist largely of fantasy from constructions that consist of less.

Burn into your consciousness that *all* explanations must contain concepts like these, even though they may be wrong. You have to start with an assumption before you can make observations that make sense. If you don't make sensible observations, you don't have anything to explain.

Note, too, that concepts like these constitute the building blocks of explanations. However you define "religion," "equality," "violence," or "entrepreneurship," all subsequent observation and analysis must make reference to the subject of study identified by the conceptual definition. The parts of an explanation that identify variables tell us not only what exists but also how they vary. For example, a child may be abused or he may not be. A husband and wife may interact on the basis of equality or not. Some children may be more abused than others, and some couples may display more violent interaction than others. By implication, if you change the conceptual definition, you change all subsequent observation and analysis.

Don't make the mistake of thinking that your initial conceptual definition will dictate your findings, however. On the contrary, QE's basic research question is: How good is what I start with? Answer this question, and judge the validity of your data and findings by reference to whether or not, or the degree to which, specific mental constructions correspond with specific observations.

Don't forget that the elaborate suppositions you've built about what you will look at in the field may bear no relation to what you find once you arrive. So, don't panic. Be flexible. Change your initial conceptual definition in light of new information. Your best assumption is that your initial conceptual definition is not the best possible definition. Critically analyze it as you collect data. Go out of your way to look for information that might invalidate it. Anticipate being able to think about old subjects in new ways. New assumptions imply new variable definitions. New definitions improve our explanations because they point to dimensions in the world of experience we did not see before. They tell us to measure variables differently and to look for connections we never before suspected. You will open up whole new realms of research and analysis to find the limitations on the new set of assumptions.

Recognizing that all you may have done is to create an elaborate figment of your imagination, however, does not vitiate your obligation to begin, somewhere. QE tells you to assume error. Deal with it in the field when you will have access to corrective information. In the meanwhile, *choose.* Do *something.* And do it *now!*

3

Management Begins *Now!*

QE's Field Preparation Rule No. 2 states:

Murphy's Law understates the facts; it *will* go wrong even when it *can't*.

Management has to begin before you get to the field if you want to improve fieldwork productivity. Confusion inheres in doing good fieldwork. It requires you to select and complete an extraordinary number of tasks—and to coordinate each task with all the others. One set of inefficiencies in ordinary ethnography comes from the lack of a clear vision of where you are going. Focus variables provide you with that vision.

A second set of inefficiencies comes from the lack of a clear vision of how you might best get there. To create a clear vision of how to get to where you need to go, identify the ends you need to reach to complete your project. Then select the appropriate research tools for each end. Integrating the two creates a research design that addresses the two questions at the heart of all research:

- Did I get it right? (internal validity)
- To whom, if anyone, can I generalize? (external validity)

A third set of inefficiencies comes from getting lost along the way. *Iterative* data collection distinguishes good ethnography from bad. Collect some data, analyze it, and use your new understanding to help you choose what data next needs collecting. Design each observation and question to test at least one part of your theoretical understanding. Note errors. Ask for clarification. Rethink the theory. Link microlevel observations and interviews with historical records and macrolevel trends that only time-series data can reveal. Try again. As you do, your fieldwork tasks will acquire complex linkages. Minimize your chances of getting lost by using detailed Gantt charts and PERT (Program Evaluation Review Technique) charts to coordinate the necessary iterations efficiently.

ORGANIZE WITH FOCUS VARIABLES

Identify the ends you need to reach by organizing data collection tasks according to your project's focus variables. Once you identify a set of data collection tasks, go get the data, analyze it, and move to the next task! Don't confuse yourself by organizing your project into a long list of tasks. You won't be able to keep track of more than about five at a time. If you try for more, you only achieve a dramatic increase in the chances of losing track of what you are doing and how it fits into your overall project goals.

For example, figures 3.1, 3.2, and 3.3 show partial organization charts that illustrate, respectively, ways to organize studies of prostitution and entrepreneurship, stress and the health of Native Americans, and a needs assessment for an elderly population. Prostitution taken to be a form of entrepreneurship tells you to focus on (1) how prostitutes initiate firms, (2) how they run them, (3) how and under what conditions prostitute firms change (expand, contract, or cease business), (4) the identities they construct and how those identities influence each other and shape social relationships of different kinds, and (5) how their working identity (as an "entrepreneur"?) may influence how they run their businesses. In figure 3.1, the central variables (1, 2, and 3) yield a description of "de fas life" (as people called it in Barbados). Project components (4, 5) bearing on identity issues come up in each of the three central components: starting a firm, conducting business, and changing business operations. To contextualize a study of prostitution and entrepreneurship entails complementary studies of gender relations, sexuality and sexual behavior, the health-care system, and so forth. Make context variables separate realms of inquiry and organize each into appropriate subsidiary focus variables.

Figure 3.2 organizes the project components for a study of stress and health among Native Americans: (1) morbidity and mortality indices, (2) ceremonial and ritual, (3) participants and the duration and character of

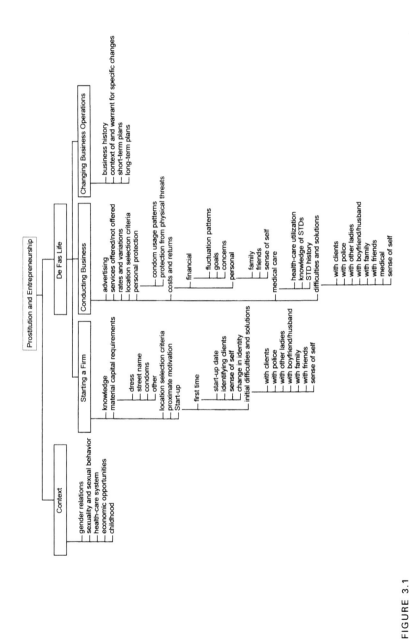

FIGURE 3.1
Prostitution and Entrepreneurship in Barbados

their participation, (4) nonparticipants, and (5) stressors and social supports and both cohort and historical change in their character and intensity. The ethnographic component of a study that looks at the hypothesis that *cases* exist of people who, for up to thirty years, may have experienced improved health from the social integration provided by their participation in community ritual and *controls* of people who may have experienced poor health because they did not consists of three components: (1) community ceremonial and ritual, (2) historical and cross-sectional variation in morbidity and mortality, and (3) stressors and social supports. The first task in data collection for the community ceremonial and ritual component requires that you document the various kinds of ceremonial and ritual, their historical disappearance and resurgence, and the emergence of new forms of community ceremonial and ritual. For each, characterize the participants and, for each, the character and history of their participation, including how their participation shapes their identity and sense of self. Which rituals are practiced, by whom, and how often? How do contemporary rituals and participants differ from those of the past? Have new ritual configurations appeared? How is the emergence of new interest in traditional rituals tied to population movements, the dissemination of information technologies, or changing political and economic relationships among social groups in specific regions? Study of stressors and social supports requires that you examine both cohort and historical change in both structural and day-to-day interaction sources of stressors and social supports. Local manifestations of stress, stressors, and social support and their continuing evolution reflect growth in the world economy, ongoing structural change in its components, and revolutionary changes in social relations and modes of interaction among populations that, themselves, experience ongoing social change and cultural evolution.

To properly contextualize a study of stress may entail a study of global changes stemming from the industrial revolution two centuries earlier. Growth in the world economy spurred by the industrial revolution was marked by increasing numbers of resource access channels. Large numbers of resource access channels imply high levels of competition. High levels of both international and regional competition give selective advantages to technical skills and competencies and reduce power differentials between gatekeepers and resource seekers. Gender, skin color, and ethnicity have become less important determinants of social position. We shall look back at this time in history, I suspect, and see a transition from sharply stratified to more egalitarian global and regional relationships, despite the complexities of the leveling process and exceptions at specific times and places. This specific study looks at parts of the leveling process.

Figure 3.3 organizes a needs assessment for an aging population with information on five variables: (1) activities of living, (2) functional skills and disabilities, (3) personal resources, (4) community services and resources, and (5) knowledge and use of community services and resources. Frame research on variable 4 to provide information on the set of assumptions from which existing services and resources follow as a logical consequence. Research findings on variables 1, 2, 3, and 5 provide evidence bearing on the assumptions that rationalize existing services and resources and may point to assumptions that do not now guide the provision of community services and resources. Once you identify living activities, which may vary dramatically regionally and with age and other social identities, you can identify the functional skills necessary to carry out those activities, as well as how you might best measure functional skills and disabilities. This information provides a foundation for knowing which personal resources might bear on living activities and functional skill limitations and which community services and resources fit with these needs (and that now don't exist). For example, information on rates of functional disabilities of specific kinds suggest specific gaps in the provision of primary or tertiary care. How should primary care providers change how they assess and treat mood disorders? How many new hospital beds will be called for to meet the expected demand for patients with diabetes or its complications? Information on variation in knowledge and use provides your foundation for recommendations bearing on how to improve existing service delivery, as well as how new services can most effectively be integrated into a restructured system designed to serve a growing elderly population. If service delivery assumes the primacy of government polyclinics but patients prefer home remedies and private physicians, what change in existing service delivery meets these needs?

A needs assessment for the elderly is properly contextualized by pointing out that this population and these needs reflect broader health transition phenomena. Fertility transitions began about one hundred years after

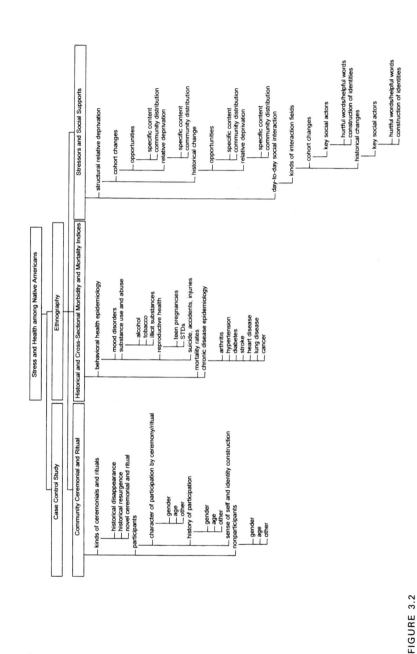

FIGURE 3.2
Stress and Health among Native Americans

England's industrial revolution. Today, below-replacement fertility characterizes North America and much of Eurasia. Below-replacement fertility
also dramatically changes the social landscape. For example, teen pregnancies become a social issue despite the fact that fertility at ages fifteen to
nineteen almost always is lower after below-replacement fertility than it
was before. Populations no longer grow without migration, and immigrants can more rapidly change the composition of a society, threatening
entrenched political and economic interests. The proportion of elderly
grows, which changes the composition of the labor force, consumer interests and spending habits, and the health care needs of a society. Whether
or not you put such a historical contextualization in depends on your con-
tractual obligations and the wishes of the contracting organization.

SELECT DIFFERENT METHODS FOR DIFFERENT GOALS

For purposes of ethnographic research, *culture* refers to the systems of
mental constructions that people use to interpret and respond to the
world of experience and to behavior isomorphic with those systems of
meaning. More specifically, culture consists of three phenomena:

- Labels, names, which identify the existence of distinct configurations of
  phenomenal experience;
- Definitions, which, however ambiguous in specific cases, differentiate
  one thing from another; and
- Intellectual and emotional associations, which give mental constructions
  distinctive meaning.

Remember: (1) the culture that specific people use to live their lives
constitutes an evolving configuration of cognition, emotion, and behavior
unique to themselves, and (2) *a* culture consists of an evolving configuration of cognition, emotion, and behavior at the intersection of individually unique cultural sets. The central problem for ethnography thus consists of identifying and describing that intersection (or *those intersections*).
To do so, you must accurately identify, describe, and characterize:

- variables (Xs and Ys, the labels that identify the components of cultures,
  the criteria that distinguish one from another, and the intellectual and

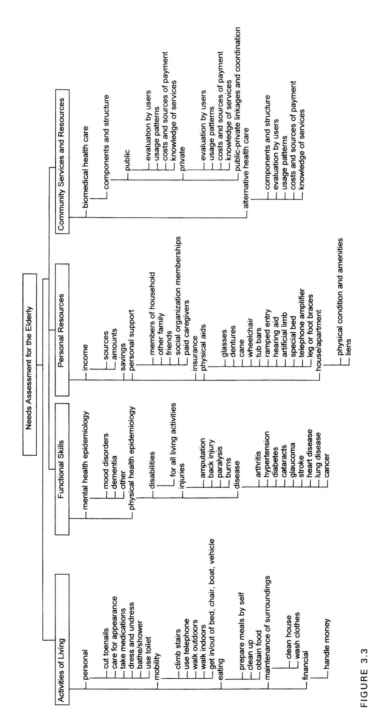

FIGURE 3.3

Needs Assessment for the Elderly

emotional associations that give specific components their meaning), and

- relationships between and among variables (the intersections among individually unique cultural sets and the life experiences that create, maintain, and change them).

Make your first priority the collection of text data from informal and semistructured observations and interviews. Then introduce rigor. Use findings from your analysis of text to formulate structured interviews to nail down key comparisons. Use these comparisons to establish the construct validity of key multidimensional variables, like the culture or cultures you study. Then examine and try to explain intracultural and intercultural variation. Employ the principles of experimental design (see further on, "Introduce Rigor"). A *Posttest Only Control Group Design* ordinarily suffices. The Posttest-Only Control Group Design works like this:

1. Randomly assign people to two groups, a control group and an experimental group.
2. Introduce a specific event or experience to the people in the experimental group.
3. Measure the variable of interest for all people and evaluate whether or not people in the experimental group give different answers or act differently than people in the control group.

Random assignment of study participants guarantees that the control and experimental groups differ only by chance prior to the introduction of the event or experience that may produce differences between the groups. Random assignment makes it a true *experimental* design, but random assignment rarely fits well into ethnographic research. Use a quasi-experimental variant—substitute explicit measurements of internal validity confounds for randomization.

Your First Priority

Text data collected through informal and semistructured observations and interviews give you insight into the assumptions that your informants use to understand and respond to the world of experience, the components of that world, and how those components are organized to form social and behavioral ecosystems. Answers require effective participant-observation. But participant-observation is not itself a method of collecting data. Participant-observation consists of many kinds of data collection tools, each of which achieves specific ends (e.g., DeWalt and DeWalt 1998). Create multiple lines of evidence to assess the construct validity of your findings by using a variety of informants, different methods of data collection and analysis, and different questions bearing on the same issue.

Use informal conversations (which will range from chaotic to reasonably controlled interchanges) to create and build personal relationships. In the process, you will learn how informants feel, think about the world, make decisions, act, see new alternatives (or not), and identify and evaluate the pragmatic and moral dimensions of relationships, behavior, knowledge, feelings, and options. Informal interviews make ideal circumstances for asking informants to free-list components of specific cultural domains. This highly flexible interview format lends itself to highly personal one-on-one interviews, as well as it does to focus groups. It also yields the best data on the key social relations and social actors in a person's life. Observation makes it possible for you to evaluate what people claim that they and other people believe, feel, and do; to discover what they may know but take for granted; and to provide data for an independent evaluation of what people do or say they do (Johnson and Sackett 1998). Explicit apprenticeships allow quick cultural immersion.

Identify life history events and processes that people find significant, as well as the nature of their significance. Collect documents, written by informants, elicited by you or not (e.g., letters), or assembled by governments or other organizations. Supplement these materials with person- or family-centered case studies, which make great stories that personalize and highlight key findings (e.g., Levy and Hollan 1998). Use semistructured interviews, carried out face-to-face or in focus groups, to discern the range of variation in perceptions, feelings, and understandings about experiences of various kinds.

But All Data Contain Errors

The *constructs* you use to formulate questions and behavioral observations will contain errors, and the *observations* you make of informant responses and behavior will embody two sources of error. The first kind of error—*measurement error*—comes from the means by which you transform sensory information into intelligible mental constructions (text or numbers or both). The second kind of error consists of either random (*sampling error*) or systematic (*selection bias*) error implicit in the subset of all possible times, places, and people, at which you actually make your observations. To assure high levels of internal and external validity, create multiple lines of evidence bearing on each dimension of your project. Avoid or eliminate the measurement error and selection biases you can identify, and randomize what remains.

Construct error is built into the assumptions you must make to begin and carry out research. Your assumptions contain biases that mirror everything you have experienced and everything you have not experienced over the course of your life. Hence, your mental constructions consist, at least partly and perhaps largely, of *fantasy,* figments of your imagination. To distinguish mental constructions that consist largely of fantasy from constructions that consist of less—in Campbell's (1970) words, to distinguish between what's there and what you put there—aim to construct a matrix consisting of data measured in many different ways for each variable and each relationship between or among variables. Think of *validity* as a relationship between the definitions of specific mental constructions and your observations. Assess data and finding validity with reference to whether or not, or the degree to which, specific mental constructions correspond with specific observations and discriminate those observations from others.

Box 3.1 lists some common sources of measurement error in ethnographic data. Before you can avoid or eliminate error, you have to see it. Make sources of measurement error part of your consciousness and take them into all interview and observation situations. Listen actively. Intersperse silent probes with both verbal ("yes!") and nonverbal (smiles, questioning expressions) forms of encouragement and acknowledgment. Ask your informants to elaborate with examples from both past and present circumstances. Ask for clarification. Summarize your understanding and ask if you got it right. Check regularly with your informant, and cross-check for variability between informants.

Don't assume that you speak the same language as your informant, *par-*

Box 3.1   Common Sources of Measurement Error

Reactivity
  ■ Informant-investigator (status, gender, race, ethnicity)
  ■ Context (e.g., public, private)

Questions
  ■ Ambiguity
  ■ Offensiveness
  ■ Biased phrasing
  ■ Make no sense to informants
  ■ Mean something different to different informants
  ■ Inaccurate translation

Interview format
  ■ Overly long
  ■ Confusing

Respondent
  ■ Disinterest
  ■ Fatigue
  ■ Lack of time
  ■ Etiquette, embarrassment
  ■ Traumatic topic or experience
  ■ Memory (bias, confusion, decay)
  ■ Threatened
  ■ Ignorance, lack of awareness or insight
  ■ No common reference standard among informants

Ethnographer
  ■ Perceptual biases and filters from prior experience
  ■ Memory (confusion, decay)
  ■ Perceptual errors of observation or recording of data
  ■ Electronic file coding errors
  ■ Absence of empathy, active engagement with informants
  ■ Failure to speak the same language

ticularly if you both speak English, Spanish, Russian, or Igbo. All speech reflects individually variable life experiences, as well as local and time-specific cultures. What warrant do you have for thinking that the meaning your informant attributes to a word or phrase matches yours? Anticipate getting your best data by appearing a little stupid.

Communicate empathy. Share personal experiences when appropriate. If you want to see what it looks like through another person's eyes, let that person see what it looks like through your eyes. Being open, making yourself vulnerable, elicits the same from others.

Internal validity confounds (box 3.2) apply to descriptive ethnography, as well as to laboratory experimental designs. *Instrumentation* constitutes a form of measurement error. As you gain experience in the field, you'll ask better questions. Fieldnotes taken at the beginning of your study won't be comparable to those taken later. Similarly, your informants will respond to you and your research activities. What they tell you and what they do will change in ways that reflect increasing knowledge of you and your project. These changes constitute *testing* artifacts. Usually, these forms of instrumentation and testing confounds help your study by yielding better and better data as your research progresses. But they may not. In either event, their presence warns you not to treat as comparable fieldnotes on a particular topic that come from different periods of research, even for six-week projects.

Other internal validity confounds complicate your attempt to interpret your data. Your fieldnotes will contain random error merely because you asked a specific informant a specific question at a specific time and place. People lie, sometimes reflexively rather than intentionally. People forget. People rationalize what they do. People do things for many reasons. People aren't aware of all, or even most, of the influences on what they do. People may be completely *unaware* of the most important influences on what they do, particularly when those influences are historical, macrolevel phenomena that can't be perceived clearly in the minutiae of day-to-day living. What they make conscious varies from one time and place to another. People misjudge the relative importance of their reasons, intentions, or motivations. They change their evaluations. The constantly changing context of fieldwork and social interaction brings into play all of these possibilities. They thus introduce random error into your measure-

---

Box 3.2   Internal Validity Confounds for Ethnography

Instrumentation confounds consist of intra- or intercultural variation that comes from differences in how you made your observations.

Diffusion confounds consist of intra- or intercultural variation that comes from communication among informants.

Testing confounds refer to intra- or intercultural variation in time-series data that comes from informant responses to your questions and observations.

Regression confounds consist of intra- or intercultural variation that comes from random fluctuations.

Mortality confounds consist of intra- or intercultural variation that comes from losing informants over the course of your study.

Maturation confounds consist of intra- or intercultural variation that comes from increasing age and experience.

History confounds consist of intra- or intercultural variation that comes from events and experiences other than the one(s) you look at.

Selection Bias confounds consist of intra- or intercultural variation that comes from excluding a nonrandom subset of informants.

---

ments. Repeated questioning or observation introduces *regression*. Pay attention to the *reliability* of your measurements. Low levels of reliability make it hard to see nuanced differences and confound the problem of distinguishing what's there from random error.

Increasing age and experience introduce *maturation* confounds. What an informant tells you at the beginning of your study may change at the end because that person has grown older and more experienced and has greater, or different, insight. Death or migration over the course of your study introduces *mortality* confounds. Everything that your informants experience over the course of your study, as well as everything your informants experienced earlier in their lives, introduces *history* confounds.

The socially constructed nature of cultural phenomena means that any one person who knows about a particular cultural phenomenon participates with other experts in its construction. In short, cultural phenomena inescapably embody *diffusion*—what statisticians call spatial and temporal autocorrelation. In seeking to understand people from the inside, looking out, aim to accurately characterize spatial and temporal autocorrelation, not correct for it. This poses a confound for explaining cultural variation, however, because intracultural or intercultural variation may merely reflect the structure and communication properties of social networks. The commonality in experience that leads to similarities and differences among informants may merely come from growing up in the same family or living in the same village. This form of the diffusion confound complicates interpretation when you try to explain intracultural or intercultural variation by reference to variables like "economic opportunities" or "ethnic violence." Its converse complicates interpretation when you document and describe intracultural or intercultural variation and confuse similarities that reflect "economic opportunities" or "ethnic violence" for similarities owing to growing up in the same family or living in the same village.

Introduce Rigor

Text data provide insight into the variables that compose cultures—how informants construct things like "families," "gender," and "age"; how they identify these things and discriminate one kind of thing from another; and how they identify, discriminate, and experience things like "power," "competition," and "cooperation." But even highly detailed case studies—of individuals, families, or communities—contain no comparisons and, hence, no evidence of relationships among variables or informants. Findings from hours and hours of an interview with a poor Native American woman don't warrant statements about identity formation at the intersection of ethnicity, class, and gender, for example. You must design comparisons into your study to assess relationships. Selected case studies of people who are both poor and rich, Native American and not, and women and men provide the necessary comparisons. But the expense of case studies compared to more focused data collection methods means that you can't collect enough to warrant generalization.

By virtue of the interview and observation formats through which you collect such data in the form of texts, however, every informant contributes a piece of the cultural puzzles, and none contributes to all of them. Informal and semistructured interviews, too, provide no basis for comparison among informants and give you only the barest hints about what's common and what's not, what's unusual and what's not. They leave you guessing about what goes with what. Ethnography rarely (e.g., Gil-White 2000) lends itself to the application of experimental designs that rule out internal validity confounds. You can't eliminate the internal validity confounds in your data until you measure them explicitly.

You can't even know if you have one or more cultures in your data, much less know where one ends and another begins. For any given domain of meaning and behavior, keep in mind that variation in your data may reflect four conditions:

- random variation around a single cognitive, emotional, or behavioral pattern that characterizes the domain or some aspect of it, which may be weak or strong;
- subpopulation differences in the strength of the pattern,
- two or more qualitatively different sets of meanings and behavior, which may differ little or constitute polar opposites; or
- no patterning in the domain or some aspect of it.

The first three conditions signal the presence of one or more *cultures*, specific configurations of cognition and emotion and isomorphic configurations of behavior generally shared among a set of people. The first condition indicates the absence of *cultural boundaries* (after Keesing 1994) within a given population and, thus, the existence of a single culture. The second condition identifies the existence of important forms of (intracultural) variation within that culture. The third condition identifies the existence of two or more cultures. The fourth condition signals the presence of individually unique configurations of cognition, emotion, and behavior. You can't look at the nuances of intercultural and intracultural variation without measuring them in a way that allows you to see them.

To help yourself distinguish constructions that exist nowhere outside your imagination from those that may exist in the world of experience, use *explicit* methods to identify the variable(s) that comprise the phenomenon you study. Explicitly *measure* each variable, explicitly assess *construct validity,* and explicitly measure the *effects* of your explanatory variable(s). This procedure helps you avoid covert tautologies, requires that you think out the implications of particular choices and, so, helps you find your more obvious mistakes and at least some of the more subtle ones. Think of data analysis as a process of discriminating sets of data with structure from sets of data with none. The more subtle the variation, the harder you will find it to distinguish structure from randomness. Explicit numerical analysis helps you see what you otherwise might miss.

Then, ask for help. You help the people who try to help you when you use explicit methods—it makes it easier for them to find your errors. Asking for help constitutes the *only* means available to escape the limitations of your own past experience—it gives you access to the experiences of other people. Draw on the expertise of people with very different life experiences, whom you will meet in the course of your research. Your initial data will help you correct mistakes you made before you arrived in the field. As you proceed in data collection and analysis, you will begin to think about old subjects in new ways. New assumptions imply new variable definitions. New definitions improve your explanations because they point to dimensions of the world you did not see before. They tell you to measure variables differently and to look for connections you never before suspected.

Use structured interviews (e.g., Weller 1998) to collect the data necessary for making comparisons among informants and, so, to address the analytical tasks of explicitly identifying cultures, cultural variation, and cultural change. Structured interview formats like yes/no—true/false questions elicit information on the properties of cultural domain items. Rating scales elicit information on their relative importance by one or another criterion. Pile sorts yield data on the relative similarity of domain items and so provide information about the structure of meaning and the organization of activities in particular cultural domains. Collect structured data in ways that allow for the historical (time series) and cross-sectional analyses you need to contextualize your cultural data with pertinent macro- and microlevel historical and regional antecedent experiences and events.

Explicit comparisons made with means, medians, proportions, or correlations identify differences between or among sets of informants. Explicit comparisons made with correlation coefficients or other measures of similarity or dissimilarity measure how strongly any two informants agree. Statistical tests tell you how often you can expect to find those differences or correlations merely by chance and thus provide a warrant for inferring that differences or relationships are *real,* not merely figments of your imagination. They can't provide a warrant for inferring that a relationship between culture and antecedent events and experiences is *determinant* until you can rule out internal validity confounds.

The classic means to solve this problem takes four steps:

1. Randomly assign people to two groups, a control group and an experimental group.
2. Measure the variable of interest for all people.
3. Introduce a specific event or experience to the people in the experimental group.
4. Remeasure the variable of interest for all people and evaluate whether or not people in the experimental group give different answers or act differently than people in the control group.

These steps yield what's called a *Pretest-Posttest Control Group* experimental design. Much intervention-outcome evaluation research employs a variant of the Pretest-Posttest Control Group design because it measures the variable of interest both before and after the people who take part experience the intervention. In the absence of randomization, this design becomes the quasi-experimental design called a Panel design. Posttest differences between the control and experimental groups reflect the effect of the intervention, assuming that both groups experience equivalent testing effects.

But Pretest-Posttest differences necessarily contain unmeasured testing artifacts that may or may not affect the outcome in the posttest measurements. In the absence of randomization, the usual state of affairs in evaluation research, Pretest-Posttest differences also contain regression effects (negative correlations with pretest scores). Variants of the *Solomon Four-*

Group Design solve this problem with an added set of experimental and control groups:

1. Randomly assign people to four groups, two control groups and two experimental groups.
2. Measure the variable of interest for the people in only one of the control groups and one of the experimental groups.
3. Introduce a specific event or experience to the people in both the experimental groups.
4. Remeasure the variable of interest for the people in only one of the control groups and one of the experimental groups.
5. Measure the variable of interest for the people in the second control group and the second experimental group.
6. Evaluate whether or not people in the experimental groups give different answers or act differently than people in the control group.

Thus, the Solomon Four-Group Design solves the problem of testing artifacts and regression by measuring differences between control and experimental groups selected independently and not subjected to pretest observations.

The latter constitutes the *Posttest-Only Control Group Design* mentioned earlier in this chapter:

1. Randomly assign people to two groups, a control group and an experimental group.
2. Introduce a specific event or experience to the people in the experimental group.
3. Measure the variable of interest for all people and evaluate whether or not people in the experimental group give different answers or act differently than people in the control group.

As in other forms of ethnographic research, the Posttest-Only Control Group Design achieves intervention-outcome research goals elegantly and with low costs. Random assignment to control and experimental groups assures comparable initial groups. In the absence of random assignment, rigorous matching on informant characteristics that correlate highly with posttest observations may achieve the same results, albeit usually at high cost. Cost-effective solutions usually employ explicit measurement of potential confounds and the application of appropriate forms of multivariate regression. Multiple regression models implement quasi-experimental time-series designs or cross-sectional designs equivalent to the Posttest Only Control Group experimental design. These research designs test for variation in life experiences that may account for intracultural and intercultural variation, controlling for internal validity confounds. If you're stuck with a Pretest-Posttest (Panel) design, include pretest scores as a separate independent variable in later analyses to control for regression effects (Markus 1979).

HOW TO FIND INFORMANTS
I found my best informants

- through colleagues,
- through Peace Corps Volunteer teachers,
- through a "women in development" job training and placement service,
- through a restaurant owner,
- through friends, and through friends or relatives of friends, and
- by striking up a conversation in a bar, in a taxi, at an airport, at a shop, and on the street corner.

Look for potential informants everywhere. Talk to anyone or everyone. You can't collect ethnographic data if you don't. And you won't begin your project until you do.

Sample Cultural Experts
Talk with the people who know about the topic you want to study—cultural experts and the people with whom they interact to construct their expertise (see Johnson 1990). If you want to know about farming, talk with farmers—and with the other people who make up farmers' key social relations: their parents, siblings, partners, children; their suppliers and their buyers; their friends; and others whose lives mesh with farmers', including farm workers, farm extension agents, bankers, tax assessors, and county planning commissioners. If you want to know about prostitution,

talk with prostitutes—and with the other people who make up prostitutes' key social relations: their parents, siblings, partners, children; their suppliers (if any) and clients; their friends; and others whose lives mesh with prostitutes, including the police. If you want to know about parental involvement in their children's education, talk with parents—and with the other people who make up key social relations for parents, including their own parents, their children, and teachers. If you want to know about stress among Native Americans, talk with Native Americans—and with the other people who constitute key actors in their lives, like bosses, co-workers, partners, children, parents, in-laws, and others.

For many realms of life, nearly everyone constitutes a cultural expert. All women constitute experts about being women; all men constitute experts about being men. Everyone living in the United States constitutes an expert on life in the United States. Of any group of cultural experts— men or women, old or young, poor or not, of whatever ethnic identity— whom should you select to interview and observe? Anyone willing to teach you what you need to know.

If your informants don't agree, you might wonder who's the expert. Here's the answer: *everyone is an expert in what he or she knows.*

When you begin your study, however, you can't know who knows what or who is a cultural expert at what. Remind yourself that people construct the way they look at the world by reflecting on events they experience at particular points in their lives and by working through the meaning of those events through specific interactions with specific people. Don't expect all farmers or all prostitutes, all women or all men to take the same point of view. At the beginning of your study, you're still looking in from the outside. People who look the same from an outsider's perspective— like farmers or prostitutes, women or men—may work with different, even conflicting, understandings about the topic you want to study. Pay close attention to cultural variation and seek out its sources.

Remember, too, that cultural differences reflect variation in internal processes of development and maturation, the time in human history when people live, the region(s) in which life stories take place, and the details of the gender, intergenerational, and intra- and intergroup relationships in which they take part. Search for concrete events and circumstances in people's lives that may shape the understandings they now work

---

Box 3.3   Protect Your Informants

Anticipate your responsibilities to the people who try to enlighten you, who give you their time and energy to help you complete your research (see Jorgensen 1971). The U.S. Department of Health and Human Services regulations exempt from formal Human Subjects regulation all research that meets the following criterion (among a set of six):

- research involving the use of survey, interview, or observation procedures in which information obtained is recorded in such a manner that human subjects cannot be identified, directly or through identifiers linked to the subjects.

To meet this criterion, precede all interviews with

- an explanation of the research goals,
- a request for an interview,
- an explanation that you want people to participate only if they feel they can do so openly and honestly; otherwise, to please tell you so you can end the interview or move to another question,
- an explanation that informants and survey respondents will be free to refuse the interview, to stop an interview, or to say that certain information they provided should not subsequently be reported,
- a request that informants and survey respondents feel free to ask any questions they want to at any time, and
- an assurance of anonymity.

Maintain anonymity. Don't record the names of people you interview. Go further. With informal and semistructured interviews, make sure you do not include codes that identify individuals uniquely in your written fieldnotes. With survey interviews, make sure that even the person who administers a particular interview cannot associate individual questionnaires with individual respondents. One simple solution is to ask survey respondents to fill out questionnaires either in your absence or in ways that you cannot know their answers. Then, ask respondents to seal completed questionnaires in unmarked envelopes. Finally, carry big bags that contain a minimum of six equivalent envelopes; ask respondents to mix their envelope with those already in the bag.

Some research designs require individual identifiers, of course. With the advent of voice analysis technologies, tape-recorded interviews contain their own unique identifiers. Consult the head of your Institutional Review Board for advice on informant protection whenever your research design or data collection tools will contain individual identifiers. But remember:

"Human Subjects Protection" too often takes the form of regulations and procedures designed to protect sponsoring organizations, not the people you ask to teach you. Outline procedures to protect the people who help you before you leave for the field. Once there, ask people you interview about their concerns. Change your procedures accordingly.

---

with. What people think and do must reflect not only their individual life histories but broader regional and global histories of people, events, and social interaction into which they were born and in which they grew up. So try to identify events, circumstances, and processes that provide one set of choices to some people and a different set of choices to others. Ask individuals to identify life experiences that were significant to them and to help you understand why those experiences were significant. In the process, keep track of life experience markers that people identify as important, as well as those that might be important.

Design sampling frames for cultural data in ways that encompass regionally and historically situated life experiences that may influence the patterns of social interaction through which people construct cultural phenomena. This strategy implements the explicit measurement of internal validity confounds that must accompany a Posttest Only Control Group design without randomization. *Maturation* confounds include age and the duration of any social event or process—like marriage, business, or ceremonial participation. *History* confounds include variables like gender, class, and ethnicity. A generic sampling frame appropriate for cross-sectional, descriptive research in many parts of the contemporary world might track the age of your respondents, their gender, class background, and ethnic (and other pertinent) identities. A fully nested sampling frame—one that allows you to look for differences in knowledge for each combination of life experience markers, like young Euro-American men from poor families or old Native American women from middle-class families—appears in table 3.1.

Don't count on these variables making a contribution to either intracultural or intercultural variation or cultural change—variables like economic opportunities at age twenty, migration, or family cohesion might exert far more important and interesting effects. Design informal and

TABLE 3.1 Generic Nested Sampling Frame for a Cross-Sectional Descriptive Study (EA = Euro-American, NA = Native American)

Gender	Men								Women							
Age	Young				Old				Young				Old			
Class	Poor		Not Poor		Poor		Not Poor		Poor		Not Poor		Poor		Not Poor	
Ethnicity	EA	NA	EA	NA	EA	NA	EA	NA	EA	NA	EA	NA	EA	NA	EA	NA
# of Interviews*	3–36	3–36	3–36	3–36	3–36	3–36	3–36	3–36	3–36	3–36	3–36	3–36	3–36	3–36	3–36	3–36

*Sample size depends on the average level of agreement among informants. See Weller (1997) or Weller and Romney (1986).

semistructured interviews to elicit information on the adequacy of the distinctions that you start with. Ask informants if they know people who think differently, and interview people who take different points of view. Actively search for sources of cultural difference. Change the criteria by which you select informants and the life experiences you measure to reflect knowledge you gain during the course of field research.

Demeaning remarks directed at, and restricted opportunities provided for, members of ethnic minorities (e.g., Native Americans) by members of a dominant ethnic majority constitute two forms of traumatic stress experienced in childhood that may exhibit dramatic effects on later behavior. Table 3.2 shows a fully nested sampling frame for a retrospective study of continuity and change in the meaning of social interaction between members of majority and minority ethnic groups. People in their sixties in 2000 can tell you what they remember about native–non-native interaction in the 1960s, when they were in their twenties. People in their forties in 2000 can tell you what they remember about native–non-native interaction in the 1980s, when they were in their twenties. People in their twenties in 2000 can tell you what they remember about native–non-native interaction at that historical period.

Table 3.3 shows a fully nested sampling frame for a case-control study, a design widely applicable to outcomes-evaluation research. Outcomes-evaluation research tests the efficacy of interventions designed to induce specific forms of cultural change. Judgments about the efficacy of interventions require information on whether or not or the degree to which people who started with one culture ended with another. Cultural differences between participants (cases) and nonparticipants (controls) that cannot be explained by other potential confounds, like gender and age, constitute evidence of a successful intervention.

TABLE 3.2   Generic Nested Sampling Frame for a Retrospective Study

Aged 20 in Historical Period	1960s		1980s		2000s	
Gender	Women	Men	Women	Men	Women	Men
Native—non-Native	N nN	N nN	N nN	N nN	N nN	N nN
# of Interviews*	3–36 3–36	3–36 3–36	3–36 3–36	3–36 3–36	3–36 3–36	3–36 3–36

*Sample size depends on the average level of agreement among informants. See Weller (1987) or Weller and Romney (1986).

TABLE 3.3   Nested Sampling Frame for a Case-Control Study

Intervention Gender	Cases				Controls			
	Women		Men		Women		Men	
Age	<20	>20	<20	>20	<20	>20	<20	>20
# of Interviews*	3–36	3–36	3–36	3–36	3–36	3–36	3–36	3–36

*Sample size depends on the average level of agreement among informants. See Weller (1987) or Weller and Romney (1986).

Samples Aren't Populations

The problem of external validity resolves into this—you *observe* samples, arrive at findings (e.g., analytical descriptions, or computed *statistics*), and *estimate* population parameters (see box 3.4). To whom, if anyone, can you generalize? To the population defined by the geographically and historically bounded set of life experiences you studied. Don't push your generalization into the future. Culture evolves. What you found may change next year or next month.

Internal validity confounds other than *maturation* and *history* don't make useful sampling criteria. They may produce intracultural and intercultural variation nonetheless. Posttest Only Control Group designs ordinarily eliminate *regression* and *mortality* confounds from your structured interview data. But the design you employ may contain both. Check. Test for *instrumentation* effects on the cultural variation you find by looking for the influence of different sources of data (e.g., interviews by different research assistants). Test for *diffusion* by looking for the influence of growing up in the same family, the same village, or the same region.

Pay close attention to your sampling criteria and the internal validity confounds you measure. *They determine to whom you can validly generalize.* The sample you actually select may allow generalization only to a population that differs considerably from the one you originally targeted (Berk 1983). For example, if you want to infer the different kinds of identity college students construct, a sample drawn from a large lecture session of Anthropology 100 excludes a large subset of informants. Do you have enough athletes or engineering or pharmacy majors? What about college seniors? International students? The absence of people with these life experiences introduces sample selection bias into your study. If you want to study prostitution and entrepreneurship, don't forget to interview *for-*

mer prostitutes about their business experiences—or point out the sample selection bias to your readers and amend your interpretation of findings accordingly.

Ask yourself how your chosen sampling method might unintentionally exclude an important subset of informants and how that exclusion may affect your findings. Health studies that draw clinic samples miss all the informants who don't attend the clinic in question or, more generally, don't seek care during the study. Cheltenham's (1992) study based on a clinic sample, for example, found that elderly Barbadians rarely used bush teas and home remedies. In a needs assessment for Barbados's elderly population, a national sample that included informants who did not necessarily attend clinics or seek care outside the home (Handwerker 1992) revealed that the use of bush teas and home remedies constituted a pervasive cultural pattern among elderly Barbadians. Forty percent of the Barbadians who used bush teas and home remedies *substituted* these alternative sources of health care for biomedical prescriptions. A clinic-based study of women's breast cancer and mammography concerns may help the clinic improve its service delivery to existing patients. But it misses women who don't have mammograms, so it can't give much insight into how the clinic can extend services to people who need them but don't currently use them.

When to Draw a Random Sample

The socially constructed nature of cultural phenomena means that any one person who knows about a particular cultural phenomenon participates with other experts in its construction. Cultural phenomena thus inescapably embody what statisticians call spatial and temporal autocorrelation. What one cultural participant does or tells you will correspond closely to what any other cultural participant does or tells you. The errors you make in predicting what one cultural participant will do or say will correspond closely to the errors you make predicting what any other cultural participant will do or say.

This conclusion means that a random sample of people does not constitute a random sample of culture. The culture of an individual consists of configurations of cognition, emotion, and behavior that intersect in multiple ways the culture or other individuals. Hence, random samples of

---

Box 3.4   The Basics of Sampling and Inference

1. Parameters and populations define each other. All the following constitute parameters and their associated populations, for example:
   - the *percentage* of students at a university who believe we need to
     preserve wilderness areas.
   - the *incidence* of child abuse in Barbados.
   - the *average* number of children born to women in England by age
     50.
   - the *degree* to which U.S. couples share child care and household
     responsibilities equally.
   - the *proportion* of women employed in the professions in the
     United States.
2. We identify parameters with Greek letters like β (beta), α (alpha),
   ϵ (epsilon), ϱ (rho), and σ (sigma),
3. Samples, by contrast, yield statistics, which we identify with Latin letters and words (like b, median, percentage, mean).
4. Each statistic constitutes a *point estimate* of a parameter—your single
   best guess about the value of the parameter.
5. Large samples estimate parameters very *precisely* because they contain little sampling error; small samples contain large amounts of sampling error because randomly selected extreme values exert greater
   effects.
6. Sample precision is measured by the size of *confidence intervals.* Confidence intervals contain the parameter a given proportion (ordinarily
   95 percent) of the time.
7. Statistical test findings apply to samples of all sizes because they incorporate into their results the degree of sampling error contained in samples of different sizes.
8. Statistics from both large and small samples thus estimate parameters
   equally accurately, but only if the sample from which they come is reasonably *unbiased.*
9. *Unbiased* samples are those in which all members of the population
   had an equal chance for sample inclusion.

individuals will yield a random sample of the intersecting configurations of cognition, emotion, and behavior (i.e., the cultures) in a population. But random samples (defined by case-independence) of cultural phenomena (which necessarily contain case-dependence) cannot exist: they constitute mutually exclusive alternatives. To understand people from the inside, looking out, aim to accurately characterize spatial and temporal autocorrelation, not correct for it. This is the point of sampling frames that encompass regionally and historically situated life experiences that may influence the patterns of social interaction through which people construct culture and that include explicitly measured internal validity confounds. In ethnography, randomly select informants (Kish 1965; see Bernard 2001) only when you want to estimate the frequency with which different cultures occur in a population.

When to Conduct a Power Analysis

Your attempt to trace intracultural or intercultural variation and change to specific antecedent life experiences depends on your ability to detect the influence of one variable on another, if the effect is real. So does your attempt to rule out the influence of specific internal validity confounds. *Powerful* research designs allow you to detect the real relationships between one variable and another confidently. An essential component of research design thus consists of an explicit evaluation of the power you might expect for different effects in samples of different sizes (Wilkinson et al. 1999; for details, see chapter 6). You will waste your time if you don't put in the effort to select a sample large enough to estimate parameters with the requisite precision.

HOW TO COORDINATE FIELDWORK ITERATIONS

Iterative data collection distinguishes good ethnography from bad. Design each observation and question to test at least one part of your theoretical understanding. Note errors. Ask for clarification. Rethink the theory. Link microlevel observations and interviews with historical records and macrolevel trends that only time-series data can reveal. Try again.

As you do so, your fieldwork tasks will acquire complex linkages. For example, you *must* complete some fieldwork tasks before others can start—you have to select a specific fieldsite before detailed data collection can begin; you have to know where to contact potential research assistants before you can build a research team. Many fieldwork tasks require that one begins before another or that one can't be completed until another begins. For example, don't expect to conduct a good domain analysis until you are well into the process of collecting data through semistructured interviews of various kinds. If you attempt to put together questionnaires or question schedules to test hypotheses bearing on variation in life experiences before the collection of cultural data is well underway, you guarantee that they will contain major design flaws that "pretests" will not uncover.

Moreover, good iterative data collection requires that your task schedule contain explicit feedback loops at specific points in time. For example, if you assemble and analyze an aggregated time series at the end of your field research or after you return, you may discover important historical events and processes that you neglected to ask about. Assemble and analyze aggregated data at the beginning of your field research. Use that information to select informants, design sampling frames, and pursue lines of inquiry that might never have emerged otherwise. Similarly, selecting a research site and building a research team requires input from primary informal interviews and observations, but informal interviews and observations continue alongside these tasks.

So does reflection on where you've come from and where you still need to go. Periods of reflection, together with informal interviews and observations, will provide the key pieces of information that allow you to move from one research task to another—and back again. Max Gluckman (1963) pointed out the significance and the importance of your informants granting you access to gossip. Your most valuable insights will likely come from informal interviews in which your informants gossip freely, albeit subject to some direction on your part—an interview format I call *controlled gossip*. Periods of reflection and planning make ideal times for controlled gossip interviews, and I distinguish key periods of reflection, planning, and further cultural data collection by talking about "First Order Gossip," "Second Order Gossip," "Third Order Gossip," and so forth. A 90-day, 12-week project should contain at least 6 distinct periods of reflection, planning, and further cultural data collection. A 30-day, 4-

week project should contain at least 3 such periods and would benefit significantly from 6.

Creating a clear vision of where you want to go and how to get there thus does not mean you won't get lost along the way. Minimize your chances of getting lost by using detailed Gantt charts and PERT (Program Evaluation Review Technique) charts to coordinate the necessary iterations efficiently.

Figure 3.4, for example, shows a Gantt chart included in chapter 1, which organizes data collection tasks for a 90-day summer field project (June, July, and August) into three components: (1) Building a Foundation, (2) Building Your Data Base, and (3) Fine-Tuning Your Findings. Note the component overlap. Begin "Building a Foundation" the moment you arrive and complete this task by the end of your third week in the field. Begin "Building your Data Base" during your second week in the field and complete this component *at least* two weeks before you leave. Begin "Fine-Tuning Your Findings" just after the midway point in "Building Your Data Base." Finish the day you leave. Create Gantt charts for each research component (e.g., see figures 4.1, 5.1, and 8.1). Use PERT charts (e.g., figure 8.2) to remind yourself of key data collection iterations. Shorter (4- and 6-week) field projects call for design modifications, such as the 30-day, 4-week project shown in figure 3.5. *Don't* alter the basic components, and *don't* alter the placement of feedback loops and periods of reflection, planning, and further cultural data collection. Instead, use more focused research questions about cultural phenomena. If you absolutely must collect data for parameter estimation for life experience variables, draw smaller samples.

Three-day projects call for a more specialized approach, which you'll find in chapter 10.

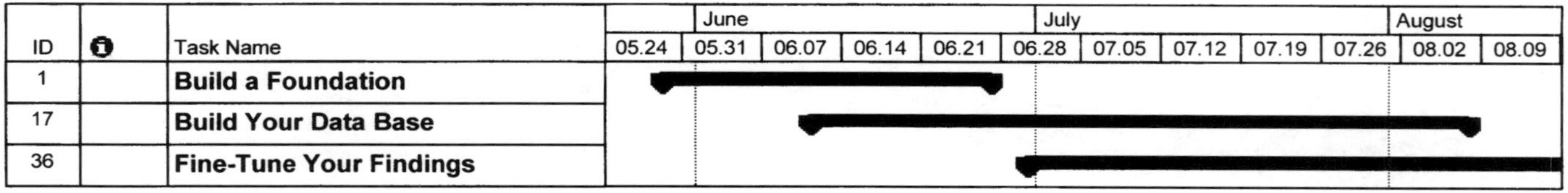

ID	🕐	Task Name	June					July				August		
			05.24	05.31	06.07	06.14	06.21	06.28	07.05	07.12	07.19	07.26	08.02	08.09
1		**Build a Foundation**												
17		**Build Your Data Base**												
36		**Fine-Tune Your Findings**												

FIGURE 3.4
Gantt Chart for a 90-Day Project

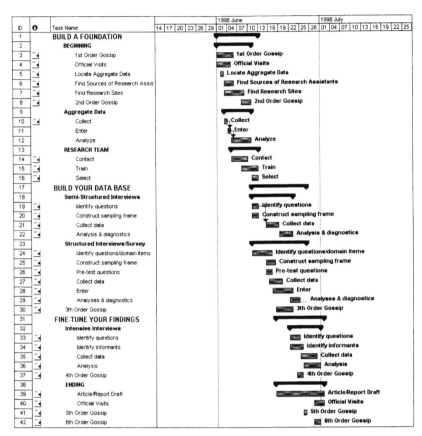

FIGURE 3.5
Gantt Chart for a 30-Day Project

4

How to Build a Foundation

Build the foundation for a 90-day (3-month) project by completing 3 major tasks within your first 3 weeks in the field (see figure 4.1, which focuses on this part of your project): (1) beginning tasks, (2) aggregated data collection, and (3) research team assembly (see chapter 9). Initiate informal and unstructured observations and interviews the moment you arrive. Take notes about *everything*. Allow plenty of time for write-up and analysis of interview and observational data—perhaps three to four hours of write-up for every hour spent talking and observing. Do initial write-ups immediately. Don't move directly from one talking and observation session to the next. Indeed, don't conduct more than three intensive ethnographic interviews per day. If you do, you won't have enough time for reflection and write-up. Feel free to talk about any subject that arises. Better, and if possible, engage in controlled gossip interviews. Keep your project goals in mind. Sit around (or stand around or lie around, as the case may be) and look around you and talk with people you meet. But look for ways to learn something about your focus variables. Exert some control over the subjects of conversation and observation.

USE INFORMAL INTERVIEWS TO INTRODUCE, EXPLORE, AND CONFIRM

> Get an informant onto a topic of interest and get out of the way.
>
> Russ Bernard, 2001

Text data collected through informal and semistructured observations and interviews give you insight into the assumptions that your informants

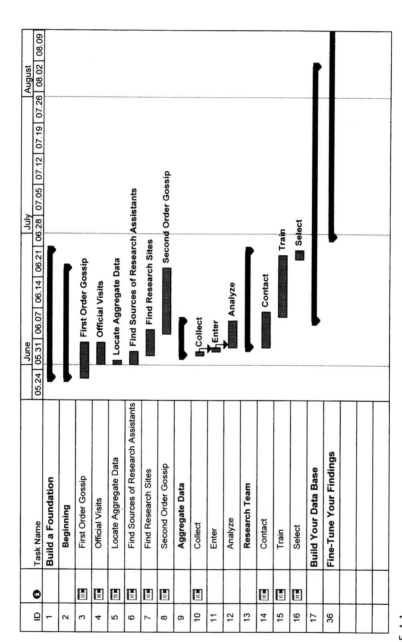

FIGURE 4.1
Building a Foundation

use to understand and respond to the world of experience, the components of that world, and how those components are organized to form
social and behavioral ecosystems. Of the two kinds of interview formats,
the first is by far the most important. Informal interviews range from
casual conversation about anything and everything from the weather to
the purpose of life, to what I characterize as *controlled gossip*. Look to controlled gossip to yield your best data and most important insights. You
must interact intensively and create personal relationships with the people
you want to understand. Spending time getting to know someone opens
the only door available for you to learn what that person sees and what it
means when he or she looks out at the world. This calls for the personal
sensitivity and creativity to allow people to feel comfortable with you, to
communicate clearly to people whom you ask for assistance that you are
nonthreatening.

Being a good listener helps. This means to listen *actively*. Intersperse
silent probes with both verbal ("yes!") and nonverbal (smiles, questioning
expressions) forms of encouragement and acknowledgment. Ask your
informants to elaborate with examples from both past and present circumstances. Ask for clarification. Summarize your understanding and ask
if you got it right. Check regularly with your informant, and cross-check
for variability between informants. To repeat: Don't assume that you
speak the same language as your informant, *particularly* if you both speak
French, English, Chinese, or Swahili. All speech reflects individually variable life experiences, as well as local and time-specific cultures. What warrant do you have for thinking that the meaning your informant attributes
to a word or phrase matches yours? Anticipate getting your best data by
appearing a little stupid.

Sharing yourself helps even more and provides the most reliable access
to the gossip through which much cultural sharing and evolution take
place (see Gluckman 1963). Communicate empathy. Share personal experiences when appropriate. If you want to see what it looks like through
another person's eyes, let that person see what it looks like through your
eyes. Being open, making yourself vulnerable, will elicit the same from
others.

To prepare for controlled gossip interviews, write out your guesses
about what cultural domains make up your study phenomenon and their

constituent variables. To collect information necessary for understanding how people create, maintain, and change meaning as they interact with other people, design your initial interviews to elicit information on the key social actors in the lives of the people on which your project focuses (e.g., "prostitutes," "clients"). Use subsequent interviews and observations to elicit information about the similarities and differences among these relationships and how the relationships are experienced both by the focus person and each kind of social actor. The result will yield a description of the key components of the social ecosystem in which people live their lives.

Begin with what James Spradley (1969) called Grand Tour questions. For example, to begin a study of stress among Native Americans, ask informants to tell you about a typical day, from beginning to end. Make a list of the events, activities, locations, and participants. Identify participants by pertinent social labels. Ethnicity, gender, and age make good starting points, but make sure you find out if and how your informants find these labels pertinent. Ask about others you should know about, like boss, neighbor, friend, husband, daughter, and stranger. Ask how this typical day changes over the course of the week, month, and year. Ask about wonderful days, weeks, and months. Ask about disastrous days, weeks, and months. Ask about particularly wonderful events, activities, and interactions and about particularly traumatic events, activities, and interactions. Make sure you record specific details, including words, behavior, and social actors. Clearly identify the criteria people use to discriminate wonderful from disastrous. Fill in the gradations between the two. Once you can paint a picture of one person's life, actively search for variation so your picture includes, at least in broad outlines, the complexity found in your study community. While you paint your word picture, add details from your observations of specific events, activities, locations, and participants. Ask how what you see compares to what you hear. Where are the discrepancies? What do *those* discrepancies tell you? Make sure you talk to both interaction participants (or all, depending on the character of particular events and activities).

In a study of prostitution, ask informants (prostitutes, clients, and others) to list all the different kinds of sales they know about. Ask where the sales are made, where the services are performed, what exactly is sold, what different services cost, how fees are decided, how long services take, who the participants may include, the risks involved, and what they do to minimize the risk. Ask about concrete instances and examples. Visit sales locations. Ask to sit or stand with the seller. Ask the seller to describe what happens (more or less) when it happens. How do sellers' reports compare with what you see? Similarly, ask clients where they make purchases, what they purchase, where services are made, how much it costs, how costs are decided, how long it takes, who the participants may include, the risks involved, and what they do to minimize the risk. Accompany clients and ask them to describe what happens (more or less) when it happens. How do their reports compare with what you see?

Ask prostitute informants to talk about what kinds of activities they engage in and what kinds of relationships they have in their lives and who is significant to them (such as "husbands," "boyfriends," "girlfriends," "children," "friends," "clients"—who else?). What differences do prostitutes see between what they do to earn money and other kinds of activities? What do these different kinds of activities have in common? Do prostitutes see some kinds of relationships as restricted to a single field of activities (e.g., "clients")? What kinds of relationships extend to different kinds of activities? As the context changes from one activity to another, do prostitutes express differences in the meanings of particular activities or relationships? Within each kind of activity, as if different kinds of relationships of particular kinds exist? For example, do prostitutes distinguish between different kinds of clients or different kinds of professional colleagues? What makes one different from the others? How are they all alike?

To place prostitution within the broader context of gender relations and sexuality, ask equivalent questions directed toward noncommercial relationships. For example, ask women to talk about the various kinds of relationships they form. Ask for each who is significant to them (such as "husbands," "boyfriends," "children," "friends," or "lovers" (men or women?), how that person is significant, and why. What makes one kind different from the others? How are they all alike?

To understand *meaning,* elicit information on the intellectual and emotional associations that specific (labeled) understandings, feelings, actions, events, processes, and identities evoke in the person or people you interview. The phenomenal elements that constitute these associations and the relationships among those elements constitute the basis by which people interpret and respond to themselves, the people with whom they interact, and the events and processes in which they take part. To study the social construction of meaning, be careful to elicit information about how inter- actions are experienced by *both* the focus person and each kind of social actor.

For example, *for each kind of relationship that defines the social ecosystem of a particular person:* Ask your informants how they experience specific activities and forms of interaction and what that social relationship and those experiences mean for these women's sense of who they are; and ask them what makes the experience of these different relationships different from one another. If you study identity and prostitution-as-entrepreneur- ship, ask informants what they do as "work" and what they do as partners, mothers, daughters and daughters-in-law, co-workers, and friends, for example. What does their work mean to them? What do their relation- ships as partners, mothers, daughters and daughters-in-law, co-workers, and friends mean to them? How clear is the boundary between work and other important activities and relationships? Indeed, is there a boundary? If so, what is it, exactly, and how do they know it? What ambiguities exist? In what contexts or social relationships does the boundary shift location or definition? What does interaction based on different definitions and/or boundaries between "work" and "nonwork" mean to these women's sense of who they are? Finally, ask each woman to talk about what she believes different kinds of social actors believe about her, about how her feelings about herself correspond or conflict with her understanding about how others see her, and about how she experiences that correspondence or conflict.

Conversely, ask the clients of your informants to explain the different kinds of relationships they have with service providers. What kinds of rela- tionships are there? What makes one kind different from the others? How are they all alike? *For each kind of relationship:* Ask them how they experi- ence their work and what that social relationship and those experiences mean for clients' sense of who they are. *For each client:* Ask him to talk about the activities involved in being a "client" and the activities involved in being a "boyfriend/husband." What do his activities as a "client" mean to him? What does his relationship as a boyfriend or husband mean to him? How clear is the boundary between client and being a boyfriend/ husband? What is the boundary, exactly, and how does he know it? What ambiguities are there? In what contexts or social relationships does the boundary shift location or definition? What does interaction based on different definitions and/or boundaries between "client" and "boyfriend/ husband" mean to these men's sense of who they are? Also, ask each client to talk about what he believes his wife/girlfriend and service providers believe about him, about how his feelings about himself correspond or conflict with his understanding about how these others see him and how he experiences that correspondence or conflict.

In a study of stress among Native Americans, ask equivalent questions of partners, parents, in-laws, co-workers, and bosses. Ask informants what they do as Indians and what they do as partners, fathers, daughters and sons-in-law, co-workers, and friends, for example. What does Indian mean to them? What do their relationships as partners, mothers, daughters and daughters-in-law, co-workers, and friends mean to them? How clear is the boundary between Indian and other important activities and relationships? Indeed, is there a boundary? If so, what is it, exactly, and how do they know it? What ambiguities exist? In what contexts or social relationships does the boundary shift location or definition? What does interaction based on different definitions and/or boundaries between Indian and non-Indian mean to their sense of who they are? Finally, ask the informants to talk about what they believe different kinds of social actors believe about them, about how their feelings about themselves correspond or conflict with their understandings about how others see them, and about how they experience that correspondence or conflict.

Conversely, ask non-Indians who interact with your informants to explain the different kinds of relationships they have with Indians. What kinds of relationships are there? What makes one kind different from the others? How are they all alike? *For each kind of relationship:* Ask them how they experience that relationship and what that social relationship and those experiences mean for their sense of who they are. *For non-Indians:* Ask them to talk about the activities that distinguish themselves from Indians and what those activities mean to them. How clearly do they see the boundary between Indian and non-Indian? What is the boundary, exactly, and how do they know it? What ambiguities are there? In what

contexts or social relationships does the boundary shift location or definition? What does interaction based on different definitions and/or boundaries between Indian and non-Indian mean to their sense of who they are?
Also, ask the clients to talk about what they believe Indians believe about
them, about how their feelings about themselves correspond or conflict
with their understanding about how these others see them, and how they
experience that correspondence or conflict.

Place data from interviews like these within an encompassing regional
and historical context. To place stress among Native Americans within the
broader context of their lives, ask informants to tell you how things were
different at earlier points in their lives. What changes did they experience
at what points in their lives? For each, fill out the details of these life histories. Ask them to describe typical days and how these changed over the
course of the week, month, and year. Ask about wonderful days, weeks,
and months. Ask about disastrous days, weeks, and months. Ask about
particularly wonderful events, activities, and interactions and about particularly traumatic events, activities, and interactions. As you did with
your data on contemporary life and living conditions, make sure you
record specific details, including words, behavior, and social actors.
Clearly identify the criteria that people used to discriminate wonderful
from disastrous. Fill in the gradations between the two. Once you can
paint a picture of one person's life, actively search for variation so that
your picture includes, at least in broad outlines, the historical complexity
found in your study community.

Ask prostitutes what they did as "work" before they worked in "de fas
life" and what they did as partners, mothers, daughters and daughters-in-
law, co-workers, and friends. What did that work mean to them and, if the
meaning of work changed, when and why? What did their relationships as
partners, mothers, daughters and daughters-in-law, co-workers, and
friends mean to them? If the meaning of specific relations changed, when
and why? How clear was the boundary between work and other important
activities and relationships? If a boundary existed, what was it, exactly, and
how did they know it? What ambiguities existed? In what contexts or
social relationships did the boundary shift location or definition? What
did interaction based on different definitions and/or boundaries between
"work" and "nonwork" mean to these women's sense of who they are?

Finally, ask each woman to talk about what she believed different kinds of social actors believed about her, about how her feelings about herself corresponded or conflicted with her understanding about how others saw her, and about how she experienced that correspondence or conflict. Plan to collect or construct time-series data that can help you understand the historical circumstances in which these experiences occurred.

To place prostitution within the broader context of gender relations and sexuality, ask equivalent questions directed toward noncommercial relationships. Ask women to talk about the experiences that they have in different types of relationships and what that social relationship and those experiences mean for these women's sense of who they are. Include questions like: What does it mean when you (what do you like, dislike, feel?) take part in or are subject to different forms of sexual activity? How is the experience different between a girl-/boyfriend, wife/husband, girlfriend/ girlfriend, or prostitute? In the context of having sex, what does _____ mean to you? How are they alike? How different? (Use terms elicited in earlier interviews, like *Intimacy, Violence, Pleasure,* and *Loving.*) What is the boundary between these experiences? What ambiguities are there? In what contexts or social relationships does the boundary shift location or definition? What do these different forms of sexual activity mean to women's and men's sense of who they are? Ask women and men to talk about what they believe their partners believe about the different kinds of sexual activity, about how their feelings correspond or conflict with their understanding about how others see the sexual activities, and how they experience that correspondence or conflict.

LOOK FOR THE ASSUMPTIONS
Aim to accumulate notes on a wide variety of subjects by the end of your first week in the field (Johnson and Johnson 1990, Emerson, Fretz, and Shaw 1995). This first stage of building fieldnotes will give you some general insight into the variables that compose cultures—how informants construct things like "families," "gender," and "age"; how they identify these things and discriminate one kind of thing from another; and how they identify, discriminate, and experience things like "power," "competition," and "cooperation." Approach analysis of your fieldnotes as an exercise in discriminating structure from randomness (Bernard and Ryan

1998, Ryan and Bernard 2000). Look for themes by asking yourself two questions:

- What do people say/do?
- What does this say about the assumptions they make about themselves and the world around them?

Use your imagination! Infer a series of assumptions *from which your informants' words and behavior follow as logical consequences.*

Reflect first on the words and phrases people use in response to specific questions and the behavior you see in particular sets of circumstances. Note key life-experience markers for each informant, like age and gender. Assemble a codebook for your analysis, and sort observations and quotes from informants in ways that correspond with each code. Text analysis software helps immensely. Anticipate the need to code specific words, phrases, sentences, paragraphs, or longer text segments at multiple hierarchical levels and for different content areas. Your inferred assumptions used by your informants to rationalize their words and behavior will suggest relationships among the kinds of behavior and words used by your informants. Take a day to reflect on where you've come. Then, plan and, by the beginning of your second week in the field, initiate the collection and analysis of aggregated data.

INTEGRATE FIELDNOTES WITH HISTORICAL EVENTS AND TRENDS

Create a timeline for documented historical changes to anticipate potentially important experiences and life events. For example, use Lexis Diagrams like the one presented in figure 4.2 to keep in focus the maturational and historical influences on different cohorts of informants. In Barbados, for example, people over age seventy in 2000 grew up at a time when women looked forward to having large families and children readily accepted obligations to help their aging parents. Their parents usually worked as field laborers or other menial occupations or left the island seeking work. Contraction of overseas work opportunities and the absence of work in Barbados led to widespread rioting in the mid-1930s. After World War II, the effect of labor unrest in the 1930s led to the political demise of the plantocracy that had ruled the island since settlement in 1625. Change in political leadership led to significant structural change in the Barbadian economy beginning about 1960. Their children, consequently, grew up at a time when women looked forward to careers and small families and actively resisted demands for assistance by elderly parents. Their grandchildren, by contrast, grew up at a time when illicit substances like crack cocaine became widely available on the island. Historical change in the experiences of successive cohorts bears on the needs of Barbadian elderly, the capacity of their children to meet those needs, and the expectations that different cohorts place on politicians and the national health system.

Collect pertinent aggregated data bases, construct appropriate variables, and use scatterplots for time-series data to acquaint yourself with important historical trends in macrolevel phenomena. Figure 4.3, for example, shows historical scatterplot of trends in key sectors of the Antiguan economy between 1953 and 1985.

Figure 4.4 shows the same time trends but overlays them and expresses

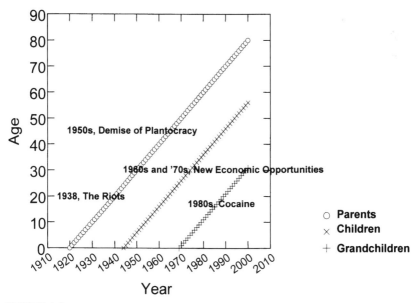

FIGURE 4.2
Lexis Diagram for Sequential Cohorts in Barbados

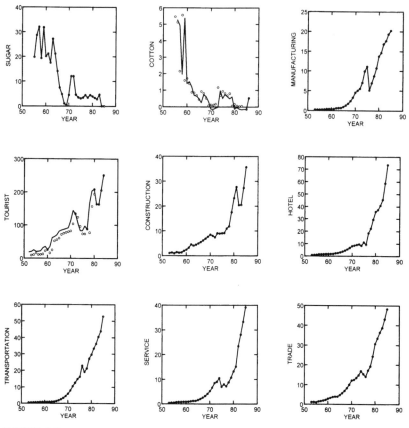

FIGURE 4.3
Macroeconomic Time-Series Plots for Antigua, West Indies

the value of each variable as a logarithm (base 2), to make it easier to compare rates of change.

The divergent historical trends in figure 4.4 signal dramatic change in the Antiguan economy. They also produce information overload, like any eyeball analysis of multiple variables. In the late 1980s, any Antiguan could tell you that the nation's economy had changed dramatically since the 1950s. Sugar was out. Tourism and manufacturing were in. That's as much as you get from figures 4.3 and 4.4, and I found it much more interesting and fun talking with Antiguans than trying to make sense of these time plots. Multivariate icon analysis integrates all this information as pictures

Sugar   ○
Cotton   ×
Manufacturing +
Tourist   ◁
Construction ▷
Hotel   ▽
Transportation △
Service   □
Trade   ◇

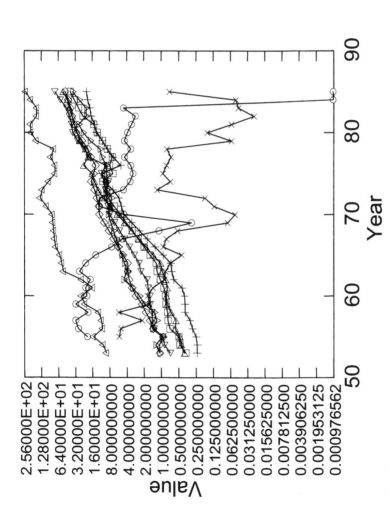

FIGURE 4.4
Overlaid Macroeconomic Time-Series Plots

to give you important information not otherwise available, however. It pinpoints the dates of change with an explicit empirical analysis.

Figure 4.5 presents a Fourier blob icon analysis that integrates the macroeconomic time series for Antigua, West Indies, shown in figures 4.3 and 4.4. I find Fourier blobs (polar coordinate Fourier waveforms) particularly helpful in identifying significant historical events and changes in historical processes. You may prefer Chernoff's faces or stars, suns, weather vanes, arrows, or other icons. All yield the same graphical information. In a set of historical time series like those analyzed for figure 4.5, each case blob corresponds with a specific year. The shape of each blob is generated by Fourier transforms of the standardized variables that characterize a particular year. The variables used for this analysis included: a real wage index, tourist arrivals, sugar production levels, cotton production levels, and national income derived from manufacturing, services, and so forth. Years with similar values across all variables exhibit similar shapes. Years with different patterns of variation exhibit different shapes. The blob analysis in figure 4.5 shows that the Antiguan economy changed little from 1955 through 1964. By 1985, however, the literal as well as the figurative shape of the Antiguan economy had changed dramatically. The earliest phases of change appear as growth in the bulge on the right side of the blobs, which begins in 1965. Fundamental changes, seen in the increased differentiation of the left side of the blobs, were well underway by 1970 and took the following decade to work themselves out. By 1980, the shape of the new Antiguan economy began to resolve itself. Examination of the data that were used to generate these blobs reveals a structural change in the Antiguan economy—a shift from an economy based largely on sugar production to one dominated by tourism and industrial manufacturing.

Incorporate this new information into all subsequent work. For Antigua, the blob analysis suggests not only that social relations and cultural categories and meanings may have changed dramatically between the 1950s and the 1980s, it also suggests who to talk to, to understand the processes of social and cultural change, and a retrospective sampling frame of the kind described in chapter 3. People who grew up in the 1950s and early 1960s can provide firsthand accounts of the early years, how their world changed, and how they experienced those changes. People who grew up during the period 1965–1975 can provide firsthand accounts of

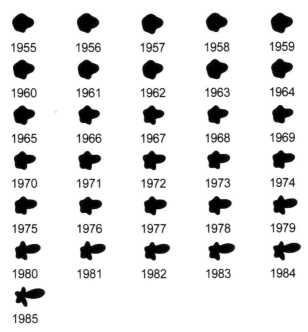

FIGURE 4.5
Icon Analysis of Macroeconomic Time Series for Antigua, West Indies

the transition years, the conflicts that arose, and how they came to be
resolved (if they were). People who grew up during the 1980s can provide
firsthand accounts of what life is like now that the structural changes have
clarified themselves and how they see themselves differ from people in the
older cohorts. What cultural boundaries, if any, separate these cohorts? If
the cohorts exhibit distinct cultures, are these cohort agreements a function of aging, of historical change, or both?

Simultaneously, use Second-Order Gossip interviews to ask about
questions that arose during your initial interviews; and ask more specific
questions to expand your knowledge of phenomenal components and,
where possible, meaning and cultural variability. Go back to your informants, and find new ones. Summarize your evolving understanding and
ask if you got it right. Check regularly with your informants. Cross-check
for variability between informants.

Make initial (and informal) assessments of informant agreements and
the reliability, validity, and generalizability of your data. In a study of sex-

uality, for example, ask the people with whom you've begun to build relationships if they will (and who else might) talk with you about different kinds of sexual activity, the different labels that people apply to the "same" activity, and, for each, what they like best, and what they dislike most. Start with labels you use; describe what you know of different forms of activity and ask if people know about them; ask what they call them. In a study of STDs, your initial questions may have suggested that, when sick, people can treat themselves with "bush teas" and can see private physicians or physicians in government-run health clinics. Ask people to tell you how they refer to private physicians and physicians in government-run health clinics, what the differences are, why you might choose one over the other or go to both. Ask them to tell you about specific forms of bush teas, what they are made from, and when and under what circumstances they might be used. Ask who uses these alternative sources of health care; ask if people choose one over the other, or if people may use all three at the same time—ask about specific examples.

PREPARE FOR A TRANSITION

By the second or third day in the field, initiate your introductory official visits to the local university or college and to pertinent government agencies. While you establish (or re-establish) pertinent research linkages and personal relations and receive appropriate research permissions, ask where you might acquire pertinent aggregated data bases and sources of research assistance. Ask, too, about possible research sites and their advantages and disadvantages. Visit possible research sites by your third or fourth day in the field. Select a site by the end of your first week.

By your second week in the field you need to begin the process of building a research team. Chapter 9 outlines the essentials of selecting, training, and operating a team of research assistants successfully. Here, note mainly that you should plan to complete the task of assembling a team of trained assistants by the end of your fourth week in the field. Don't treat the task of building a research team separately from other "Building a Foundation" tasks. Incorporate findings from Second-Order Gossip interviews and from your analysis of aggregate data into what you do as you contact, train, and select research team members. Treat team members as key informants, as well as research assistants. If you work in Antigua, for example, include on your team members of the three cohorts that experienced significant differences in the world in which they grew up. In a study in which you expect important regional cultural variation, as in a study of cultural change among natives in Alaska and the neighboring Russian Far East, include on your team people from each region.

USE SEMISTRUCTURED INTERVIEWS TO FIND THE LIMITS OF VARIATION

Informal interviews grade into semistructured interviews. You make the shift once you write down *and use* a series of questions to guide your interview about specific cultural domains. You make informal interviews far more efficient if you write out questions before you begin. Writing the questions forces you to think about the content of specific domains and how they may be linked to others. Use the findings of informal interviews to correct your initial guesses, to elaborate them, and to restructure your understanding. In the process, draw up additional lists of questions. Once informal interviews fail to turn up new questions, corrections to old questions, or domain boundaries that had remained hidden, shift to a semistructured interview format. Resource limitations (your time, money, and energy) mean that you can conduct informal interviews with relatively few people. Use semistructured interviews to extend the number and variety of people you talk with.

Don't confuse semistructured interviews with structured interviews. You defeat the singular utility of semistructured interviews if you try to collect comparable data for each informant. Use semistructured interviews to find the limits of variation for specific cultural domains. Collect data from focus groups and focused interviews of a large set of informants selected for their diversity.

To use semistructured interviews most efficiently with single informants,

- take a series of questions like those in box 4.1,
- assign each question its own sheet of paper, and
- ask a large set of diverse informants to respond to one to three questions each.

Your team of research assistants will collect volumes of data quickly. Add it to your field notes and the analyses you undertake with text analysis software.

Any interview of any kind undertaken with more than a single person constitutes a focus group. For semistructured interviews, however, address the task with explicit planning (e.g., Morgan and Krueger 1998). Start by selecting informants who are knowledgeable about specific cultural domains. This usually means a relatively homogenous group of people (e.g., older Native American men; young Native American women who attend college; participants in specific forms of ritual or ceremonial). If you want to explore issues related to prostitute–client interaction, select one group of prostitutes and another of clients. Aim at groups of five to ten people. Too few people and a single person can dominate the discussion. Too many creates management problems, and only one or two participants may dominate the discussion. Use your prior knowledge of social networks when selecting focus group participants. Participants who know each other well will produce a wealth of information on topics about which they share a common interest, like the significance and meaning of a particular ceremony. Participants will produce little if they feel the need to hide information they don't want to share with people who know them well. Moreover, participants who know each other well will share many realms of culture. Individual focus groups composed of such people will not extend your understanding of the limits of variation. To extend that understanding, organize a series of focus groups, each consisting of sets of informants who participate in distinctive social networks. If you tape-record focus group sessions, consider asking a research assistant to note who says what, so that you can minimize transcription confusions, and to take supplementary notes.

Start collecting data with semistructured interviews no later than your third week in the field. Reflect on the notes you took during Week Two and findings from your analysis of aggregated data. Where do you need to go now, and what questions do you need to ask to clarify the research issue of labels and definitions and their interrelationships? What questions bearing on meaning do you need to ask, of whom, and how? What life experience data do you need, how will you pose the questions, whom do

---

Box 4.1   Ethnomedical Interviews

Record Age and Gender of each informant.
F34 is a 30-year-old woman; M26 is a 26-year-old man.

Our Question: What's the most common health problem you deal with in your clinical setting?

What are the most common (important, dangerous, etc.) health problems you or people in this community experience? *Make and maintain a cumulative list of labels.*

For Each:
Diagnosis
How do you know you have it (what complaints, problems, and symptoms would you see)?
- Probe for symptoms that can't be seen.
- Probe for use and means of self-diagnosis, use of specialists (who?), criteria used when choosing who and how to do this. Probe for uncertainties. Who knows most about this problem?

Etiology and prognosis
What happens to people who get it?
- Probe for sequences.

Epidemiology
Who can have the problem?
- How do adults get it? Men? Women?
- How do children get it? Boys? Girls?
- Who never has the problem?

For Each:
Prevention
What can you do to prevent it?
- Probe for differences by age, sex, etc.
- Probe for problems (emotional, social, physical, etc.) people encounter when they use one or another means of prevention.

Cure
What can you do to get rid of it?
- Probe for differences by age, sex, etc.
- Probe for problems (emotional, social, physical, etc.) people encounter when they use one or another means of prevention.

---

you need to ask, and in what numbers? Formulate semistructured interviews to pursue specific questions, topics, and issues in greater depth.
Conduct focus groups to gain a deeper understanding of issues of meaning
and to explore issues of cultural variability. Use semistructured interviews
as part of the training process for your research assistants.

How to Build Your Data Base by Using Structured Interviews to Make Comparisons

Build your data base with three lines of data collection:

1. continue and extend semistructured interviews begun in the first phase of your project;
2. continue and extend informal interviews, but with key informants begin to use informal interviews to confirm, explore nuances, and add detail to findings from your semistructured interviews; and
3. conduct structured interviews so that you can make the explicit comparisons necessary to meet project goals (see figure 5.1, which focuses on this phase of your project).

Use a period of Third Order Gossip for reflection and planning, as well as analysis of semistructured interviews and preliminary analyses of data collected through structured interviews and observations, to design more detailed data collection. By the end of your fourth week in the field, data collected through informal and semistructured interviews will raise new questions. But they will also provide a foundation from which you can prepare effective structured interviews to pursue ever more specific questions about identity and meaning, and cultural consensus and variability.

The same data will permit you to formulate well-designed questionnaires (which you hand to informants to fill out) or question schedules (on which you record answers to the questions you ask) with which to collect pertinent life experience data.

Use structured interviews to collect data on the properties of domain items and the structure of domain items and activities. Use your project goals to decide if you should conduct one or several highly focused sets of structured interviews, integrate several data collection goals into a single survey, or both. To make this choice, keep in mind that one general rule governs all structured interviews—keep your respondents' attention! To do so and thus make an immense contribution to the collection of valid, reliable data, apply several more specific ones.

REMEMBER THAT STRUCTURED INTERVIEW RESPONDENTS, LIKE KEY INFORMANTS, ARE YOUR TEACHERS

Ask them to help you in much the same way that you'd approach a potential key informant. Devote the first page of your questionnaire or question schedule to an explanation of your goals and how the person you approach for an interview can help. Give your respondents an idea about the kinds of questions they will be asked, how you'd like them to respond, and how long it will take to complete the interview. Let them know that you're concerned about their privacy and what you plan to do to protect it. Tell your respondents clearly that you will respect their wish to stop the interview prior to its completion. Encourage your respondents to ask questions. Give them a means to contact you later, should concerns or questions arise after you (or your research assistant) complete the interview and leave. Box 5.1 illustrates a set of questions bearing on historical change in gender relations.

KEEP IT SHORT 'N' SWEET

Keep survey questionnaires or question schedules to a length that can be completed within about thirty minutes, on average. Trim questionnaires or interview schedules to their *absolute essentials.* Don't begin to formulate questions until analysis of informal and semistructured interviews yields clear ideas about the assumptions that your informants used to under-

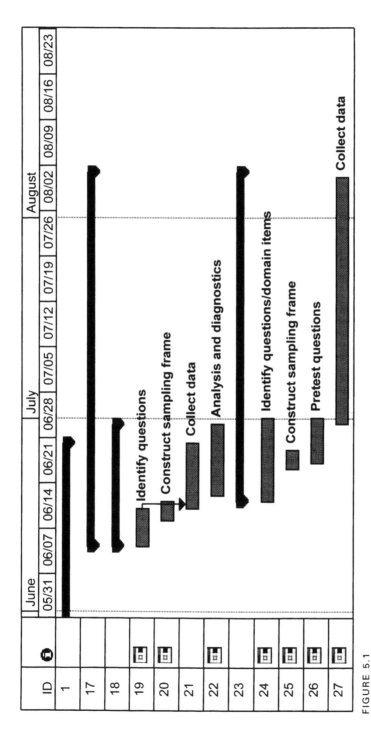

FIGURE 5.1
Building Your Data Base

Box 5.1   Example Explanation for a Structured Interview

The questions on the following pages ask you to tell us about some of your experiences with men and how your experiences, feelings, and thoughts may be different from those of your mother. Your answers will help us better understand how relationships between men and women have changed over the last forty years. We want you to participate only if you can do so openly and honestly. You are free to stop the interview or to say that certain information you tell us should not be reported later.

You can answer most of the questions in one of two ways. First, some questions ask you to fill in a blank space with the answer that is right for you. Second, some questions already have answers that you can choose from. You can answer these by drawing a circle around the response that is right for you. Please, feel free to write any additional information that you feel is important for us to know. Some of the questions ask you to write short explanations. It takes about fifteen to thirty minutes to answer all the questions.

We want to make sure that no one but you will know what you told us. We are particularly concerned because some questions ask about private events and feelings. Here is what you can do to make sure your answers remain private:

1. Don't write your name on this form.
2. When you complete all the questions, place this form inside the attached envelope and seal it.
3. We will collect your envelope in a large envelope or bag that has many other envelopes already inside it. Mix your envelope with the others so we cannot tell which is yours.

If you have any questions, please feel free to ask them at any time. If you have a question later, please contact me at _____.

---

stand and respond to the world of experience, the variables that comprise the cultural domains you study, and ways you might best measure them. Once you do, state questions simply and clearly. Make clear transitions between survey sections, if you integrate several structured interview components into a single survey, so that the *order* of your questions makes sense to your informants.

For example, the pregnancy history questions in box 5.2 begin with a question about any past pregnancies, move to the question of the number of past pregnancies, ask about current family size and composition, then consolidate with specific questions about each pregnancy and its outcome. The pregnancy history ends with a set of questions that summarizes and asks for corrections.

ASK QUESTIONS FOR WHICH INFORMAL INTERVIEWS HAVE ALREADY GIVEN YOU ANSWERS

Don't put questions that explore unknown domains on structured interviews. Questions like the following—which only ask for labels people apply to categories of experience—belong on surveys:

- How old were you when you first had sex? _____
- How old was your first sexual partner? _____
- Did you freely choose to have sex this first time?   1 yes   0 no
- How often do you protect yourself from getting a disease when you have sex?
     4 all the time   3 almost all the time   2 sometimes   1 rarely   0 never
- How often do you use condoms when you have sex?
     4 all the time   3 most of the time   2 sometimes   1 rarely   0 never

Questions like the following *don't* belong on structured interviews—ask them during informal or semistructured interviews:

- What is sexual abuse? What things would a man do that would be sexually abusive to a girl? To a woman? What makes the difference between things that are sexually abusive to girls and things that are sexually abusive to women?
- Tell me about the different kinds of acts and language you think of as "violent." When do these acts occur? What makes them "violent"?
- What do you know about breast cancer? Have you, a friend, or a family member ever had breast cancer? If so, what was the experience like for the person who had the cancer? How did her friends and family respond?
- What kinds of behavior do kids display toward one another in the classroom? On the playground? For each, when was the last time you saw

Box 5.2   Pregnancy Histories

Have you ever been pregnant?   1 Yes   2 No
If yes, how many times have you been pregnant, even if the
pregnancies lasted only a week or so? _____

How many (biological) children do you have? _____
How many children have you adopted? _____
And how many have you given out for adoption? _____

	Age Preg.	Month Preg.	Miscarriage Stillbirth Livebirth	Live Birth Date	Boy or Girl	If DIED: Months Lived	Months B.Fed
1	_____	_____	M S LB	_____	M F	_____mo	_____mo
2	_____	_____	M S LB	_____	M F	_____mo	_____mo
3	_____	_____	M S LB	_____	M F	_____mo	_____mo
13	_____	_____	M S LB	_____	M F	_____mo	_____mo
14	_____	_____	M S LB	_____	M F	_____mo	_____mo
15	_____	_____	M S LB	_____	M F	_____mo	_____mo

** Have live birth dates been verified from a baptisimal book?
1 Yes   2 No

Have you ever had trouble getting pregnant?—i.e., a medical or biological
condition that made it difficult or impossible to get pregnant: 1 Yes   2 No
If yes, explain:

To check to see if I understand you correctly, this means when you were
(give age range), you experienced (add number from top of page) and give
a response catagory _____ pregnancies, miscarriages, etc.

	P	M	SB	LB	Infant Deaths
− 19	_____	_____	_____	_____	_____
20–24	_____	_____	_____	_____	_____
25–29	_____	_____	_____	_____	_____
30–34	_____	_____	_____	_____	_____
35–39	_____	_____	_____	_____	_____
40–44	_____	_____	_____	_____	_____
45–49	_____	_____	_____	_____	_____

How many of these pregnancies did you plan? _____

that? What happened, exactly? That is, can you tell me the sequence of events, what one kid said or did, how the other responded with words or acts? Who were the participants (probe for gender, age, grade similarities and differences)?

- Lead me around the clinic and tell me what's here, who the different people are, why they're here, what they do.

USE BINARY RESPONSES TO IDENTIFY THE PROPERTIES OF PEOPLE AND THINGS

Use binary response (yes/no—true/false) questions to elicit information on the properties that might distinguish different kinds of clients, different kinds of sexual services, different kinds of social interactions, or different kinds of life events. Box 5.3 illustrates with questions bearing on the sources of disability and potential needs for an elderly population. Box 5.4 illustrates with questions bearing on sexual abuse.

USE RATING SCALES TO ASSESS RELATIVE IMPORTANCE

Use ordinal rating scales to elicit information on the relative importance of different kinds of clients, different kinds of sexual services, different kinds of social relations, or different properties of social interaction. Box 5.5 illustrates with questions that assess informants' ability to carry out basic living activities.

USE PILE SORTS TO ASSESS RELATIVE SIMILARITY

Many methods yield information on the relative similarity of things that bear on your research topic—triads, paired comparisons, and pile sorts, to name only a few (see, e.g., Bernard 2001, 2000). The most flexible and parsimonious of these is a simple ("free") pile sort (for a comparison among methods, see http://www.anth.uconn.edu/faculty/boster/nih/methcomp.htm). Construct a set of items (photographs, implements, plants or plant parts, or slips of paper with names on them), and ask your informant to create piles of things that go together.

Pile sorts actively engage informants, who usually find them interesting, even fun. But free pile sorts elicit vastly different quantities of information from different informants. At the extremes, for example, of two infor-

---

Box 5.3   Sources of Disability for the Elderly and Potential Needs

Do you have difficulty doing any of these things without help because of any of the following conditions?

Diabetes	0 no	1 yes	Arthritis	0 no	1 yes
Severe burns	0 no	1 yes	Nerve problems	0 no	1 yes
Amputation	0 no	1 yes	Back injury/problem	0 no	1 yes
Paralysis	0 no	1 yes	Circulation problems	0 no	1 yes
Eyesight problems	0 no	1 yes	Chronic lung problems	0 no	1 yes
Heart problem	0 no	1 yes	Cancer	0 no	1 yes
Hearing	0 no	1 yes	Other: _____	0 no	1 yes
Stroke/passover	0 no	1 yes			

Please tell me which of the following you want (1), and which you have (2)?

		WANT	HAVE			WANT	HAVE
Cane	0 no	1	2	Special bed	0 no	1	2
Night chair	0 no	1	2	Telephone amplifier	0 no	1	2
Crutches	0 no	1	2	Tub bars	0 no	1	2
Dentures	0 no	1	2	Walker	0 no	1	2
Glasses	0 no	1	2	Wheelchair	0 no	1	2
Hearing aid	0 no	1	2	Ramped entry	0 no	1	2
Artificial limb	0 no	1	2	Leg/foot braces	0 no	1	2

---

mants who sort the same 26 items, one might create 2 piles and the other might create 20. Boster's (1994) successive pile sort retains the flexibility and parsimony of the method and solves the lumper-splitter problem in a way that yields very finely grained comparisons. It's the method of choice for collecting similarity data. As a bonus, you can collect these data either in one-on-one interviews or in focus groups!

Here's how: Construct a set of items and ask your informant or set of informants to

- sort a set of items into piles that represent the basic similarities and differences among the items;
- successively *merge* the initial piles on the basis of similarity until only two groups remain; and

---

Box 5.4   Assessing Sexual Abuse

How old were you when you first had sex? _____
How old was your first sexual partner? _____
Did you freely choose to have sex this first time?   1 yes   0 no

CIRCLE if this first sexual experience occurred with
father   step-father   mother's boyfriend
other family member, Who? _____

CIRCLE if any later sexual experience occurred with
father   step-father   mother's boyfriend
other family member, Who? _____
How old were you when this happened?

Has anyone threatened you, whether this person actually used the words or not, to get you to have sex with him or her? The threat could have applied, for example, to a job, to your physical welfare, or even to your feelings or a relationship.

Were you threatened?		Did you have sex when you did not want to? How old were you?		
**by a boss	0 no 1 yes	0 no	1 yes	_____
**by a teacher	0 no 1 yes	0 no	1 yes	_____
**by a sexual partner	0 no 1 yes	0 no	1 yes	_____
**by a friend	0 no 1 yes	0 no	1 yes	_____
**by your father	0 no 1 yes	0 no	1 yes	_____
**by your step-father	0 no 1 yes	0 no	1 yes	_____
**by your mother's boyfriend	0 no 1 yes	0 no	1 yes	_____
**by a stranger	0 no 1 yes	0 no	1 yes	_____
**by a male relative	0 no 1 yes	0 no	1 yes	_____
Who?				

- successively *split* the initial piles on the basis of dissimilarity until every pile consists of a single item.

Boster created an elegant cut-card method for collecting successive pile sort data (see box 5.6). Boster's method assumes that information about similarities and differences is contained in the *order* in which an informant

Box 5.5   Disability and Disease

How well can you do these things *by yourself:*

	Without Any Help	With Physical Aids	With Some Help of a Person	Completely Unable
*dress and undress	0	1	2	3
*care for your appearance	0	1	2	3
*bathe or shower	0	1	2	3
*use toilet	0	1	2	3
*get in/out of a bed/armless chair	0	1	2	3
*get into and out of a car	0	1	2	3
*climb stairs	0	1	2	3
*walk easily indoors	0	1	2	3
*walk easily outdoors	0	1	2	3
*eat	0	1	2	3
*use telephone	0	1	2	3
*prepare meals by yourself	0	1	2	3
*do housework	0	1	2	3
*do laundry	0	1	2	3
*go shopping	0	1	2	3
*handle your own money	0	1	2	3
*use public transportation	0	1	2	3
*take your medications or injections	0	1	2	3
*cut your toenails	0	1	2	3

makes piles, and he defines relative similarity as the ordinal distance between any one cut and another. Boster wrote software specifically designed to manage and analyze data collected on the basis of these assumptions, which is free for the asking. To get the software, contact him at: boster@sp.uconn.edu.

I assume that all pertinent information about similarities and differences is contained in the final set of merged and split piles, which is the same as assuming that the order in which an informant makes the piles

---

Box 5.6   Boster's Successive Pile Sort
http://www.anth.uconn.edu/faculty/boster

- Obtain a collection of stimuli and a set of $(N-1)$ number cards. If there are 25 items, then you need 24 number cards. Each stimulus item should be identified with a letter of the alphabet.

- Lay the stimuli in random order in front of the informant and say something like the following: Here is a set of 25 cards, each with the name of a different kind of disease [or whatever]. Please sort them into piles according to which diseases you think are most similar to one another. You can sort them according to whatever characteristics of the diseases you like and into as many piles as you like.

- After informants have finished the sort, leave the stimuli as they are and record the number of piles. This number of initial piles is the number "N" throughout these instructions. Next say: Now please tell me which of these piles of diseases [or whatever] are the most similar to one another? That is, if you could only make $[N-1]$ piles, which piles would you join together? [For example, if the informant made 7 piles, ask which of the 7 he or she would join if he or she had to make only 6 piles.]

- Take the piles that the informant indicates as being most similar and move them next to each other, if necessary. Place the number card $[N-1]$ between the pair of piles the informant says that he or she would join. Now say: Treating the piles you have just joined as a single pile, now which piles of diseases would you join?

- Place the number card $[N-2]$ between this pair of piles. Again, move the piles around if necessary. Continue this process until there are only two piles and place the number card 1 between them. Now say: Returning to your original piles, split the pile that contains the diseases that are most different from one another. That is, if you had to make $[N+1]$ piles, which pile would you split and HOW?

- The informant has almost as much freedom in choosing how to split the piles as she or he has in the initial sort. For example, although an informant can only split a pile into two, he or she may choose to split a pile with 6 items into piles of 1 and 5, 2 and 4, or 3 and 3. Place the number card $[N]$ between the piles that have just been split apart and say: Again, split the pile that contains the diseases that are most different from one another. That is, if you had to make $[N+2]$ piles, which pile would you split?

Box 5.6   (Continued)

- Place the number card [N+ 1] between the pile that is split. Continue this process until there is only one pile remaining to be split, and place the number card 24 (25 items − 1) between the remaining two items. You should now have a sequence of items (stimuli) and number cards that alternates: item, number card, item, number card, . . . item. Record the informant's successive sorting of the items by writing down the sequence of item identifiers (letters of the alphabet) and the numbers on the number cards (e.g., B 2 A 4 D 1 F 3 E 5 C).

At the end, record the number of original piles and an identifier of the informant.

---

contains no useful information about similarities and differences. I define relative similarity as the relative number of times an informant places any two items in the same pile and in different piles (i.e., by a Simple Matching coefficient), or the relative number of times an informant places any two items in the same pile (Jaccard's coefficient). If you accept these assumptions, you can collect and analyze successive pile sort data with the software you currently use, like SPSS, SAS, or SYSTAT.

First, elicit the hierarchy of relative similarities using the technique described earlier. For example, a study designed to understand how parents, teachers, and students experience and respond to violence in schools might examine the kinds of interaction that take place between students. Informal and semistructured interviews or observations might reveal the following set of eighteen items, describing different forms of student–student interaction: pushing, stealing, hitting, name-calling, rolling-of-eyes, angry looks, blaming, using foul language, slapping, touching-to-annoy, yelling, positive and supportive words, negative and demeaning words, hugging, smiling at, laughing at, laughing with, and spitting. Create a set of eighteen numbered cards or slips of paper with the words on one side and numbers 1–18 on the other. Find a location where your informants can spread out the entire set of items. Then:

- Ask your informants to sort the eighteen items into piles that represent the basic similarities and differences among the items. Record the items in each pile. Begin to create a coding sheet that lists the items in each pile in successive lines, like that in box 5.7. The informant's initial set of piles (circled items) appears in a large font and in bold print in the middle of box 5.7 (the identifiers Pile 4, Pile 7, and Pile 15 refer to the order in which I recorded the final set of merged and split files; see box 5.8).

- Ask your informants to merge two of the existing piles, on the basis of similarity. Record the items in the new pile. In box 5.7, the informant merged the pile with items 1, 3, 9, and 10 with the pile that contained item 18.

- Continue to ask them to merge two of the existing piles, on the basis of similarity, until all the items are in two piles. As your informant or informants create successive new piles, record the items in each new pile. In Box 5.7, the informant merged the pile with items 1, 3, 9, 10, and 18 with the pile that contained item 2. The informant then merged this pile (items 1, 3, 9, 10, and 18) with the pile that contained items 4, 6, 7, 8, 11, 13, and 16. The informant merged the initial pile that contained items 12, 15, and 17 with the initial pile that contained item 14. The informant thus created two piles from the original eighteen items.

- When all the items have been placed into two piles, ask your informants to return to the initial set of piles and split one of them, on the basis of dissimilarity. Record the items in each of the new piles. In box 5.7, the informant split the pile that contained items 12, 15, and 17 into two piles, one containing items 15 and 17, and one containing only item 12.

- Continue to ask your informants to split each pile on the basis of dissimilarity until every pile consists of a single item. The informant first returned to the pile that contained items 1, 3, 9, and 10 and split it into two piles: one that contained items 3 and 9, and one that contained items 1 and 10. The informant then returned to the largest initial pile (4, 5, 6, 7, 8, 11, 13, and 16) and split it into two piles: one that contained only a single item (5) and one that contained the rest (items 4, 6, 7, 8, 11, 13, and 16). The informant continued to split the latter pile by removing a single item at a time.

The informant whose pile sort appears in the coding sheet in box 5.7 created sixteen piles that contained two or more items (the identifier Pile

Box 5.7   Example of a Successive Pile Sort Code Sheet for Use with SYSTAT

Items PUSH1 STEAL2 HIT3 NNAMES4 ROLLEYES5 ANGLOOK6 BLAMEO7 FLANG8 SLAP9 TANNOY10 YELL11 POS12 NEG13 HUG14 SMILE15 LAT16 LWITH17 SPIT18

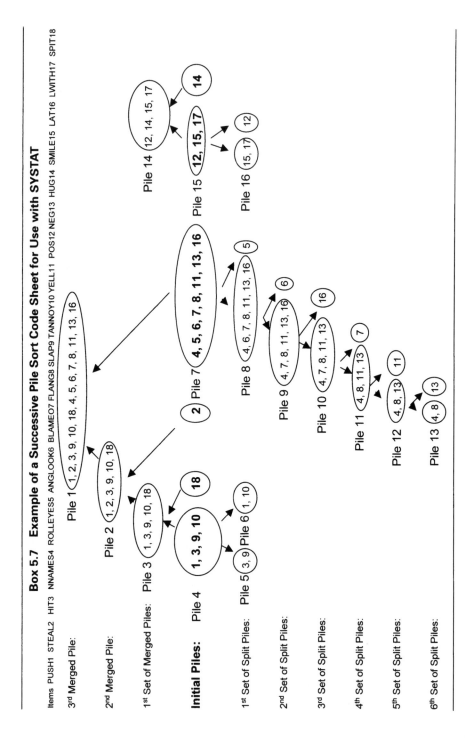

3rd Merged Pile:

Pile 1 (1, 2, 3, 9, 10, 18, 4, 5, 6, 7, 8, 11, 13, 16)

2nd Merged Pile:

Pile 2 (1, 2, 3, 9, 10, 18)

1st Set of Merged Piles: Pile 3 (1, 3, 9, 10, 18)

Initial Piles: Pile 4   **1, 3, 9, 10**   **18**

1st Set of Split Piles: Pile 5 (3, 9) Pile 6 (1, 10)

Pile 7   **2**   **4, 5, 6, 7, 8, 11, 13, 16**

Pile 14 (12, 14, 15, 17)

Pile 15   **12, 15, 17**   **14**

Pile 16 (15, 17)   (12)

Pile 8 (4, 6, 7, 8, 11, 13, 16)   (5)

2nd Set of Split Piles:

Pile 9 (4, 7, 8, 11, 13, 16)   (6)

3rd Set of Split Piles:

Pile 10 (4, 7, 8, 11, 13)   (16)

4th Set of Split Piles:

Pile 11 (4, 8, 11, 13)   (7)

5th Set of Split Piles:

Pile 12 (4, 8, 13)   (11)

6th Set of Split Piles:

Pile 13 (4, 8)   (13)

1, Pile 2, Pile 3 . . . Pile 16). (We ignore piles that contain either one item or *N* items because piles like these do not discriminate similarity from difference.) Use this information to create a rectangular informant-by-variable matrix like that illustrated in box 5.8. The rows in box 5.7 correspond with the pile identifiers in box 5.8.

Give each informant a numerical code. For each informant, rows consist of the contents of specific piles: 1s if an item is present in a pile and 0s otherwise. You may find it easiest to fill in the 1s for specific piles and, once you've entered all the piles for all informants, use a command file like the following to fill in the 0s:

If PUSH 1 =. then let push 1 = 0
If STEAL 2 =. then let steal 2 = 0
If HIT 3 =. then let hit 3 = 0
If NAMES 3 =. then let names 3 = 0
If ROLL EYES 5 =. then let roll eyes 5 = 0
If A LOOK 6 =. then let a look 6 = 0
If BLAME 7 =. then let blame 7 = 0
If FOUL 8 =. then let foul 8 = 0
If SLAP 9 =. then let slap 9 = 0
If TOUCH 10 =. then let touch 10 = 0
If YELL 11 =. then let yell 11 = 0
If COMPLIMENT 12 =. then let compliment 12 = 0
If INSULT 13 =. then let insult 13 = 0
If HUG 14 =. then let hug 14 = 0
If SMILE 15 =. then let smile 15 = 0
If MAKE FUN 16 =. then let make fun 16 = 0
If LAUGH 17 =. then let laugh 17 = 0
If SPIT 18 =. then let spit 18 = 0

USE LIKERT SCALES FOR MULTIDIMENSIONAL VARIABLES

Multidimensional variables like *depression, stress, affection,* or *problem drinking* identify singularly important phenomena. But they pose a special problem. You can't see them, so you can't measure them directly. Use multiple indicators for multidimensional variables, but use *short* Likert

Box 5.8 Example of a Successive Pile Sort Matrix for Use with SYSTAT

Pile	INFORMANT	PUSH1	STEAL2	HIT3	NNAMES4	ROLLEYES5	ANGLOOK6	BLAME07	FLANG8	SLAP9	TANNOY10	YELL11	POS12	NEG13	HUG14	SMILE15	LAT16	LWITH17	SPIT18
1	1	1	1	1	0	1	1	1	1	1	1	1	0	1	0	0	0	0	1
2	1	1	1	1	0	0	0	0	0	1	1	0	0	0	0	0	1	0	1
3	1	1	0	1	0	0	0	0	0	1	1	0	0	0	0	0	0	0	1
4	1	1	0	1	0	0	0	0	0	1	1	0	0	0	0	0	1	0	0
5	1	0	0	1	0	0	0	0	0	1	0	0	0	0	0	0	0	0	0
6	1	1	1	0	0	0	0	0	0	0	1	0	0	0	0	0	0	0	0
7	1	0	0	0	1	1	1	1	1	0	0	1	0	1	0	0	1	0	0
8	1	0	0	0	1	0	1	1	1	0	0	1	0	1	0	0	1	0	0
9	1	0	0	0	1	0	0	1	1	0	0	1	0	1	0	0	1	0	0
10	1	0	0	0	1	0	0	1	1	0	0	1	0	1	0	0	0	0	0
11	1	0	0	0	1	0	0	0	0	0	0	0	0	1	0	0	0	0	0
12	1	0	0	0	1	0	0	0	1	0	0	0	0	1	0	0	0	0	0
13	1	0	0	0	0	0	0	0	0	0	0	0	0	0	0	0	0	0	0
14	1	0	0	0	0	0	0	0	0	0	0	0	1	0	1	1	0	1	0
15	1	0	0	0	0	0	0	0	0	0	0	0	1	0	0	1	0	1	0
16	1	0	0	0	0	0	0	0	0	0	0	0	0	0	0	1	0	1	0

Scales whenever possible—e.g., the short MAST (Pokorny, Miller, and Kaplan 1972) or CAGE (Mayfield, McLeod, and Hull 1974) inventories for alcohol abuse, the 6-item scale for depression evaluated by Berwick (Berwick et al. 1991; see box 5.9), or the 4- and 8-item scales for traumatic (violent) and supportive (affectionate) social interaction (Handwerker 1996; see box 5.10). Use scales developed in other studies to add to a comparative research base.

Check the relevance of items included in established scales. In the West Indies, for example, the CAGE scale for alcoholism might follow a question that refers specifically to the consumption of beer and rum:

Do you drink beer, rum, or drinks like that?   0 no   1 yes
   If yes, how often have you:
Never   A few times   Sometimes   Often   Lots of times
tried to cut down how much you drink?   0   1   2   3   4

Box 5.9   Example of Likert Scales
Screening Instrument for Mood Disorders

(Adapted from Berwick et al. 1991)
The next questions ask about how you have been feeling. *During the last 4 weeks*, how often have you:

	All the Time	Regu-larly	Some-times	Rarely	Never
Felt nervous?	4	3	2	1	0
Felt calm and peaceful?	4	3	2	1	0
Felt downhearted and blue?	4	3	2	1	0
Felt happy?	4	3	2	1	0
Felt so down in the dumps that nothing could cheer you up?	4	3	2	1	0
Felt tense?	4	3	2	1	0
Had difficulty concentrating?	4	3	2	1	0
Gotten angry quickly?	4	3	2	1	0
Had difficulty falling asleep/ sleeping all night?	4	3	2	1	0

Box 5.10   Example of Likert Scales

Risk Assessment Instrument for Social Stressors
(Adapted from Handwerker 1999)

Over the last month [when you were a child], how often did someone:

	All the Time	Regu- larly	Some- times	Rarely	Never
Demean or belittle you?	4	3	2	1	0
Treat you as an inferior?	4	3	2	1	0
Block your attempts to achieve?	4	3	2	1	0
Make you feel bad about yourself?	4	3	2	1	0
Treat you as an equal?	4	3	2	1	0
Help you achieve?	4	3	2	1	0
Make you feel special?	4	3	2	1	0
Show you respect?	4	3	2	1	0

Scales for Affection and Violence in Personal Relationships
(Adapted from Handwerker 1993)

How does [a specific social actor, like "your partner"] treat you?

	All the Time	Regu- larly	Some- times	Rarely	Never
Spend free time with you?	4	3	2	1	0
Make decisions with you?	4	3	2	1	0
Treat you as an equal?	4	3	2	1	0
Hug or touch you in loving ways?	4	3	2	1	0
Talk with you and respect what you say?	4	3	2	1	0
Encourage you to do special things with your life?	4	3	2	1	0
Actively help you do these things?	4	3	2	1	0
Make you feel special and important?	4	3	2	1	0
Slap or hit you to hurt or punish?	4	3	2	1	0
Beat you (slap or hit repeatedly)?	4	3	2	1	0
Hurt you physically in any other way?	4	3	2	1	0
Say things that make you feel bad about yourself?	4	3	2	1	0

gotten annoyed with people who complain about your
drinking? 0 1 2 3 4
felt guilty about your drinking? 0 1 2 3 4
had a drink when you first get up in the morning *to feel
better?* 0 1 2 3 4

In Russia, the lead question should refer to vodka rather than rum.
Similarly, the 5-point scale may not make sense to people used to thinking
in terms of qualitative rather than quantitative distinctions. In Alaska and
the Russian Far East, the following questions achieve the same goal in
terms that people found meaningful:

Have you ever felt that you can't stop drinking?   0 no   1 yes
Have you ever thought about stopping?   0 no   1 yes

Don't hesitate to alter existing scales or create new ones that utilize the
criteria used by your informants. Try out different questions and the
"same" question asked in different ways to see what kind of information
they elicit. The items in boxes 5.9, 5.10, and those for the CAGE scale ask
for 5-point ordinal ratings. If you anticipate transforming your measurements into binary codes, use a 4-point scale (0, 1, 2, 3) instead. As the
adaptation of the CAGE questions indicates, binary responses might best
suit your informants.

Formulate some questions yourself. Ask informants to formulate others. Bernard's methods text (2001) lays out steps for building Likert Scales:
(1) choose and name the variable you want to measure, (2) make up lots
of items (questions or statements) that might tap the different dimensions
of the theoretical construct you want to measure, (3) choose response categories that might be appropriate, (4) ask a sample of people to respond
to your items, (5) determine which of the original set of items elicits
responses that might constitute reliable, valid measurements of your variable, and (6) try it again on a new sample to see if scale validity and reliability hold up (see Handwerker 1996 for an example).

Verify that sufficient consistency exists in people's experiences to justify
believing that labels like *depression, stress, affection,* or *problem drinking*
possess a phenomenal substance that extends beyond your imagination.

The meaning, for example, of being hit, battered, or beaten or being subject to other physically painful actions can vary from moment to moment, from person to person, and from one social or historical context to another. However, if a single, coherent underlying phenomenon exists that we can legitimately label "violence" (or "affection," "depression," and "problem drinking"), your observations should exhibit some predictable properties. Most fundamentally, observations you make of the "same" phenomenon should cohere. The absence of coherence constitutes evidence that you were mistaken to believe, for example, that the experiences of being hit, battered, or beaten or being subject to other physically painful actions by other people can be legitimately taken as expressions of a single underlying phenomenon called "violence."

In the process, explicitly assess the content validity of your scale items! *Content* validity consists of a consensus among informants that the items you use to measure a multidimensional variable actually measure the variable. To measure "stress" among working women that they experience in the course of daily social interaction, for example, informal interviews suggested that informants consistently equated "stress" with their emotional response to dissonance between the behavior they experience and the behavior they find acceptable. The behavioral characteristics women consistently associated with emotional dissonance included words or acts, for example, that "demean or belittle you," rather than treat you with respect; as in the following:

> [A woman, a trained clinician working for a grant-funded public service foundation with uncertain continuing funding, reported a conversation with less highly qualified co-workers about their future employment prospects] One woman told me "Well, you don't have to worry, John [husband] will take care of you." I wanted to belt her. My other co-worker said "you know, top [clinicians] make more money [than you]." [During this interview, she mentioned that she also senses a general lack of empathy or support from her inner circle. In addition, she now lives in a neighborhood of mostly nonprofessional women who focus on home and family management. She senses that they think of her as inferior because she works and doesn't attend to home and family the way they do.]

Or

The vignettes that pop to mind are many: the pediatric surgeon who sought out the male resident to teach how to drain an abscess on my patient; the neonatologist who said he would "clobber" me had I not been a "lady" because he didn't like being called late in the day about a sick newborn (I guess I should be thankful I was a woman that day).

To complete your analysis of content validity, assess the construct validity of the cultural agreement you think exists (see chapter 7).

COLLECT TIME-SERIES (HISTORICAL) DATA

As with cultural data collected through informal and semistructured interviews and observations, place data collected in structured interviews in context with historical and macrolevel processes. One way to do this is to incorporate the assembly or collection of aggregated time-series data into your data collection plans. Use these data to identify macrolevel historical processes, like structural changes in regional economies. Equally important, allow for the construction of appropriate time-series variables from your survey data.

Ethnographers rarely use time series. But you should. Consider the following scenario:

Mary is a civil servant in a Third World country who was 35 in 1985, the youngest of 5 siblings. As of 1985, she had completed secondary school, and, at various times, had received further work-related overseas schooling in the United States and the United Kingdom. She had been promoted from an entry-level to a mid-level civil service position, and was up for promotion to a senior-level position after some 15 years of government service. She was also pursuing a university degree in night school to increase her chances for promotion to still more responsible positions. Although Mary dated regularly and generally had good relationships with men, she had never married and did not want to, at least in the foreseeable future. She had no children, and did not either expect or want any. She had purchased land in a middle-class neighborhood and had built a nice house, where she lived alone. Her savings had accumulated, and, periodically, she vacationed abroad. She particularly enjoyed sailing on cruise ships.

Mary's life stood in stark contrast with that of her mother, who had had only 6 years of education and who worked principally as a maid when Mary was growing up. Mary grew up in a small, moveable wood-frame dwelling situated on rented land, where she lived with her grandmother, mother, and her brothers and sisters. Mary's mother had never married; but she would have liked to, if she had found a partner who did not resort to violence to settle domestic arguments. Had she married, she would have liked to have had more children. Mary's mother had never accumulated savings and had never either lived or visited abroad. Instead, she looked forward to the day when her children might have good jobs and could help her in her old age. She was to be disappointed. For although she had shared what little she had with her own mother, only Mary and one other child gave her regular help as of 1985. The other three children lived abroad and rarely even wrote home.

The differences between the lives of this mother and daughter are shared in varying degrees by women the world over. Documenting and determining why, exactly, changes like these occur is one of the biggest challenges facing the social sciences. These tasks also pose new methodological issues, for microlevel phenomena such as those described earlier reflect, at least in part, macrolevel changes in the availability of jobs, education, and real income, to name only a few potential influences. They also may constitute macrolevel variables, as when changes in the class composition of a society induce additional demands on government, when increases in the educational level of a workforce contribute to economic growth, or when declines in the birth rate change the medical needs of a population.

Documenting and testing explanations for historical changes such as these can be done best with historical, macrolevel time series. One reason ethnographers rarely use time series is that those available through official sources rarely include the variables that most interest us. When you can't find what you want in conventional data bases, create your own. Generate time-series data for variables in which you are specifically interested, for historical periods of up to thirty or forty years from survey data. But to do so, you must plan ahead and incorporate important survey design features. Do it like this:

1. Plan to estimate parameters for age cohorts, so stratify your sample by age. Randomly sample 5-year cohorts, for example. A total sample of

around 400 cases can yield acceptably good estimates for many variables for a time span of up to 40 years, including retrospective estimates of period age-specific fertility. But samples of as few as 200 total cases may suffice, or samples of more than 1,000 may be necessary, depending on the rarity of the event that you want to estimate (e.g., large samples will be necessary for reasonable estimates of infant mortality).

2. Identify age cohorts clearly. In the best of all possible worlds, be able to discriminate people by age precisely, by birth*day*, so that someone who was born on the 3rd of October is known to be older than someone who was born on the 4th of October of the same year. For many problems, however, less precise age measurements will suffice.

3. Measure prospective time-series variables for clearly identifiable developmental reference points. For example, measure the number of years of formal schooling completed *by age 20;* or jobs held *at age 25;* or cumulative number of births *by age 30.* You can measure changes in the class composition of a society by estimating the proportion of people who were raised in lower-class homes. To create a historical time series, however, you have to relate this variable to a developmental reference point. For example, the time-series variable might be "the proportion of people who were aged 20 in 1950, 1951, 1952, . . . , 1980 who were raised in a lower-class home."

4. Sort your cases from the youngest to the oldest. The SYSTAT SORT command can do this job easily and quickly.

5. Generate LOWESS smoothed values of the time-series variable or variables (on LOWESS, see Cleveland 1979, 1981; Efrom and Tibshirani 1991). A variable like education, which is recorded as the "number of years of completed schooling," can be smoothed in its original measurements. If you are interested in the proportion of women who completed secondary school, you will have to create an appropriate dummy variable first. This task is a simple one if you use the SYSTAT module SERIES.

6. Equate pertinent developmental ages with years (e.g., assign people who were age 20 in 1950 to the year 1950).

7. The LOWESS smoothed values of "number of years of formal schooling by age 20" can then be used as estimates of the mean years of schooling at age 20 among women who, for example, were 20 in 1950,

1951, . . . , 1980. If you don't use SYSTAT and your statistical software cannot produce LOWESS smoothing, you might compute means for 5-year cohorts, assign the means to the year that corresponds to the middle of the age cohort, and assign missing values on the assumption of constant growth rates between existing values. Smooth the resulting series as appropriate.

Figure 5.2 shows a time series constructed by these procedures that reveals regionally distinctive historical trends in the proportion of native children who experienced hurtful social interaction from non-natives ("ethnic violence") in Alaska and the Russian Far East. Figures 5.3 and 5.4 reveal a time-lagged linkage between traumatic stress inflicted on native children by non-natives and late violent death. A finding that traumatic stress inflicted on native children by natives exhibits no demonstrable link to violent death ties this phenomenon uniquely to social issues having to do specifically with the distribution of power within that community and

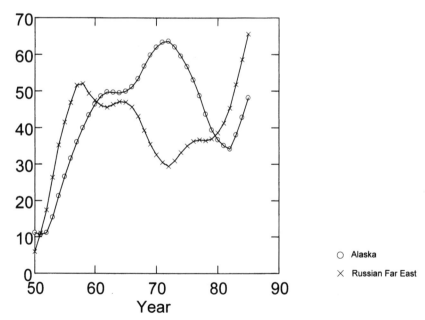

○ Alaska

✕ Russian Far East

FIGURE 5.2
Trends in Ethnic Violence toward Native Children in Alaska and the Russian Far East

intergroup competition over access to resources. Indeed, both the Alaskan and Russian time-series trends in the incidence of ethnic violence toward native children appear to correspond closely with the degree to which natives and non-natives came into overt conflict over resources. Ethnic violence rose dramatically during the 1950s as immigration by non-natives swelled the regional population. In Alaska, increasing interaction between natives and non-natives coincided with the Civil Rights Movement in the South and provided the impetus for native human and land rights claims through the decade of the 1960s and increasing rates of ethnic violence to children. The subsequent decline of ethnic violence coincides with the establishment of Native Corporations after 1971, which gave natives a position of power in Alaskan society. Collapse of oil prices in the 1980s and other events spurred an increase in ethnic violence to children.

The time lags for the effects of hurtful words heard in childhood on later violent death mean that the Alaskan time series extend beyond the limits of our data on violent deaths. These periods of time, in which we

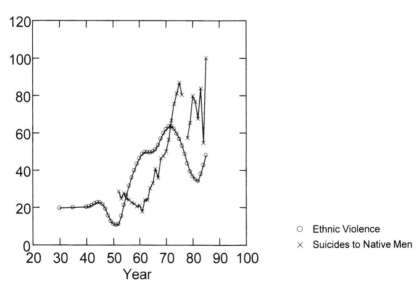

FIGURE 5.3
Time-Lagged Correlation (r = .890, p < .000) between Ethnic Violence and Violent Death to Alaskan Natives

have estimates of ethnic violence but no current data on violent deaths, permit a further test of the hypothesis that childhood experiences of ethnic violence lead to violent deaths in adolescence and adulthood.

The aggregated data you collected during the first phase of your project give you a second way to place individual data in context with historical and macrolevel processes. Use the macrolevel variables contained in aggregated sets of data to incorporate macrolevel variables into microlevel models. For example, "employment opportunities" is a difficult variable to measure for individuals. Fundamentally, it is a macrolevel phenomenon manifested as growth in jobs and pay throughout the economy. In a study of Antigua, I measured it is as a composite of three variables (Handwerker 1993a).

1. The first variable measured realized opportunities with information on sampled women's current monthly income.

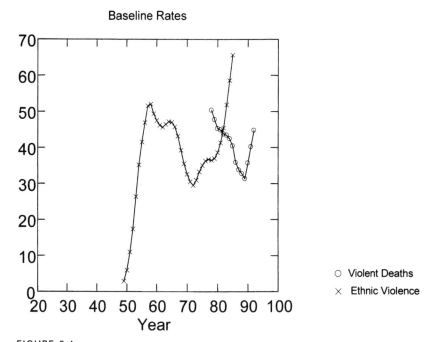

FIGURE 5.4
Time-Lagged Correlation ($r = .893$, $p < .000$) between Ethnic Violence and Violent Death to Russian Natives

2. The second variable measured the realism of employment expectations. Social class influences one's chance of finding good jobs that pay well in obvious and significant ways even today. I measure women's realism expectations with a social class indicator—their mother's level of education. Social class influences chances for advancement, as well as chances for employment. To capture potential interaction between these variables, I took the product of the social class and the realized opportunities variables.

3. The third variable reflected my expectation that macrolevel economic growth alters the effects of the interaction of social class and realized opportunities. Prior to about 1965, there was little economic growth as measured by Antigua's Gross Domestic Product (GDP), and few new employment opportunities. Employment opportunities estimated from GDP grew rapidly until they leveled off in the 1980s. Women who turned twenty during the 1980s had much the same employment opportunities. Women who turned twenty prior to about 1965 had much the same employment opportunities, albeit many fewer than were available to women who turned twenty in the 1980s. Each year between 1965 to 1980, however, women who turned twenty had increasing real job opportunities. I used a cohort variable equal to 1 for women younger than thirty in 1988, and increasing by 1 unit increments for each year of age back to about 1965, to tap the growth of job opportunities available due to macrolevel economic growth. To discount the interaction of the social class and realized opportunities indicator, I divided the cohort index into their product.

6

How to Build Your Data Base by Making Basic Comparisons Early

Data from structured interviews make possible the explicit comparisons necessary to meet project goals. If your project calls for the collection of life experience data with which to test specific hypotheses bearing on the extent to which or the likelihood that people with specific precursor life experiences employ one or another cultural models or engage in one or another pattern of behavior, plan an interactive process. Make basic comparisons early. Establish an appropriate sampling frame midway through the two- to three-week period that it will take to formulate a good structured interview. Analysis and diagnostics of your first set of data from structured interviews should lead to changes in your sampling frame and more fine-tuned data collection.

Once you begin your structured interviews, don't work on anything else. You won't have time. If you conduct a survey, don't wait until you finish to search for findings. Enter structured interview data into electronic format the day they come in. If you aim for a small sample of 20–50 cases, analyze your data at the end of data collection. If you aim for 100–200 cases, conduct a preliminary analysis after you've entered the first 50 cases. If you aim for a relatively large sample of 400–500 cases, do another preliminary analysis after you've entered about 200 cases. Use these preliminary analyses to explore your data—see the questions in table 6.1. Play with data transformations. Write batch data transformation and data anal-

ysis command files to make your final analysis go faster. Use your preliminary as well as your final field analysis of structured interview or observation data to identify questions about meaning and cultural variability that
you still need to ask.

If you know little or nothing about numerical analysis, read this chapter and the two following chapters very, very slowly. Remember that numbers contain a tremendous amount of information. If you don't take your
time, you'll become overwhelmed by the information. To avoid a panic
reaction, dissect the chapter into tiny bits. Study the interplay between
textual explanation and graphics. Create a mind game with yourself to
come up with your own examples for each data analysis question and the
statistic that can answer that question. Consult a basic textbook (e.g., Bernard 2000, 2001) to see more examples.

EMPLOY SIX NORMING AND STANDARDIZING OPERATIONS

Understanding comes from comparison, and comparison requires a common reference point. We call these points reference *norms* or *standards*.
We call the six different kinds of operations by which we create reference
points *norming* or *standardizing*.

1. Standardize *frequencies* (*f*) on the *number of observations* (*N*) to create
   proportions and *probabilities* (*f/N*). Multiply that number by 100 to create *percentages*.
2. Sum the *probability of observed values* to create *arithmetic means*.

   Means are defined as the expected value of a series of observations.
   Means thus constitute a prediction of a variable with an equation like
   this: $Y = \beta + \epsilon$. This equation says you can predict the variable Y
   with a constant β (beta). It also says that you cannot predict the variable perfectly. Some predictions will overestimate the variable. Others
   will underestimate it. Each prediction makes some degree of random
   error ϵ (epsilon). The mean thus assumes that a variable exhibits a
   specific value but that observation of the variable introduces random
   error into your measurements. The mean estimates the constant β.
   The standard deviation (*sd*) estimates the average amount of error
   when you predict a variable as its mean.

Given that the arithmetic mean is defined as the expected value of a series of observations, calculate the arithmetic mean as the sum of the probabilities of finding the observed values. If you ask nine prostitute informants how many clients they serviced during the last three hours and they give you the following set of values (0, 1, 2, 2, 3, 4, 4, 5, 12), to find the mean, multiply each observation by the probability of its occurrence (1/9), and sum the series—in short, add the numbers and divide by the number of observations.

Find the error made when you use the mean as the variable's expected value by finding the difference between each value and the mean, then sum the discrepancies between the prediction (the mean) and the observation. Figure 6.1 shows the average number of commercial sex transactions in the last three hours, plus the responses for each informant. Lines of different lengths highlight the discrepancy between specific respondents and the mean, and the size of each. Note that negative discrepancies (the mean *overestimates* the number of transactions) perfectly balances the positive discrepancies (the mean *underestimates* the number of transactions. By definition, the sum of the errors comes to zero.

To measure how much variation exists around the mean, square each discrepancy and sum the series. This operation creates the *Sum of Squares* (*SS*). This quantity becomes the variation you will attempt to explain by reference to other variables.

To measure the *average* amount of variation around the mean, divide the *Sum of Squares* (*SS*) by $N - 1$, then remove the squaring by taking the square root of this number. This operation creates the *standard deviation* (*sd*). *Note:* Use $N - 1$ (rather than N) to compute this average because the samples on which you can calculate standard deviations necessarily contain *less* variation than the entire population you sampled. The quantity ($N - 1$) corrects your *sample* estimate of the average level of variation in your target *population.*

The *mode*, by contrast, is merely the value in a distribution that occurs most often. The frequency of the modal value standardized on the total number of observations constitutes the probability of its occurrence. Distributions with 2 or more values that occur relatively frequently constitute *bimodal* or *multimodal* distributions. Sex transac-

TABLE 6.1

Answer Different Questions	With Different Statistics
What's the smallest value, the largest value, and the distance between them?	Minimum, Maximum, Range
How often does this event occur, compared to all other possibilities (i.e., what's the probability of this event)?	Proportion (f/N)
How many times out of 100 does this event occur, compared to all other possibilities?	Percentage $(f/N)*100$
How big is this value compared to that value?	Index (X_1/X_0) ■ Consumer Price Index = (Cost of Goods at Time t_{0+n})/(Cost of Goods at Time t_0) ■ Real Wage "Rages" = Average Wages/CPI
How often does this event occur compared to another?	Ratio (f_1/f_2) ■ sex ratios = $100*(f_m/f_f)$ Rates (f_y/f_x) ■ Infant Mortality = $1,000*(f_{infants-who-die}/f_{infants born})$
How much has this changed?	Proportion or percentage change $[(X_1 - X_0)/X_0$ ■ Population Growth = $(P_{1980} - P_{1930})/P_{1950}$ = (4.4 billion − 2.5 billion)/2.5 billion = .76.
How fast did the change occur, on average?	Geometric Mean (Proportion change$^{1/n}$ where n = number of time units between t_1 and t_0). ■ $1.76^{1/30}$ = 1.9 percent per year for the 30 years between 1950 and 1980.
What's the special value?	Mean (arithmetic mean = Sum of X/N)
What value splits the distribution into two equal parts?	Median (the value of the $[N/2]$nd case; the 50th percentile)
Where's the middle 50 percent of the cases?	Interquartile Range (the cases between the 25th percentile and the 75th percentile); the value of the 25th percentile is the lower hinge; the value of the 75th percentile is the upper hinge.
What's an unusual case (outlier), using the interquartile range as the basis for comparison?	All cases in the lower quartile with values smaller than the lower hinge by 1.5 *Interquartile Range, and all cases in the upper quartile with values larger than the upper hinge by 1.5 *Interquartile Range.
What value occurs most often?	Mode
How much variation is there?	Sum of Squares (SS) = Sum of (Discrepancies between Values and the Mean)^2
What's the average level of variation?	Standard deviation (sd) = $(SS/N − 1)^5$

Answer Different Questions	With Different Statistics
What's the size of this value, compared to the average level of variation?	z-score = (Discrepancy between a value and the mean)/(standard deviation)
What's an unusual case (outlier), using the average level of variation (*sd*) as the basis for comparison?	Cases with z-scores much larger than $+/-2.00$.
Is the distribution symmetrical?	Mean, median, and mode occupy the same location.
Is the distribution skewed?	Mean pulled away from the median, which is pulled away from the mode, in the direction of skew.
How often does this finding (mean, proportion, or difference) occur just by chance?	Probability given by an appropriate statistical test.

tions exhibit a bimodal distribution because two informants completed 2 and 4 transactions each, and only one informant completed 0, 1, 3, 5, and 12 transactions in the last 3 hours.

The *median* is the value of the case that falls at the 50th percentile and divides the array into two equal parts. With 9 informants, the median case is informant 5, and the value of the median case is 3; with 10 informants, the median case falls between informants 5 and 6 and the value of the median would be the midpoint of the values for 5 and 6. The *interquartile range* identifies the middle 50 percent of cases that fall between the 25th and 75th percentile. The value of the case that falls at the 25th percentile is the *lower hinge*. The value of the case that falls at the 75th percentile is the *upper hinge*. The lower and upper hinges are 2 and 4, respectively.

3. Standardize the *value of one event* (x_1) on the *value of another event* (x_0) to create an *index*. For example,

- Consumer Price Indexes express the dollar value of a set of basic commodities and services in one year as a ratio of the value of the same commodities and services in a reference point year. The 1998 U.S. Consumer Price Index for urban areas set the average costs over the years 1982–84 as equal to 100. The CPI for 1962, the year I started college, was 30.2. The CPI for 1997, the year my youngest children started college, was 160.5. Basic living expenses were

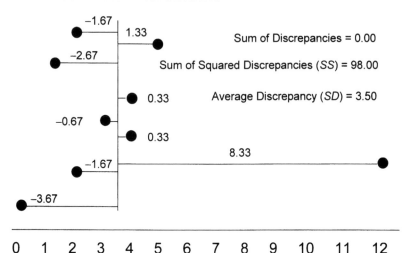

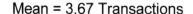

FIGURE 6.1
Identifying and Measuring Variation around the Mean

$(160.5/30.2) = 5.3$ times higher in 1997 than they were in 1962. What cost me $100 costs my children $530.

- Real Wage "Rates" express the average wage as a proportion of consumer price indexes; real wage indexes express the average wage rates in one year as a ratio of the average wage rates in a reference point year. In 1953, the real wage rate in Antigua, West Indies, was 187.8. If we set 1953 as the index year, the real wage index for 1953 becomes 100. The real wage rate in Antigua in 1985 was 417.9, so the real wage index was 2.2—in 30 years, real income had more than more than doubled.

4. Standardize the *frequency of one event* (f_y) on *the frequency of another event* (f_x) to create *ratios* and *rates.* For example,

- Divide the number of males born by the number of females born (f_m/f_f) to create a *sex ratio* at birth for a population. Multiply the *sex ratio* by 100 to find the number of males born for every 100 females born.
- Divide the number of births for one year by the total population

in midyear, then multiply by 1,000, to find a population's *Crude Birth Rate*. The result of (Births/Midyear Population) *1,000 tells you the number of births for every 1,000 people in the population.

- Divide the number of deaths for one year by the total population in midyear, then multiply by 1,000, to find a population's *Crude Death Rate*. The result of (Deaths/Midyear Population) *1,000 tells you the number of deaths for every 1,000 people in the population.

- Divide the number of infant deaths for one year by the number of live births in that year, then multiply by 1,000, to find a population's *Infant Mortality Rate*. The result of (Infant Deaths/Live Births)*1,000 tells you the number of infant deaths for every 1,000 live births.

5. Standardize *one rate or index* on an *initial rate or index* to measure the *change* in rates or indexes. The difference between a *Rate at Time 1* and the *Rate at Time 0*, divided by the *Rate at Time 0*, gives you the proportional change in rates. Multiply the proportional change by 100 to find the *percentage change* in rates. For example,

- The world's population in 1950 was approximately 2.5 billion people and grew to 4.4 billion people in 1980. The world's population grew by (4.4 − 2.5), or 1.9 billion people. The population in 1980 was (4.4/2.5), or 1.76 times larger than the population in 1950, or 176 percent larger than the population in 1950. The world's population grew from the original (100 percent) by (4.4 − 2.5)/2.5, or 76 percent.

- *Rates of change* constitute *geometric* means. To find the *average rate of world population growth* between the 30 years that elapsed between 1950 and 1980, take the 30th root of the proportional change of 1.76. $1.76^{1/30} = 1.9$ percent per year for the 30 years between 1950 and 1980. The world's population grew by an annual average of 1.9 percent between 1950 and 1980.

6. Standardize *discrepancies between observations and the mean* (observation − mean) on the *standard deviation* to express these discrepancies as a proportion of the average level of variation in your observations. Standardizing scores converts them to units of the Normal Distribution, called *z-scores*. This makes the mean = 0.00 and the standard

deviation = 1.00. As figure 6.2 shows, for example, the prostitute who did no business in the previous 3 hours expressed a level of business about the same size as the average level of variation (z-score = 1.05), but below (the z-score was a *negative* 1.05) the average of 3.67 business transactions. The prostitutes who completed 4 transactions during that 3-hour period expressed a level of business only 10 percent the size of the average level of variation, and *over* the average of 3.67 business transactions (the z-score was a *positive* .10). The prostitute who completed 12 transactions during the previous 3 hours expressed a level of business 2.38 times greater than the average level of variation in these observations, and above the average. Standard scores higher than plus or minus 2 represent unusual large discrepancies from the average level of variation and constitute *outliers*. Did this informant exaggerate? How, exactly, did she attract and service 12 clients in only 3 hours?

Standardize to make comparisons between variables measured with different scales. Standardizing variables measured with the same scale provides a convenient basis for converting scores to binary codes—all negative scores become 0s; all positive scores become 1s. Transpose your matrix to standardize on informants if you suspect that they may apply different mental scales to a set of ratings data.

USE PICTURES TO UNDERSTAND THE PROPERTIES OF FREQUENCY DISTRIBUTIONS

Frequency distributions may exhibit symmetry or *skew*. The mean, median, and mode at the same location define symmetric distributions. In skewed distributions, like the commercial transactions in figures 6.2 and 6.3, the mean is pulled away from the median, which is pulled away from the mode.

Use three kinds of pictures in combination to help you evaluate the distribution characteristics of particular variables (see figure 6.3). *Stem-and-leaf* plots partition each observation into a stem number and a leaf number and show the value of each case from the smallest to the largest distribution. Stem-and-leaf plots give you a good picture of the distribution of cases in the body of a distribution and identify outliers. They also

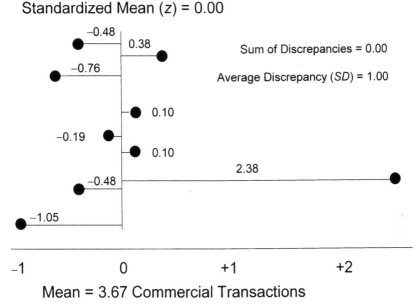

Standardized Mean (z) = 0.00

−0.48
0.38
−0.76
Sum of Discrepancies = 0.00
Average Discrepancy (SD) = 1.00
0.10
−0.19
0.10
2.38
−0.48
−1.05

−1   0   +1   +2

Mean = 3.67 Commercial Transactions

FIGURE 6.2
Measuring Variation around the Mean with Standard Scores

identify the minimum and maximum values, the median, and the lower hinge and upper hinge. Stem-and-leaf plots truncate the full range of possible scores, however. They thus give a misleading impression of the shape of the overall distribution.

Box-and-whisker plots show the shape of the entire distribution. The box contains the middle 50 percent of all cases—those between the lower hinge (25th percentile) and the upper hinge (75th percentile), and a line identifies the location of the median (the 50th percentile). Whiskers extend to cases with values lower than the 25th percentile and higher than the 75th percentile, so long as the case locations fall within 1.5 times the interquartile range (the length of the box). Cases located beyond these bounds constitute outliers.

Dot density plots show the location of each case, as well as an accurate picture of the full distribution of a variable. However, dot density plots do not explicitly identify outliers.

```
Stem and Leaf Plot of Variable:
Commercial Sex Transactions in Past Four Hours, N = 9

         Minimum:         0.000
         Lower Hinge:         2.000
         Median:          3.000
         Upper Hinge:         4.000
         Maximum:        12.000

               0   0
               1   0
               2 H 00
               3 M 0
               4 H 00
               5   0
      * * * Outside Values * * *
              12   0
```

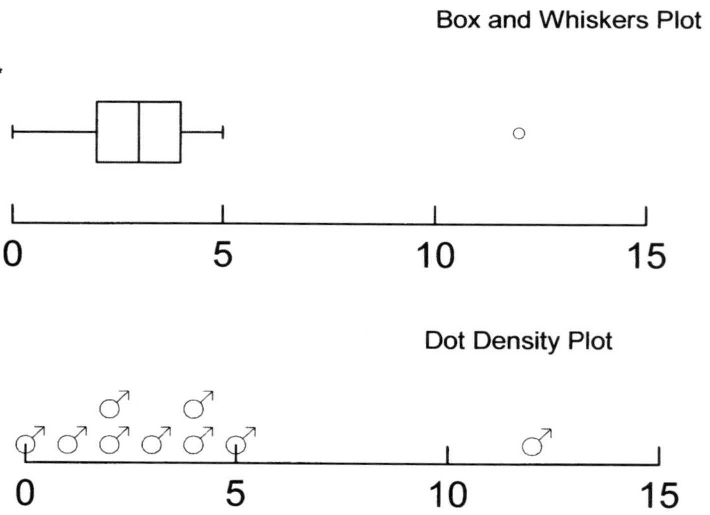

Box and Whiskers Plot
0
5
10
15
Dot Density Plot
0
5
10
15

FIGURE 6.3
Pictures for Evaluating a Variable's Overall Distribution

LOOK FOR RELATIONSHIPS BETWEEN VARIABLES

Identify relationships between two variables by looking for the way in which changes in one variable correspond in direction and magnitude with changes in the other. With variables measured with ratio or ordinal scales, z-scores make these comparisons easy to see because standardizing gives each variable the same reference points (mean $= 0$, $sd = 1$).

Z-scores of -1.00 identify informants who exhibited a value 1 standard deviation below the mean, whether the variable was "business transactions completed by a prostitute in the last 3 hours," the number of "hurtful experiences experienced by Native Americans when interacting with Yankees," or the intensity of "affection between parent and child." Two variables co-vary to the extent to which *both* variables exhibit *identical* sets of standardized scores. Two variables thus co-vary when they *share* variance. Two variables co-vary perfectly when they share an identical *pattern* of variation.

Measure *co-variation* for specific cases as the product of their set of z-scores (e.g., $-1.46 * -1.46 = 2.13$). *Pearson's r* coefficient measures the *average* amount of co-variation in a set of observations. When each set of z-scores exhibits the same sign, on average, the relationship is positive—as one variable goes up, the other goes up. If each set of z-scores exhibits the opposite sign, on average, the relationship is negative—as one variable goes up, the other goes down. In *perfect* positive relationships (see figure 6.4), when one variable changes by 1 standard deviation unit, the other changes the same amount (1), and $r = 1.00$. In *perfect* negative relationships, when one variable changes by 1 standard deviation unit, the other changes the same amount but in the opposite direction (-1), and $r = -1.00$.

Figure 6.5 shows a *scatterplot* of the relationship between the number of commercial sex transactions in the last three hours and location of the business relative to the police station.

Figure 6.6 shows the sets of standardized scores for the number of commercial sex transactions in the last three hours and the location of the business relative to the police station, and their co-variance. The *regression* line drawn among the cases identifies the best linear fit among the complete set of scores. An $r = .39$ means that when one variable changes by 1 standard deviation unit, the other changes an average of .39 standard devi-

Z(Var1)	Z(Var2)	Z(Var1*Var1)
−1.46	−1.46	2.13
−1.10	−1.10	1.20
−0.73	−0.73	0.53
−0.37	−0.37	0.13
0.00	0.00	0.00
0.37	0.37	0.13
0.73	0.73	0.53
1.10	1.10	1.20
1.46	1.46	2.13

Both Variables Exhibit the *Same* Discrepancy in the *Same* Direction, Which Means a Perfect *Positive* Relationship:

Pearson's *r* = +1.00

Z(Var1)	Z(Var2)	Z(Var1*Var1)
−1.46	1.46	−2.13
−1.10	1.10	−1.20
−0.73	0.73	−0.53
−0.37	0.37	−0.13
0.00	0.00	0.00
0.37	−0.37	−0.13
0.73	−0.73	−0.53
1.10	−1.10	−1.20
1.46	−1.46	−2.13

Both Variables Exhibit the *Same* Discrepancy in the *Opposite* Direction, Which Means a Perfect *Negative* Relationship:

Pearson's *r* = -1.00

FIGURE 6.4
Measuring Co-Variation

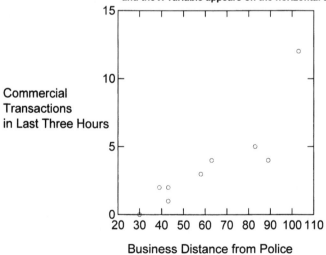

By convention, the *Y* variable appears on the vertical axis of plots and tables and the *X* variable appears on the horizontal axis.

FIGURE 6.5
Scatterplot of Commercial Sex Transactions by Distance from a Police Station

ation units. An $r = .87$ means that when one variable changes by 1 standard deviation unit, the other changes an average of .87 standard deviation units. The Pearson's r of .873 thus indicates a strong positive relationship between the level of business and distance to the police station. The Pearson's r of .89 in figures 5.4 and 5.5 reveal strong positive relationships between the time-lagged trends in childhood ethnic violence experiences and later violent death.

Note: Pearson's r applied to ordinal (rating) scores becomes the coefficient called *Spearman's Rho*. Pearson's r applied to binary scores becomes the coefficient called *Phi*. To know how much variance two variables share, calculate r^2.

Identify relationships between two binary variables (coded 1 for yes/present and 0 otherwise) by looking at the proportion of cases in cell *a*, or cells *a* and *d*, compared to the proportion of cases in the remaining cells in a 2 × 2 table like the following:

Y and *X* can represent variables, like whether or not an informant currently uses a biomedical prescription medicine (*X*), or whether or not the informant currently uses a bush tea or home remedy to prevent or treat disease (*Y*). The letters *a, b, c,* and *d* represent the number of informants who fall into particular cells of the table. For example, in a needs assessment for the elderly, the value of *a* might tell us the number of informants who currently used *both* prescription medicines *and* home remedies. The value of *d* would tell us the number of informants who used *neither* prescription medicines *nor* home remedies. Sums across rows (*a* + *b, c* + *d*) and down columns (*a* + *c, b* + *d*) yield marginal frequencies, which sum to *N*, the total number of cases.

FOR ETHNOGRAPHY, LOOK FOR RELATIONSHIPS BETWEEN INFORMANTS

Y and *X* can also represent informants, and cell frequencies can constitute counts of characteristics they share or do not share. For example, elderly informants may experience difficulty carrying out activities of living because of conditions like arthritis, severe burns, diabetes, amputations, circulation problems, back injuries, cancer, or problems with their heart, eyesight, or hearing. To see similarities and differences between informants, create a variable-by-informant matrix like the one in box 6.1.

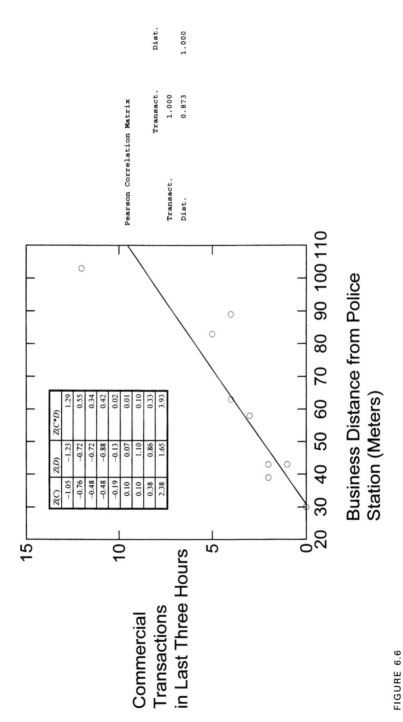

Pearson Correlation Matrix

	Transact.	Dist.
Transact.	1.000	
Dist.	0.873	1.000

Z(C)	Z(D)	Z(C*D)
−1.05	−1.23	1.29
−0.76	−0.72	0.55
−0.48	−0.72	0.34
−0.48	−0.88	0.42
−0.19	−0.13	0.02
0.10	0.07	0.01
0.10	1.10	0.10
0.38	0.86	0.33
2.38	1.65	3.93

Commercial Transactions in Last Three Hours

Business Distance from Police Station (Meters)

FIGURE 6.6
Pearson's *r* and the Regression Line for a Linear Relationship

TABLE 6.2

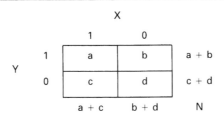

For the ten conditions measured for the two informants in box 6.1, a tabular comparison of the informants looks like this:

The letters *a, b, c,* and *d* now represent the number of characteristics shared or not shared between informants. For example, in a needs assessment for the elderly, the value of *a* would tell us the number of conditions that make it difficult to carry out activities of living shared by both informants. The value of *d* would tell us the number of conditions that make it difficult to carry out activities of living that don't affect either informant. Sums across rows $(a + b, c + d)$ and down columns $(a + c, b + d)$ yield marginal frequencies, which sum to *N*, the total number of conditions. Informant 2 has difficulty carrying out activities of living in part because he has a severe burn that Informant 1 doesn't have (cell *b*). Cells *a* and *d*

**Box 6.1   Variable by Informant Matrix to See Similarities
and Differences between Informants**

Source of Disability	Informant 1	Informant 2
Arthritis	1	1
Burn	0	1
Diabetes	0	0
Amputation	0	0
Circulation	0	0
Back injury	0	0
Cancer	0	0
Heart	0	0
Eyesight	0	0
Hearing	0	0

TABLE 6.3

		Informant 2		
		1	0	
Informant 1	1	1	1	2
	0	0	8	8
		1	9	10

contain the similarities between these informants. If you look at both cells, you find that the two informants are similar in that both have arthritis, and neither has diabetes, an amputation, circulation problems, back injuries, cancer, or problems with their heart, eyesight, or hearing. If you look just at cell *a*, you find that the two informants are similar in that both have arthritis.

Use the *Simple Matching* coefficient if you want to measure similarity by including qualities neither informant exhibits (diabetes, an amputation, circulation problems, back injuries, cancer, or problems with their heart, eyesight, or hearing); use Pearson's coefficient as an alternative. The Simple Matching coefficient expresses all agreements among informants (cells *a* + d) as a proportion of the total (cells *a* + *b* + *c* + *d*).

Use *Jaccard's coefficient* to measure similarities between informants if your comparisons should ignore qualities neither exhibits (diabetes, an amputation, circulation problems, back injuries, cancer, or problems with their heart, eyesight, or hearing) to focus on qualities both exhibit (arthritis). When you count mutual absences (cell *d*), you may produce misleading or irrelevant comparisons that make two informants appear similar mainly because of the qualities neither exhibits (the absence of diabetes, heart problems, amputations, and the like). Jaccard's coefficient measures informant similarities as the proportion of qualities both exhibit (cell *a*) as a proportion of qualities at least one informant exhibits, and as both *could* exhibit (cells *a* + b + c).

The similarity between these two informants as measured by Jaccard's coefficient is ($[a = 1]/[a+b+c = 2]$) = 0.500. The similarity between these two informants as measured by the Simple Matching coefficient is

($[a + d = 9] / [a + b + c + d = 10] = 0.900$. (The similarity between these two informants as measured by Pearson's coefficient is .667.)

BEWARE OF RANDOM ERROR

Random error occurs merely because each sample of observations differs from every other sample of observations. Figure 6.7 shows dot density plots with embedded box plots of 9 samples—3 random samples of 1,000 cases each, 3 random samples of 100 samples each, and 3 random samples of 10 cases each, along with their means. These samples come from the normal population with a parameter (β) of 0.00. Each sample of the same size differs from every other sample of the same size, and none of their means estimates the parameter of 0.00 perfectly. Note from the embedded box plots that even very large random samples may contain outliers just by chance.

Figure 6.8 shows scatterplot matrices (SPLOM) of the relationships between the three variables for each set of samples ($N = 10, 100$, and 1,000). Each pair of variables appears in a scatterplot, along with box plots of the distribution of each variable. I include their Pearson's coefficients. Pearson's coefficients estimate a parameter called *rho* (ρ). The parameter $\rho = 0.00$ in the population sampled. No Pearson's coefficient equals 0. Although the Pearson's coefficients from the largest samples come close to 0.00, the small sample gives us estimates of 0.316, 0.295, and -0.530.

Samples of different sizes give different results. Larger samples look more like each other than smaller samples. Large samples thus contain small amounts of random error, and small samples contain large amounts of random error. Means and Pearson's coefficients calculated for large samples estimate their respective parameters (β, ρ) more precisely than small samples.

Figure 6.9 shows overlaid dot density plots of the three 10-case and three 100-case samples. Successive random samples fluctuate around the population parameter of 0.00. Means or Pearson's coefficients calculated on successive random samples also fluctuate around the population parameter. Sample means or Pearson's coefficients will converge on the parameter exactly as you draw more and more samples. This holds true even for highly skewed populations.

Random error thus means that statistics fluctuate from sample to sam-

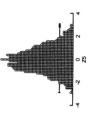

**3 Random
Samples, *N* = 1,000**

Mean = −.019   Mean = −.021   Mean = −.013

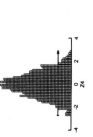

**3 Random
Samples, *N* = 100**

Mean = −.084   Mean = −.019   Mean = −.041

**3 Random
Samples, *N* = 10**

Mean = .267   Mean = −.076   Mean = −.439

FIGURE 6.7
Variation in Random Samples of Different Sizes: Distribution

Pearson Correlation Matrix

	Z1	Z2	Z3
Z1	1.000		
Z2	0.316	1.000	
Z3	-0.530	0.295	1.000

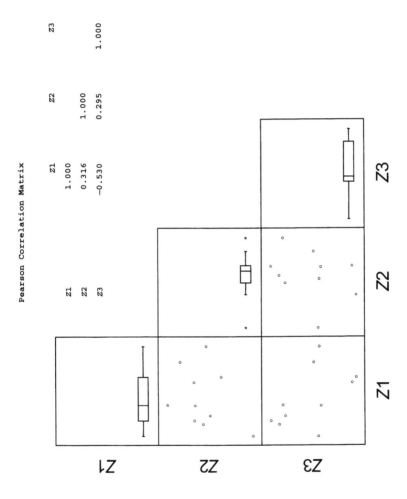

FIGURE 6.8
Variation in Random Samples of Different Sizes: Correlation

Pearson Correlation Matrix

	Z7	Z8	Z9
Z7	1.000		
Z8	-0.037	1.000	
Z9	0.037	-0.099	1.000

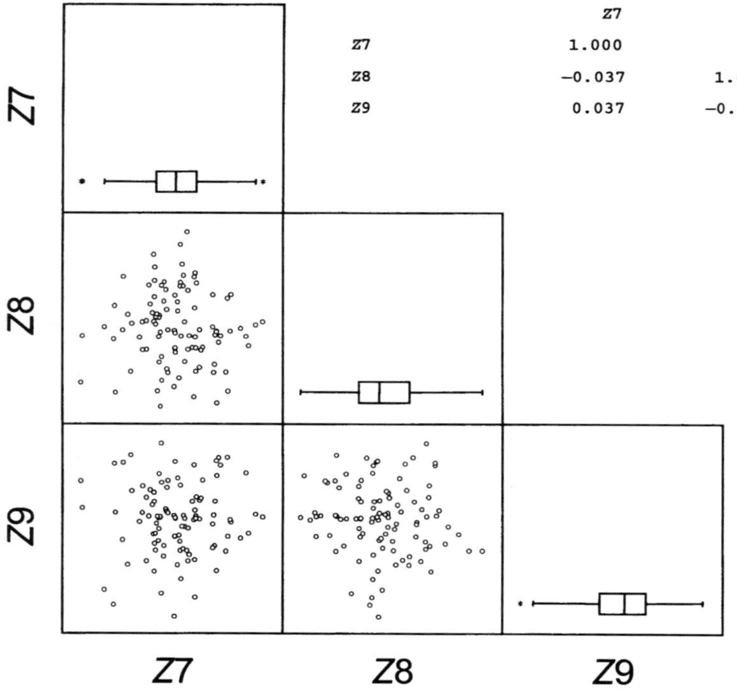

FIGURE 6.8 (Continued)

Pearson Correlation Matrix

	z4	z5	z6
z4	1.000		
z5	0.028	1.000	
z6	0.001	0.009	1.000

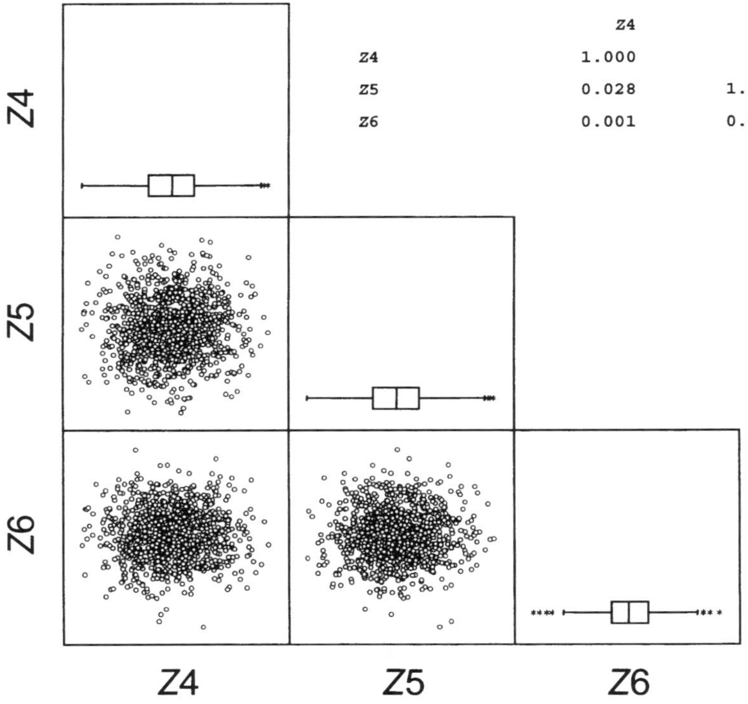

FIGURE 6.8 (Continued)

3 Random Samples of 10 Cases Each

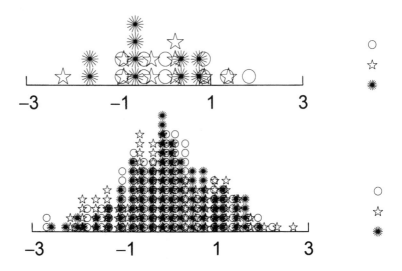

3 Random Samples of 100 Cases Each

FIGURE 6.9
Variation in Successive Random Samples

ple. Statistics fluctuate less as sample size goes up. Statistics fluctuate more as the variability in the population goes up (which we estimate with the standard deviation). The average level of error we make estimating a parameter from sample statistics is called the *standard error of the estimate (SE)*. The standard error of the mean, for example, is a simple ratio of the standard deviation to the square root of sample size *N*. To reiterate, large samples estimate population parameters more *precisely* than small samples.

We know the sampling distributions of many variables. This makes it possible to know the probability of finding a specific statistic if we draw a sample from a population with a specific parameter. Sampling distributions of means and Pearson's coefficients, for example, correspond with the sampling distribution of a variable called t, with N (k degrees of free-dom (k = number of variables). Like z-scores, t-scores measure distance from a mean set to 0.00. As N grows, the *t-distribution* converges with the *normal distribution* (see figure 6.10, which shows the slightly flattened *t*-distribution for t_{df} = 8 overlaid on a normal distribution).

With large samples, $t = z = +/-1.96$ identifies points on both sides

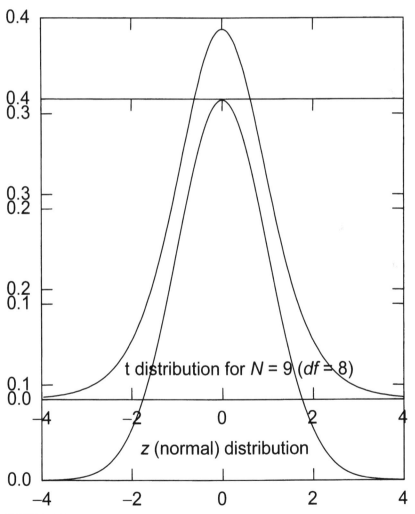

FIGURE 6.10
Overlay Plots of the Normal Distribution and a *t* Distribution

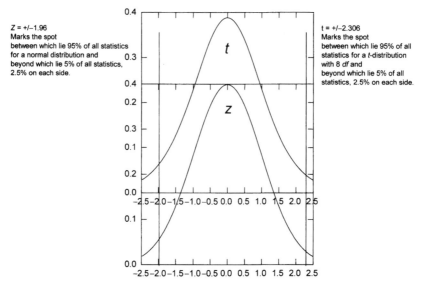

FIGURE 6.10 (Continued)

of the sampling distribution that contain 95 percent of all possible statistics drawn from successive samples from the same population. Thus, 2.5 percent of all possible statistics will *overestimate* the parameter and fall at a point higher than +1.96; 2.5 percent of all possible statistics will *underestimate* the parameter and fall at a point higher than −1.96. Smaller samples, with greater amounts of random error, make this number larger. For samples of 9 cases with ($N - k = 9 - 1$) or 8 degrees of freedom, this number becomes 2.306. Figure 6.10 identifies these points for the *t*-distribution and the normal distribution. The tails of the *t*-distribution at both points (1.96 and 2.306) contain noticeably more cases than the respective tails of the normal distribution.

TEST HYPOTHESES

Random error in your observations confounds the meaning of specific findings. For example:

- Robert Lowie (1921) looked at the possibility that Shoshone decorative rectangles employed the criterion of shape the ancient Greeks called the Golden Rectangle. The width/length ratio of 20 Shoshone rectangles averaged .660. The width/length ratio of the Golden Rectangle was .618. Lowie's average suggests that Shoshone employed an aesthetic standard different from the Golden Rectangle.

- The correlation of .873 between commercial sex transactions and business distance from the police station makes it look like business gets better the further away from police stations that business transactions take place.

Every statistic constitutes a point estimate of a parameter and thus embodies a test hypothesis (H_1)—namely, that the statistic perfectly or closely estimates the parameter. Thus, the Shoshone statistic of .660 is bigger than the Golden Rectangle parameter of .618. In short, H_1: Shoshone Mean $\neq$ Greek parameter (μ).

The Pearson's r statistic measures a real positive relationship between business transactions and distance from police stations. In short, H_1: the parameter rho $(\rho) \neq 0.00$.

But statistics fluctuate from sample to sample. Random error thus constitutes an alternative, null hypothesis (H_0)—namely, that the statistic occurred by chance.

- Maybe the Shoshone statistic of .660 is a random error; maybe the parameter from which the sample comes is .618? In short, H_0: Shoshone Mean = Greek parameter (μ).

- Maybe the correlation of .873 between commercial sex transactions and business distance from the police station is a random error; maybe the parameter from which the sample comes is 0.00? In short, H_0: the parameter rho $(\rho) = 0.00$.

You can't interpret your data unless you either reject or accept the null hypothesis. You may decide wrongly no matter what choice you make. If you accept the test hypothesis when the null hypothesis is true, you make a Type I, or alpha (α) error. If you accept the null hypothesis when the test hypothesis is true, you make a Type II, or beta (β) error. To decide this issue, you need to know the probability (p) that the null hypothesis is true.

In sum, your analysis gives you a specific *test hypothesis:*
   H_1: this finding is real.
Random error in your sample gives you a *null hypothesis:*
   H_0: this finding isn't real, it's just random error.

The probability (p) that the null hypothesis is true comes from a statistical test. There are many different statistical tests, but all yield one and only one value, p. All p's tell you the same thing: the probability that your finding occurred as a random error. Since p is the probability that H_0 is true, it also tells you how often you will be wrong to think that H_1 is true.

USE THE REGULARITY OF SAMPLING
DISTRIBUTIONS TO FIND PROBABILITIES

Use the *t*-distribution with $N - k$ degrees of freedom to find out how often you could find a statistic of .660 by random error in a sample drawn from a population with a parameter of .618. First, use confidence limits. Assume that Lowie's (1921) sample mean of .660 based on 20 cases perfectly estimates the parameter of the sampled population. For $N - k$ (20 − 1) = 19 degrees of freedom, $t = +/- 2.093$ identifies the points above and below the parameter that will contain 95 percent of all statistics calculated from samples drawn randomly from that population. Shoshone rectangles exhibit an $SE = .021$. To find the set of ratios that you could find as random error from a population characterized by a parameter of .660, add and subtract from the .660 the quantity ($SE*t = .021*2.093$), or .044. The lower limit of (.660 − .044 = .616) and the upper limit of (.660 + .044 = .704) contain 95 percent of all possible statistics calculated as random errors from 20 case samples from a population characterized by a parameter of .660. The Grecian Golden Ratio of .618 falls within these limits. Given that we don't know the parameter of the population from which we drew the Shoshone sample, and any of ratios contained by the interval constitute plausible parameters, we cannot dismiss the null hypothesis that the Shoshone mean constitutes a random error from a population with a parameter of .618.

Second, calculate the probability of finding a statistic of .660 as random error in a sample of 20 cases from a population characterized by the Grecian parameter of .618. Find $t =$ (statistic − parameter)/standard error, or $(.660 - .618)/.021 = 2.00$. For a $t = 2.00$ with N (k (19)) degrees of freedom, $p = .030$. Three percent of all statistics calculated as random errors in samples of 20 cases from a population characterized by the Grecian parameter of .618 will have ratios of .660 or larger. If you decide that the sample of Shoshone rectangles comes from a population with a parameter larger than .618, you'll be wrong 3 percent of the time.

What about the possibility that the Pearson's coefficient of .873 between level of business and distance from police stations is just a random error? The associated t-statistic of 4.743 for a sample of 9 informants with ($N - k = 9 - 2$) 7 degrees of freedom, $p = .002$. Only 2 of every 1,000 statistics calculated as random errors in samples of 9 cases from a population characterized by the parameter (π) of 0.00 will have Pearson's coefficients of .873 or larger. If you decide that the relationship between level of business and distance from police stations is *real* and comes from a population with a parameter larger than 0.00, you'll be wrong only 2 times out of 1,000.

INFORM YOUR INTERPRETATION WITH KNOWLEDGE OF SAMPLING DISTRIBUTIONS

External validity comes from properly designed sampling frames (see chapter 3). The criteria by which you select informants and the other internal validity confounds you measure determine the population to which you can validly generalize. But you will waste your time if you don't put in the effort to select a sample large enough to estimate parameters with the requisite precision. Explicitly evaluate the power you might expect for different effects in samples of different sizes (Wilkinson et al. 1999).

Power refers to your ability to detect the influence of one variable on another, if the effect is real. Power varies with the risk of a Type I or α (alpha) error that you're willing to accept, sample size, and the size of the effect that you want to be able to detect. The probability of making a Type II or β (beta) error—of *not* detecting a real relationship between variables—is $1 -$ Power. For a fixed sample and effect size, when you lower α, you simultaneously raise β. When you want to rigorously avoid concluding, for example, that distance from a police station influences the level of prostitute business transactions when, in fact, it doesn't, you might set α at .01. But when you do so, you reduce your chances of seeing a relationship that's real but weak.

Figure 6.11 illustrates the interdependencies between sample size, power, and effect size, when you set α at .01. Figure 6.12 illustrates the interdependencies between sample size, β, and effect size, when you set α at .01. As sample size goes up, your ability to detect a real relationship (*power*) goes up, and the chances that you'll miss it (β) goes down. But how power goes up and β goes down varies dramatically with the size of the effect. If the real shared variance between variables is about .06 (a Pearson's *r* of .25), you'd miss it about half the time even with a sample of 100 cases. If the real shared variance between variables is about .25 (a Pearson's *r* of .50), you'd only miss it about 9 percent of the time with a sample of only 50 cases, and you'd only miss it 1 percent of the time with a sample of 75 cases. By contrast, if the real shared variance between variables is about .76 (a Pearson's *r* of .873), you could expect to miss it only about 3 percent of the time even with a sample of only 10 cases, and not at all with only 15 cases.

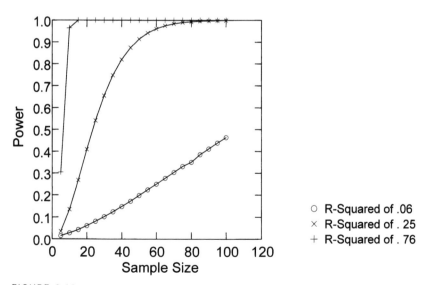

FIGURE 6.11
Relationship between Power and Sample Size for Effects of Different Sizes

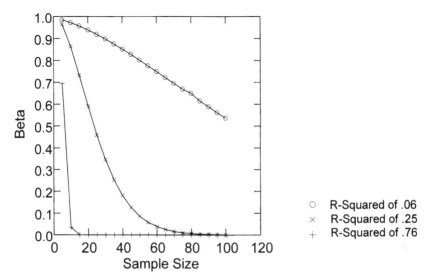

FIGURE 6.12
Relationship between Beta and Sample Size for Effects of Different Sizes

Select a sample large enough to detect the relationships you suspect might exist, and measure your variables reliably. The small amounts of random error (small standard errors) embedded in large samples with highly reliable measurements let you see small differences that you'd miss with smaller samples or less reliable measurements. Take advantage of the case-dependence built into cultural phenomena. Case-dependence produces small standard errors that classical tests overestimate. This means that ethnography requires fewer cases than other research, for the same precision. To make the most of this advantage, test hypotheses with boot-strap, jackknife, or permutation tests. If you use classical statistical tests like the t-test without corrections for case-dependence (see chapter 8), you make it harder to detect subtle forms of structure in your data. Small samples with variables measured unreliably produce the same effect—an increase in your chances of making a Type II, or beta (β) error. The power of your test just gets worse—the chance that you will fail to see effects grows (Tversky and Kahneman 1979)—when you select small samples from highly variable populations.

Explicit sampling frames (see chapter 3) stratify your sample in appropriate ways and, with specific exceptions, make huge samples unnecessary. Few field projects need structured interviews with more than 400–500 individuals. Samples of 100 suffice for many purposes; samples of 50 have their uses even when you conduct demographic research (e.g., Handwerker 1988).

How to Fine-Tune by Evaluating the Construct Validity of Cultures

The middle portion of your project will lead you to tentative conclusions about your study subject. Use the last portion of your project to validate and fine-tune these conclusions (see figure 7.1, which focuses on this part of your project). Begin by evaluating the construct validity of culture.

IS YOUR CONSTRUCT IMAGINARY?

Construct validity refers to the observed match between a set of observations and the theoretical construct it purports to measure (Campbell 1970). By virtue of being human, we *use* culture to interpret sensory input from the world of experience and use a variety of internal mental processes to alter both culture and behavior in ways that reflect variation in sensory input. One outcome consists of assumptions on which we construct our understanding of the world. Because our theories constitute cultural constitutions, they necessarily contain biases that mirror everything we have experienced and everything we have not experienced over the course of our lives. Hence make your central research objective to distinguish what's there from what you put there. *Validity* consists of a relationship between the definitions of specific mental constructions and specific observations. You cannot evaluate the validity of your data or findings without information about whether or not, or the degree to

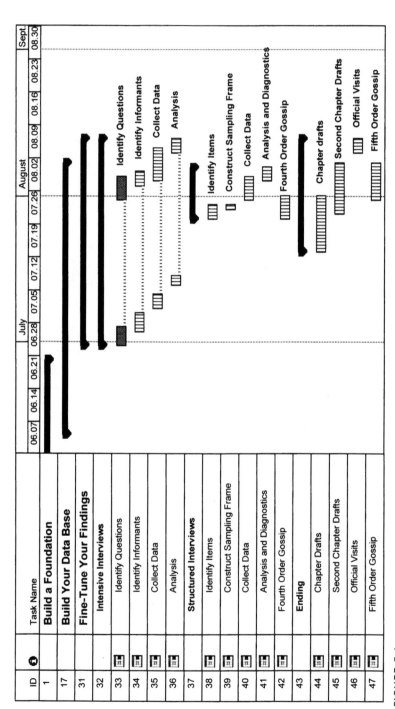

ID	❶	Task Name
1		**Build a Foundation**
17		**Build Your Data Base**
31		**Fine-Tune Your Findings**
32		**Intensive Interviews**
33		Identify Questions
34		Identify Informants
35		Collect Data
36		Analysis
37		**Structured Interviews**
38		Identify Items
39		Construct Sampling Frame
40		Collect Data
41		Analysis and Diagnostics
42		Fourth Order Gossip
43		**Ending**
44		Chapter Drafts
45		Second Chapter Drafts
46		Official Visits
47		Fifth Order Gossip

FIGURE 7.1
Fine-Tune Your Data Base

which, specific mental constructions correspond with specific observations and discriminate those observations from others.

Many critically important variables, like *stress, affection, problem-drinking,* and *perceived health,* cannot be measured directly. Indeed, we must posit their existence since we cannot see them. Measurement of multidimensional constructs like these require specific observations of a set of items, each of which constitutes an independent and imperfect measure of the otherwise unseen, underlying variable. Box 7.1, for example, lists six items that might constitute independent measures of a variable called *perceived health status.* As Campbell and Fiske (1959) point out, items that measure the same theoretical construct should correlate highly. Items that measure a second construct should not correlate as highly with the items that measure the first. If such a variable as *perceived health* exists, and if these items measure that variable, you will see it as a large intersection shared by the six items, any one of which measures *perceived health* imperfectly. A large shared variance among these items means that people who report high levels of *general well-being* should also report that they *eat, run,* and *see* well; people who report that they *eat* poorly should also report that they *hear, carry,* and *run* poorly.

USE FACTOR ANALYSIS TO IDENTIFY THE INTERSECTION AMONG SETS OF VARIABLES

Principal components analysis (e.g., Rummel 1970) provides a direct test of the hypothesis that a specific set of scale items constitutes an independent set of imperfect measurements of one and only one otherwise unseen, underlying variable. Principal components analysis constructs a

---

Box 7.1   Items for a Likert Scale Measuring Perceived Health

- In general, how would you describe your health?
- Please describe how clear your vision is.
- How clearly can you normally hear a conversation?
- How easily can you run at least 100 yards/meters?
- How easily can you carry 25 pounds (10 kilos) thirty feet (9 meters)?
- How easily can you bite and chew on hard foods?

small set of variables (*factors* or *principal components*) from additive combinations of existing similarities among variables. Each factor thus identifies the existence of otherwise unseen variables that lie at the intersection of observed similarities among variables you measured. The size of the intersection tells you the importance of the factor. Factor *loadings* (Pearson's coefficients) measure the size of the intersection. The square of a loading (r^2) tells you how much variance that a specific item shares with the unseen variable identified by each factor. Important measures of this unseen variable show loadings at or above 0.500 (25 percent shared variance). The sum of squared loadings for a factor (its *eigenvalue*) tells you how much variation *all* your cases or variables share with a factor. A factor's eigenvalue divided by the sum of eigenvalues for all factors tells you the overall size of the shared intersection identified by the factor.

The first factor or principal component identifies the largest shared intersection among a set of variables. The second factor accounts for the largest shared intersection that remains. Subsequent factors account for the largest shared intersection left by previously extracted factors.

Principal components analysis will yield 1 factor for every variable. Six items will form a 6*6 similarity matrix and will yield 6 factors, for example. Evidence of a *single* valid factor consists of (1) a first factor with an intersection that accounts for 50 percent of the variance in the matrix (or more), (2) a sharp scree fall between the eigenvalue for the first and second factor (first factor approximately 3 or more times larger than the second), (3) the eigenvalue of the second factor lies at the top of the scree, (4) there exist no (or inconsequentially small) negative loadings on factor 1, and (5) there exist no (or inconsequentially small numbers of) high ($+/-.50$) loadings on factor 2. Pay close attention to the last condition. As Rummel notes (1970:373), because the first factor is fitted to the data to account for the maximum variance, when two independent clusters of interrelated variables exist, factor 1 may be located between them. All variables may load highly on factor 1. But the variables will also load highly on factor 2, and the variables that comprise each independent cluster will exhibit different signs on factor 2.

Evidence of these five conditions showed that people who live dramatically different lives—the descendants of former plantation slaves who make a living in tourist economies in the West Indies and people who

continue to hunt, gather, and herd in the Alaskan and Siberian Arctic—
agree about experiences that comprise unitary phenomena, otherwise
unseen, legitimately called *violence* and *affection* (Handwerker 1997). Similar evidence showed that, irrespective of ethnic identity (European American, Latino American, African American, and Native American), working
women agree about experiences that comprise unitary phenomena, otherwise unseen, legitimately called *stress* and *social support* coming from daily
social interaction, and *depression* (Handwerker 1999b).

Use scree plots to differentiate data with structure (valid factors) from
random data. *Scree* refers to the jumble of rocks and soil that accumulates
at the bottom of cliffs. A scree plot shows the size of the eigenvalues for
all factors beginning with factor 1. Just by chance, sample items may show
great similarity. Factor analysis of matrices filled with random data will
find some eigenvalues over 1.0 and some high loadings just by chance. But
matrices that contain no real factors will generate random distributions of
eigenvalues and loadings. Half the eigenvalues will be over 1.00, half will
be under 1.00, and you'll see no perceptible scree. Figure 7.2 shows you
what scree plots for random data coming from samples of different sizes
look like. Note the effects of sample size—larger samples contain less random error and yield more precise pictures of the sampled population and
have flatter scree plots; small samples contain lots of random error and
yield pictures of the sampled population that might suggest the presence
of real factors. The telling clue is the absence of a dramatic scree fall
between the eigenvalue of factor 1 and factor 2, even among random data
from tiny ($N = 10$ cases) samples.

Contrast figure 7.2 with figure 7.3, which shows a dramatic scree fall
(from 5.268 to 0.344). The eigenvalue of the first factor is more than 15
times larger than the eigenvalue of the second, which lies at the beginning
of the scree. The dramatic scree fall, together with the absence of any
eigenvalue located above the scree, confirms the presence of a single valid
factor. The average loading on factor 1 was nearly .94. These findings
come from a principal components analysis of responses to the 6 items in
box 7.1 from informants in Alaska and the Russian Far East. The average
loading of about 0.94 means that these 6 items share (.94*.94) about 88
percent of their variance. If we imagine that a circle represents the variability among informant responses for any one variable, the 88 percent

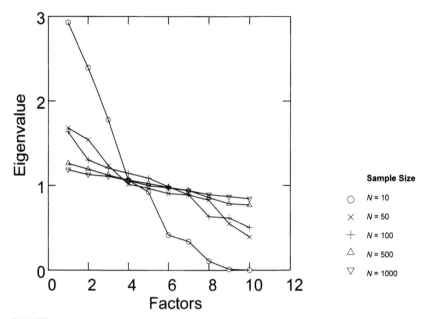

FIGURE 7.2
Scree Plots of Eigenvalues from Matrices That Show No Structure, for Samples of Different Sizes

shared variance means that 6 circles overlap nearly perfectly. This very large shared intersection among these items confirms that *perceived health* measured with these items possesses a phenomenal existence independent of my imagination.

These findings establish the construct validity of the scale for *perceived health,* but they don't establish that these items measure the variable *reliably. Reliability* refers to the extent to which two or more attempts to measure the same variable yield the same results (Cronbach and Meehl 1955). Each item used to construct a scale constitutes an attempt to measure a given variable. Thus, the issue of construct validity overlaps the issue of reliability. The preceding evidence of construct validity implies that the variables consist of reliable measurements.

But we can adduce independent evidence of the reliability of these scales. Items of reliable scales should correlate highly with each other. So, too, sets of items should correlate highly with other item sets. Split-half coefficients measure the correlation between the items comprising each scale, once they are divided into two sets. Cronbach's α (alpha, also called

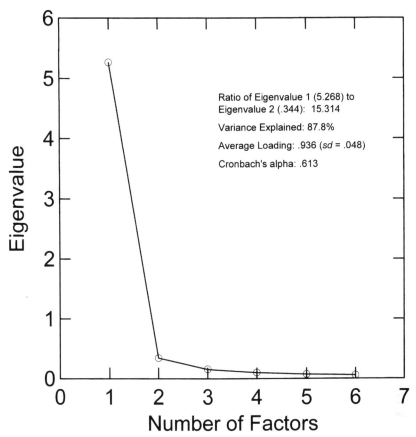

Ratio of Eigenvalue 1 (5.268) to
Eigenvalue 2 (.344): 15.314

Variance Explained: 87.8%

Average Loading: .936 (*sd* = .048)

Cronbach's alpha: .613

FIGURE 7.3
Scree Plot of Eigenvalues from a Matrix with Structure (a Single Factor)

the Kuder-Richardson coefficient, the output from the Spearman-Brown
Prophesy Formula) estimates the average of all possible split-half reliability coefficients. Look for scale reliability scores of .75 or higher. The low
reliability coefficient of about .61 means that we might miss subtle relationships between *perceived health* and other variables.

FOR ETHNOGRAPHY, USE FACTOR ANALYSIS TO IDENTIFY THE INTERSECTION(S) AMONG SETS OF INFORMANTS

You can easily answer questions like "Do Iñupiat Eskimo give answers or
act in ways that differ from West Indians?" but, as Keesing (1994) pointed

out, the answers beg the question of the location of cultural boundaries. Questions like these impose cultural differences by assumption rather than evidence. To avoid this error and to pinpoint cultural boundaries, if they exist, use principal components to establish the construct validity of the culture or cultures in your data. Findings from such an analysis will tell you whether or not or the extent to which cultural boundaries correspond with social labels like Nuer or Navajo, men or women, or old and young.

You can't see *cultures. Cultures* consist of configurations of cognition and emotion and an isomorphic configuration of behavior that form the intersection of configurations unique to individuals within a specific set of people. A culture thus constitutes a multidimensional variable, just like variables such as *stress, affection, problem-drinking,* and *perceived health.* Validate the construct by demonstrating that specific people share a specific configuration of cognition, emotion, and/or behavior. The construct validity of a culture requires that what some informants tell us or do correlates highly with what other informants tell us or do. Informants who have constructed and participate in a different culture will say things and/ or act in ways that correlate highly among themselves, but what they say or do will not correlate as highly with the first set of informants. Conduct a standard construct validity analysis and look for evidence that cultural variation in your data displays:

- random variation around a single cognitive, emotional, or behavioral pattern that characterizes the domain or some aspect of it, which may be weak or strong (*a single culture*);
- significant subpopulation differences in the strength of the pattern (*intracultural variation*),
- two or more qualitatively different sets of meanings and behavior, which may differ little or constitute polar opposites (*multiple cultures*); or
- no patterning in the data or some aspect of it (*random data*).

To carry out such an analysis on a standard informant-by-variable matrix:

- Transpose the matrix (make it a variable-by-informant matrix) so you can see and measure the similarities and differences among your informants.
- Produce and SAVE a similarity matrix for your informants. Use Pearson's r for ratio or ordinal scores. Use either the Simple Matching or Jaccard's coefficient for binary variables, depending on the similarities you want to measure. In SYSTAT, you must open the matrix you just created and SAVE AS a correlation matrix.
- Conduct a principal components analysis of the similarity matrix that solves for 2 factors; save the factor loadings.
- Plot the loadings on factor 2 by the loadings on factor 1 to identify patterns of cultural variation. In the presence of a single valid factor, factor loadings tell you how much individual informants participate in the culture identified by that factor.
- For two or more cultures, disaggregate the matrix and re-run the analyses to identify intercultural variation or cultural change (see further on).

Remember that factor 1 captures the broadest range of commonalties among your informants. Loadings on factor 1 will tell you the degree to which the responses given by particular informants correspond with that shared intersection. Factor 2 captures the broadest range of commonalties among your informants *on all the variance not captured by factor 1*. Loadings on factor 2 will tell you the degree to which the pattern of responses given by particular informants corresponds with that secondary range of commonalty. A plot of the loadings on factor 2 by the loadings on factor 1 gives you a picture of the overall patterns of agreement among your informants.

To complete your analysis, calculate Cronbach's alpha (the Spearman-Brown Prophesy Formula) to measure the reliability and validity of your findings (see Weller 1987).

Successive Pile Sort Data

Successive pile sort data call for two kinds of primary analyses. The first primary analysis assesses the construct validity of cultures in the data with a principal components analysis of the similarities among items as seen by the entire set of informants. To carry out this analysis, you will measure the similarities among items as seen by any one informant with a triangular similarity matrix, convert that matrix to a single column of numbers (a vector), do this for all informants, and construct a file that consists of one column of similarity coefficients for each informant.

The second primary analysis, carried out separately for each culture, identifies the cultural construction of similarities and differences with a cluster analysis, multidimensional scaling analysis, and/or a correspondence analysis. This analysis requires the construction of a set of stacked similarity matrices—each matrix expresses how a particular informant looked at the set of items, and the matrix for any one informant is stacked on top of (or below) the matrix for another informant. Here are the steps for your informant-by-variable matrix:

- SELECT by informant and generate and SAVE an item similarity matrix for each informant, using a Simple Matching coefficient ($S4$) or Jaccard's coefficient ($S3$). Use a command file like this, for Simple Matching coefficients (for Jaccard's coefficients, substitute $S3$ for $S4$):

      CORR
      SELECT INFORMANT = 1
      SAVE "C:\WINNT\Profiles\Administrator\Personal\Systat\ED2000\
          MAT1.SYD"
      S4 PUSH1 STEAL2 HIT3 NAMES4 ROLLEYES5 ALOOK6 BLAME7
      FOUL8 SLAP9, TOUCH10 YELL11 COMPLIMENT12 INSULT13
      HUG14 SMILE15 MAKEFUN16 LAUGH17, SPIT18

      SELECT INFORMANT = 2
      SAVE "C:\WINNT\Profiles\Administrator\Personal\Systat\ED2000\
          MAT2.SYD"
      S4 PUSH1 STEAL2 HIT3 NAMES4 ROLLEYES5 ALOOK6 BLAME7
      FOUL8 SLAP9, TOUCH10 YELL11 COMPLIMENT12 INSULT13
      HUG14 SMILE15 MAKEFUN16 LAUGH17, SPIT18

- Convert each triangular similarity matrix into a single column, or vector (without the diagonal elements), and SAVE the vector file. Use a command file like this:

```
MATRIX
USE
"C:\WINNT\Profiles\ADMINISTRATOR\Personal\Systat\ED2000\
    MAT1.SYD"
MAT VECMAT1 = STRING(MAT1,0)
SAVE VECMAT1
CLEAR


USE
"C:\WINNT\Profiles\ADMINISTRATOR\Personal\Systat\ED2000\
    MAT2.SYD"
MAT VECMAT2 = STRING(MAT2,0)
SAVE VECMAT2
CLEAR


USE
"C:\WINNT\Profiles\ADMINISTRATOR\Personal\Systat\ED2000\
    MAT3.SYD"
MAT VECMAT3 = STRING(MAT3,0)
SAVE VECMAT3
CLEAR
```

▪ Successively MERGE the vectors into a master data file for a construct
validity analysis. Use a command file like this:

```
SAVE "C:\WINNT\Profiles\Administrator\Personal\Systat\ED2000\
    VECMAT12.SYD"
MERGE
"C:\WINNT\Profiles\Administrator\Personal\Systat\ED2000\
    VECMAT1.SYD" "C:\WINNT\Profiles\Administrator\Personal\
Systat\ED2000\
    VECMAT2.SYD"


SAVE "C:\WINNT\Profiles\Administrator\Personal\Systat\ED2000\
    VECMAT123.SYD"
```

```
MERGE
"C:\WINNT\Profiles\Administrator\Personal\Systat\ED2000\
    VECMAT12.SYD"
"C:\WINNT\Profiles\Administrator\Personal\Systat\ED2000\
    VECMAT3.SYD"

SAVE
"C:\WINNT\Profiles\Administrator\Personal\Systat\ED2000\
    VECMAT1234.SYD"
MERGE
"C:\WINNT\Profiles\Administrator\Personal\Systat\ED2000\
    VECMAT123.SYD"
"C:\WINNT\Profiles\Administrator\Personal\Systat\ED2000\
    VECMAT4.SYD"
```

- Conduct your construct validity analysis with the master data file with a
  vector for each informant.
- Once you determine the number of valid cultures in your data, *for each
  culture,* successively APPEND informant similarity matrices into a master file that contains 1 item similarity matrix for each informant in the
  culture. Use a command file like this:

```
SAVE
"C:\WINNT\Profiles\Administrator\Personal\Systat\ED2000\
    AP12.SYD"
APPEND
"C:\WINNT\Profiles\Administrator\Personal\Systat\ED2000\
    MAT1.SYD"
"C:\WINNT\Profiles\Administrator\Personal\Systat\ED2000\
    MAT2.SYD" / MATCH

SAVE "C:\WINNT\Profiles\Administrator\Personal\Systat\ED2000\
    AP123.SYD"
APPEND
"C:\WINNT\Profiles\Administrator\Personal\Systat\ED2000\
    AP12.SYD"
```

"C:\WINNT\Profiles\Administrator\Personal\Systat\ED2000\
MAT3.SYD" / MATCH

SAVE
"C:\WINNT\Profiles\Administrator\Personal\Systat\ED2000\
AP1234.SYD"
APPEND
"C:\WINNT\Profiles\Administrator\Personal\Systat\ED2000\
AP123.SYD"
"C:\WINNT\Profiles\Administrator\Personal\Systat\ED2000\
MAT4.SYD" / MATCH

- Open the fully appended stacked similarity matrix file you just created
  and SAVE AS a correlation matrix. Apply multidimensional scaling
  (MDS), cluster and/or correspondence analysis to this file to identify the
  cultural construction of relative similarities among the items.

Evidence of a Single Culture

Figure 7.4 illustrates the fundamental output possibilities for your initial principal components analysis. A scatter of points that corresponds
most closely with the location of 1s, with high loadings on factor 1 and
low loadings on factor 2, constitutes evidence of a single culture. Factor 1
will account for around 50 percent of the variance in the matrix (or more),
and you will find a sharp scree fall between the eigenvalue for factor 1 and
factor 2 (factor 1 approximately 3 times or more larger than factor 2),
no (or inconsequentially small) negative loadings on factor 1, and no (or
inconsequentially few) high positive or negative loadings on factor 2.

Evidence for important forms of intracultural variation consists of
cases that trail off from the central cluster with either increasing negative
or positive loadings on factor 2. Examination of the central tendencies
(modes, medians, modes) of the variables will tell you what your informants agree about in their behavior or ideas or both. A regression analysis
of the loadings on factors 1 and 2 using the variables you analyze will point
to sources of cultural variability and suggest the nature of factor 2 (see
chapter 8).

For example, look at data that illustrate a single culture from a study

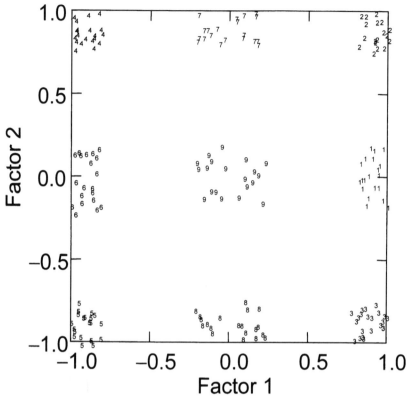

FIGURE 7.4
Scatterplot of the Fundamental Principal Components' Output Variations

of the meaning of stressors and social supports among working women (Handwerker 1999b). Informants include 90 working women who exhibited a wide range of ages, educational levels, class backgrounds, and historical origins (ethnicities). Women of African origin living in Barbados and Connecticut constitute 24 percent of the sample; women of northwest European origin living in Connecticut and Massachusetts constitute 50 percent of the sample; women of Hispanic origin living in Puerto Rico and Connecticut constitute 9 percent of the sample; women of American native origin living on California's North Coast constitute 17 percent of the sample. Informant ages range from 18 to 78 (mean = 40.7, sd = 13.7). Educational attainment ranges from a completed primary school education (6 years) to a completed graduate education (Ph.D., M.D., coded as 21 years even if took longer). The mean level of educational attainment of 15.6 years (sd = 3.2) represents just under a completed college education. Informant ages and educational attainment are comparable among women of all ethnic groups, with the exception of the oldest African American women, who left school after the primary grades due to limited educational opportunities. Forty-one percent of the sample grew up in poverty. European Americans (Odds Ratio [OR—see the section logistic regression in chapter 8] = 1.00) and Hispanic Americans (OR = 2.0, 95 percent Confidence Interval [CI] = 13.4 to .3) exhibited an equivalent likelihood of growing up in poverty, controlling for age. African American informants were approximately 6 times more likely to report growing up in poverty (OR = 5.7, 95 percent CI = 17.8 to 1.9). Native American informants were 44 times more likely to report growing up in poverty (OR = 44.6, 95 percent CI = 280.7 to 7.1).

Initial informal and semistructured ethnographic interviews yielded information on the nature and components of stress experienced by working women and potential cultural variation by age, ethnicity, educational attainment, and class background. Informants consistently equated "stress" with their emotional response to dissonance between the behavior they experience and the behavior they find acceptable. The behavioral characteristics women consistently identified as stressful (rather than supportive) included words or acts that

- "make you feel bad about yourself," rather than make you feel special and important;
- "treat you as an inferior," rather than treat you as an equal;
- "block your attempts to achieve," rather than help you achieve; and
- "demean or belittle you," rather than treat you with respect.

Subsequent structured interviews yielded 4-point ratings (from 0 = "never acceptable" to 3 = "always acceptable") for each set of complementary items.

Figure 7.5 shows the dispersion of cases that emerged from the initial principal components analysis when plotted by their loadings on the first two factors. Case labels come from the historical origins of study participants (A = African American; H = Hispanic American; E = European

American; and N = Native American). Virtually all cases form a tight cluster on the right center of the scatterplot, showing high-to-very-high loadings on the first factor and low loadings on the second factor. To make the scatter of informants visible, I jittered the points by adding a small amount of random error to each observation. The agreement was so high that, without the jitter, all you'd see on the plot would be a tiny dot. (When informants appear to have loadings greater than 1.00 in later plots, it's only because I jittered the plots so you could see the informants.)

Informants thus expressed a strong consensus that certain words or acts are *always* acceptable (rating of 3 on the 0-1-2-3 scale) and other words or acts are *never* acceptable (rating of 0 on the 0-1-2-3 scale). The first factor of agreements among informants was 23.951 times larger than the second and accounted for 88.5 percent of variance among informants. The average factor loading was .93 (sd = .16). Factor 1 pointed to an informant agreement that words or acts that imply respect, equality, active assistance, or otherwise make one feel special and important are *always* acceptable and function as social supports; and that words or acts that imply inferiority, impede achievement, or otherwise make one feel bad about oneself are *never* acceptable and function as stressors. A tiny number of informants expressed some tolerance for behavior that the vast majority of informants found totally unacceptable.

Evidence of Multiple Cultures

Any other scatter of cases constitutes evidence that your matrix contains two or more cultures. A scatter of cases that corresponds with the placement of 1s and 9s in figure 7.4 suggests not only that some informants (the 9s) do not participate in the same culture as other informants (the 1s), but that you may not have measured the variables pertinent to understanding their culture or the differences between the culture of 1s and the culture of 9s. For example, figure 7.6 shows findings from an analysis of similarity judgments about items that go into the construction of meals. The items included: white potatoes, rice, beans, pork, beef, garlic, hot peppers, sweet peppers, greens, sugar, corn, chicken, wheat, tomatoes, sweet potatoes, and fish. Informants included people who self-identified themselves as members of Puerto Rican, Ukrainian, and South Asian ethnic communities in Connecticut, as well as people who did not, here identi-

(Cases identified by historical origin: A = Africa, E = Northwest Europe, H = Hispanic, N = American Native)

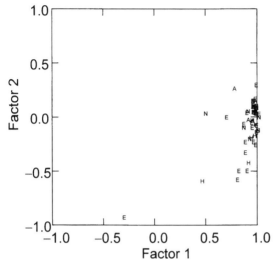

FIGURE 7.5
Scatterplot of the Stressor and Social Support Culture

fied merely as "Euro-Americans" (case-labels in figure 7.6 identify informant ethnicities). Initial analysis revealed a factor 1 nearly 5 times larger
than factor 2, which accounted for 76.5 percent of the variability in informant responses. This finding pointed to a broad agreement among informants about the similarities and differences among meal components.

Note the large number of informants in figure 7.6 who show very low
loadings on factor 1, however. This finding led to further interviews that
revealed that people who identified themselves as members of distinctive
ethnic communities generally constructed meals with elements like
"beans," "potatoes," "tomatoes," and "greens." By contrast, however,
Euro-Americans (and a few members of distinctive ethnic communities)
constructed meals with elements like "pizza," "hamburgers," and "salad."
When I disaggregated the original set of data and redid the analysis, Euro-
American responses to questions about similarities and differences among
items like "beans," "tomatoes," and "greens" showed the random variation that comes from not having a clue about the domain we asked them
about—a first factor only 1.1 times larger than the second, which
accounted for only 15.7 percent of matrix variance, and loadings on factor

(Cases identified by ethnic community: PR=Puerto Rican, EA=European American, UKR=Ukranian, SA=South Asian)

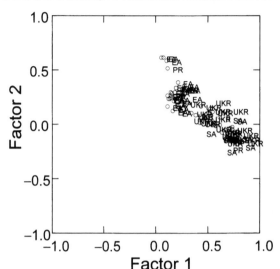

FIGURE 7.6
Scatterplot of Agreements about Similarities and Differences in Meal Components

1, which averaged 0.03 ($sd = .40$) and ranged from $-.73$ to $+.65$. Although some people who self-identified themselves as members of minority ethnic communities appeared to be just as clueless, analysis of the responses from Puerto Ricans, South Asians, and Ukrainians, by contrast, revealed a first factor more than 8 times larger than the second, which accounted for 83 percent of the variability among informants.

All other case scatters suggest that you have correctly identified variables that make comparisons meaningful. Clusters in the upper and lower right quadrants of the scatterplot (the 2s and 3s) identify the high positive and negative loadings on factor 2 that signal that factor 1 was placed between two independent clusters of informants. Depending on how many cultures exist in your matrix and their relationship to each other, you may see some combination of informant clusters in the upper and right halves of the scatterplot (the 1s and 7s), in the lower right and upper left quadrants (the 3s and 4s), or all of these possibilities.

Select each distinct cluster of cases for independent principal components analyses. Each subsequent analysis should reveal that factor 1 will account for around 50 percent of the variance in the matrix (or more), and you will find a sharp scree fall between the eigenvalue for factor 1 and factor 2 (factor 1 approximately 3 times or more larger than factor 2), no (or inconsequentially small) negative loadings on factor 1, and no (or inconsequentially few) high positive or negative loadings on factor 2. Examination of the central tendencies (modes, medians, modes) of the variables will tell you what each set of informants agrees about in its behavior or ideas or both, and how its members differ from informants who belong to the other set or sets. If one or more of these secondary analyses reveal intracultural variation, a regression analysis of the loadings on factors 1 and 2 using the variables you analyze will point to sources of cultural variability and suggest the nature of factor 2 (see chapter 8). If one or more of these secondary analyses reveals two or more independent cultures, select each distinct cluster of cases for independent tertiary principal components analyses. Conduct independent principal components analyses until you exhaust the possibilities.

Keep in mind that not all cultural variation may show coherent patterning. Some individuals may exhibit cultural patterns unique to themselves. These outliers may reflect genuine differences or measurement error. In these subsequent analyses, move the data on outlier informants to a separate file. Analysis of this final set of informants will reveal that there exists no large first factor and an average factor loading that approximates 0.00.

Evidence of Two Cultures: An Outcome Evaluation of a Student Identity Intervention

Evaluation research, as I pointed out in chapter 2, tests the efficacy of interventions designed to induce specific forms of cultural change. Example interventions, you will remember, include bicycle safety programs designed to increase the chances that a child will use a helmet while riding, training of health-care providers designed to improve their ability to carry out accurate physical examinations, and training of prospective college students in what it means to be a college student. Interventions assume the existence of, and teach, "correct" answers—riding with, not without helmets; the correct way to conduct physical examinations; the components of college student identity necessary for a successful college career, which include *contemplating* and *discussing important ideas.*

People who attend college bring with them an identity as *student* and elaborate that identity with experiences accumulated over their college careers. An intervention that targeted people admitted to the university with low SAT scores might aim to provide pre–first semester experiences that produced people for whom their identity as a college student included meanings like *contemplating* and *discussing important ideas,* not merely getting to class on time. Judgments about the efficacy of interventions like this one require information on whether or not or the degree to which people who started with one culture ended with another. Principal components analysis provides a direct test of the hypothesis that a set of informants tells us the same things or acts in the same way. If the informants do, specific verbal or behavioral responses constitute an independent set of measurements of one and only one otherwise unseen variable (culture). A direct answer to an outcomes-evaluation question thus comes from a factor analysis carried out on a matrix that includes the

- intervention-defined "correct" answers coded as 1 (correct),
- the answers given by cases coded as 1 (if correct) or 0 (if not), and
- the answers given by controls coded as 1 (if correct) or 0 (if not).

Transpose your standard informant-by-variable matrix and produce a similarity matrix among informants using either a Simple Matching or Jaccard's coefficient, depending on the pertinent similarities. Remember that, in SYSTAT, you must open the similarity matrix you just created and SAVE AS a correlation matrix. Proceed through the standard construct validity procedures.

Figure 7.7 shows a scree plot from an outcomes-evaluation study of student identity. The plot shows a sharp scree fall between factor 1 and factor 2, which identifies the presence of a large shared understanding of what it means to be a student. The plot shows also, however, that the eigenvalue of factor 2 lies above the scree. The data thus contain evidence of a second culture of student identity.

Figure 7.8 shows a scatterplot of loadings on factor 2 by the loadings on factor 1. All informants load highly (>0.500) on factor 1. Factor 1 thus identifies a general consensus about some components of student identity. Some informants, however, also load highly (>0.500) on factor 2. The high positive and negative loadings on factor 2 signal that factor 1 was

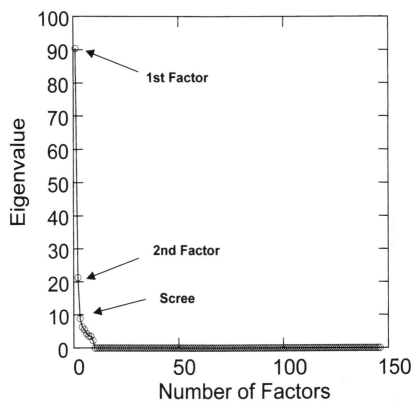

FIGURE 7.7
Scree Plot of Eigenvalues from a Matrix with Structure (2 Factors)

placed between two independent clusters of informants. Factor 2 thus identifies an independent consensus about other components of student identity. Table 7.1 shows the differences between the two cultures.

Most informants constructed what I call the Basic Student Identity. What it means to be a student consists of (1) accepting responsibility and (2) getting to class on time. Informants don't agree on whether or not time management is an important component of being a student. They don't see contemplating and discussing important ideas, studying regularly, participating in class, or reading books outside of class as important components of their identity as *students.*

A small number of informants saw their identity as *students* very differently. The students who had constructed what I call a Serious Student

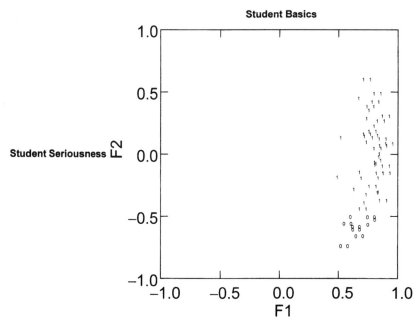

FIGURE 7.8
Scatterplot of Factor 2 * Factor 1

Identity split over whether or not reading books outside of class was important. But they agreed that important components of their identity as students included, in addition to accepting responsibility and getting to class on time, (1) contemplating and (2) discussing important ideas, (3) time management, (4) studying regularly, and (5) participating in class.

TABLE 7.1   Different Cultures of Student Identity (% Agreeing with Intervention-Defined Correct Evaluations)

	Contemplate Important Ideas	Discuss Important Ideas	Accept Responsibility	Manage Time	Study Regularly	Participate in Class	Get to Class Ontime	Read Books Outside of Class
Basic Student Identity	33.6%	9.2%	65.5%	50.4%	31.1%	10.9%	71.4%	4.2%
Serious Student Identity	96.3%	81.5%	100%	100%	92.6%	66.7%	100%	48.1%

A separate analysis carried out on the majority of informants who load highly on factor 1 but not on factor 2 reveals a single valid factor: (1) a first factor that accounts for approximately 50 percent of the variance in a matrix (or more), (2) a sharp scree fall between the eigenvalue for the first and second factor (first factor approximately 3 or more times larger than the second), (3) the eigenvalue of the second factor lies at the top of the scree, and (4) no (or inconsequentially small) negative factor loadings on the first factor (see figure 7.9). Figure 7.10 shows a scatterplot of loadings on factor 2 by the loadings on factor 1 that reveals no cultural variation suggesting the presence of an alternative culture (no loadings much larger than $+/-0.500$ on factor 1).

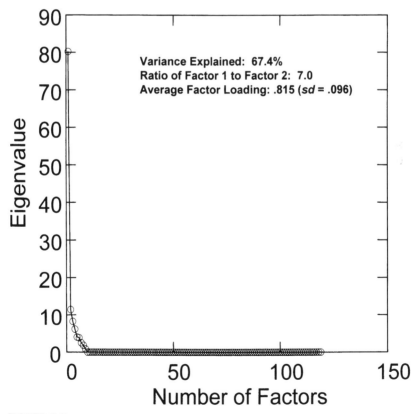

FIGURE 7.9
Scree Plot for Basic Student Culture

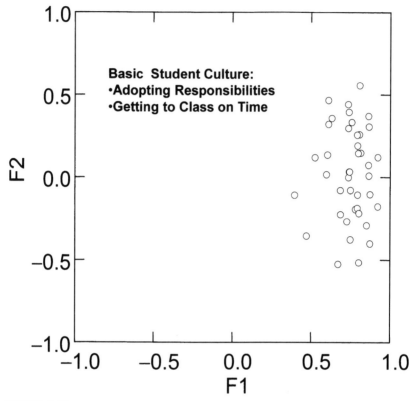

FIGURE 7.10
Scatterplot for the Basic Student Culture

A separate analysis carried out on the minority of informants who load highly on both original factors also reveals a single valid factor: (1) a first factor that accounts for approximately 50 percent of the variance in a matrix (or more), (2) a sharp scree fall between the eigenvalue for the first and second factor (first factor approximately 3 or more times larger than the second), (3) the eigenvalue of the second factor lies at the top of the scree, and (4) no (or inconsequentially small) negative factor loadings on the first factor (see figure 7.11). Figure 7.12 shows a scatterplot of loadings on factor 2 by the loadings on factor 1 that reveals intracultural variation but no cultural variation suggesting the presence of an alternative culture (no loadings much larger than ± 0.500 on factor 1).

These findings confirm the existence of two cultures of student identity.

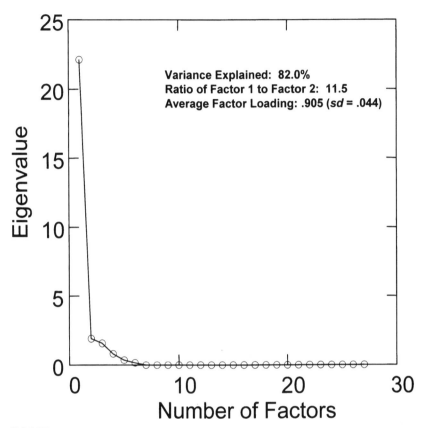

FIGURE 7.11
Scree Plot for Serious Student Culture

One conforms to the intervention-defined "correct" answers constructed by college faculty and administrators. It remains to determine whether or not students who went through the intervention program responded by changing their culture of student identity (see chapter 9).

Evidence of Cultures of Violence and Affection, with Significant Intracultural Variation

Data from a study of the violence and affection experienced during childhood by Barbadian men (Handwerker 1996) illustrate two cultures, one with significant intracultural variation. Data analyzed here come from an island-wide random sample of 145 informants aged 20–45 in 1990. The

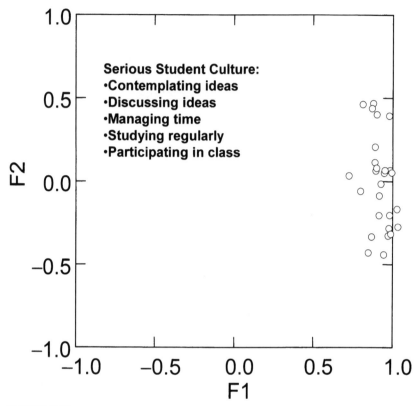

FIGURE 7.12
Scatterplot for the Serious Student Culture

random selection of informants allows us to estimate the relative frequency of cultures, in the presence of more than one. Approximately 38 percent of these men come from homes that contained both biological parents from their birth through their 16th birthday; 14 percent lived with a stepfather for 2 or more years; and 27 percent experienced interaction with one or more of their mother's visiting partners. Sixteen percent were raised by foster parents, mostly grandparents or aunts and uncles. Only 1 percent were raised by unrelated foster parents. Approximately 81 percent of these men come from working-class homes, in which parents left school after completing the primary grades and worked men's occupations like farmer, mason, stevedore, and mechanic and women's occupations like farmer, fishboner, hawker, maid, garment worker, hairdresser, and midwife. Approximately 17 percent came from middle-class homes, in which one or more parent had at least some secondary education and worked at men's occupations like foreman, supervisor, bookkeeper, accountant, and newswriter and women's occupations like secretary, clerk, receptionist, nurse, and teacher. About 2 percent of the sample came from upper-class homes, in which parents had completed a college education and worked at men's occupations like bank supervisor, restaurant owner, or solicitor and women's occupations like government officer and who hired household help (maids, gardeners).

I measured violent and affectionate interactions with parents with items that, with one exception, were identical to those that emerged in the more recent study of stressors and social supports (see box 5.7, chapter 5). The exception is that I asked this set of informants about physical forms of violence (stressors) and affection (social supports). The scale measuring the intensity of violence experienced in childhood from mothers ranged from 0 to 14 (mean = 2.661, sd = 2.524). The scale measuring violence experienced in childhood from fathers ranged from 0 to 16 (mean = 1.966, sd = 2.783). The mean for both parents represents an average of less than 1 ("rarely") for each violence scale item. Thus, on average, Barbadians reported experiencing little violence from either parent. Following the recommendation of Barbadian judges, I classified a child as abused if he or she experienced any form of violence that occurred "regularly" or "all the time." By this criterion, about 16 percent of these informants experienced abuse by their mother; about 15 percent experienced abuse by their father (or other male caretaker). Overall, one person in four reported experiencing physical and emotional violence as children.

The two scales measuring affection experienced in childhood from mothers and fathers ranged from 0 to 20. The mean for mother–child relationships was 13.688 (sd = 5.083), which constitutes an average close to 3 ("most of the time") for each affection scale item. The mean for father–child relationships was 10.300 (sd = 6.176), which constitutes an average of about 2 ("sometimes") for each affection scale item. A matched samples t-test yields a t = 10.711, $p<.001$. This finding warrants the inference that sons experienced more affection from their mothers than from their fathers. I identified relationships between a parent and child as marked by affection only when the summed score averaged 3 ("most of the time") or

higher. By this criterion, 30.5 percent of boys experienced openly affectionate relationships with parents (boys experienced the same likelihood
of an affectionate relationship with both male and female caregivers [Chi-
squared derived $p = .059$]).

To examine the cultural patterning in these data, I analyzed a trans-
posed matrix that contained informant ratings for the full set of measures
of violence (stressors) and affection (social supports) experienced during
childhood. I also created factor score measures of the balance of stress and
social support that informants experienced from their fathers (and other
male) and mothers (and other female) caregivers. By definition, factor
scores have means of 0 and standard deviations of 1. Factor scores that
approximate 0 identify informants who experience levels of stress and
social support that balance each other from one or another parent or other
caregiver. Positive scores identify informants who experienced relationships marked by affection. Negative scores identify informants who experienced relationships marked by violence. Factor scores for mothers (and
other female caregivers) ranged from -3.6 to $+1.7$. Factor scores for
fathers (and other male caregivers) ranged from -2.9 to $+1.4$.

Figure 7.13 shows the dispersion of cases that emerged from the initial
principal components analysis when plotted by their loadings on the
unrotated first two factors. Factor 1 identifies a dimension of abuse (low
loadings) and affection (high loadings). Factor 2 identifies a dimension of
similarity (low loadings) and dissimilarity (high loadings) in the character
of interaction between sons and their mother and father. The dispersion
of informants reveals two distinct cultures and important forms of intracultural variation for the numerically dominant culture. For the dominant
culture, a secondary independent principal components analysis revealed
a first factor eigenvalue 4.65 times larger than the second, a first factor
that accounted for 64.8 percent of matrix variance, and an average factor
loading of .780 ($sd = .198$) with no negative loadings. For the minority
culture, a secondary independent principal components analysis revealed
a first factor eigenvalue 3.09 times larger than the second, a first factor
that accounted for 72.4 percent of matrix variance, and an average loading
of .831 ($sd = .163$).

I set case size in the scatterplots of figure 7.13 proportional to the balance of affection and violence measured by the factor score variables and

(Cases identified by factor scores that measure the balance of affection [positive scores] and violence [negative scores] in parent–child interaction)

Father's Treatment of Son

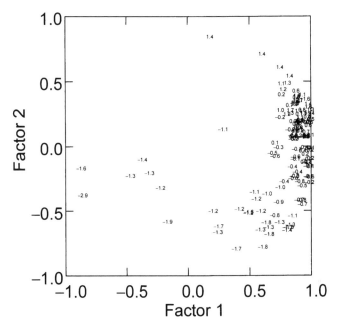

FIGURE 7.13
Scatterplot of Cultures of Violence and Affection

used female and male symbols to distinguish mother–child from father–child interaction. The tiny symbols in the lower left quadrant of both scatterplots show that minority culture constitutes a "culture of violence," in which children experienced high levels of violence from both fathers and mothers. The much larger symbols in the right half of the scatterplots show that the majority culture constitutes a "culture of affection," in which children generally experienced little violence and much affection from both parents. Contrasts in the size of symbols for mothers and fathers show important forms of intracultural variation. Mothers showered affection on their sons far more consistently than did fathers. The very large male symbols and small female symbols in the upper right por-

Mother's Treatment of Son

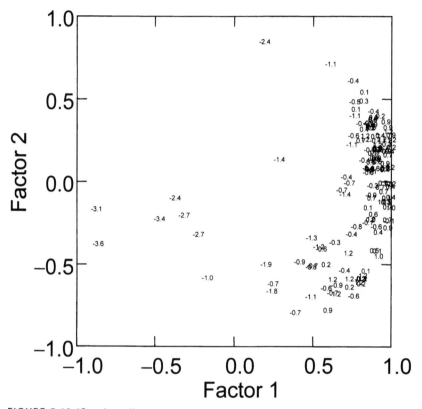

FIGURE 7.13 (Continued)

tion of these scatterplots identifies a small number of cases in which fathers showered much affection on sons who experienced relationships with their mothers that tended toward abuse. The very large female symbols and small male symbols in the lower right quadrant identify a small number of cases in which mothers showered much affection on sons who experienced abusive relationships with their fathers. This analysis thus points to four distinctive sets of family dynamics to explore in depth through additional informal, semistructured, and structured interviews.

Evidence of Six Cultures of Substance Use and Abuse

Data from a random sample of 211 men aged 15 to 86 in 1993 who lived in Chukotka and Kamchatka in the Russian Far East and in the Aleutians and the NANA region of Alaska (Handwerker, Kraus, and Richards under review), illustrate evidence of six cultures. These data consist of all of the men interviewed out of a total sample of 720 men and women collected in hub towns and affiliated villages in four study regions as part of an extensive study of social, cultural, and health transition in the North. Research participants in Alaska (53 percent of the sample) included Aleut and Iñupiat Eskimo natives and Euro-American immigrants. Research participants in the Russian Far East (47 percent of the sample) included Chukchee, Yupik Eskimo, Koryak, Itelmen, Kamchadal, and even natives and Euro-Russian immigrants. Seventy-seven percent of the sample were natives. These men ranged in age from 15 to 86 (mean $= 38.6; sd = 13.8$), and reported 0–18 years of formal schooling (mean $= 9.7, sd = 2.4$).

Human communities in the Arctic currently find themselves in the midst of profound changes in culture and social relations, which affect and are effects of equally profound changes in the relations among human communities and the biological and physical systems that comprise the Arctic ecosystem (National Research Council [NRC] 1989). Dramatic changes in mortality rates and in the configuration of sources of mortality and morbidity were integral parts of these changes in culture, social relations, and ecology. Nutritional deficiencies and infectious disease have been replaced in importance by the use and abuse of tobacco, alcohol, and illicit substances; sexually transmitted disease; suicide; and the other forms of violence now familiar to the rest of the world (McNabb 1990a; Desjarlais, Eisenberg, Good, and Kleinman 1995).

In 1993, we measured two closely related sets of behavioral health variables: (1) indicators of potentially life-threatening risk-taking behavior (being subject to physical violence in the past year, current injuries that impaired daily activities, and current sexually transmitted disease), and (2) substance use and abuse (cigarette smoking, alcohol use, alcohol abuse, and illicit substance use and abuse). In 1993, 18.8 percent of our informants reported being subject to violent acts during the preceding year; 24.5 percent reported current injuries or (rarely) illnesses that impeded their daily activities; and 10 percent reported a current sexually transmit-

ted disease. Cigarette and alcohol consumption constitutes a broad cultural pattern in these Northern communities: 64.4 percent of our informants reported that they smoked cigarettes; 77.0 percent reported alcohol
consumption. We measured problem drinking with the modification of
the CAGE inventory reported in chapter 5 and counted as a problem
drinker anyone who responded positively to both items. By this criterion,
19.0 percent of our informants were problem drinkers. Illicit substances
used in our research communities included glue sniffing and the use of
marijuana ("hash") and crack cocaine ("coke"). Nearly one in three of
our informants (28.4 percent) reported current use of one or more of
these substances.

Figure 7.14 shows the dispersion of cases that emerged from the initial
principal components analysis when plotted by their loadings on the
unrotated first two factors. Factor 1 identifies a dimension of both alcohol
and cigarette consumption (high loadings) or its absence (low loadings).
Factor 2 identifies a dimension of the use of illicit substances (high loadings) or its absence (low loadings). The initial principal components analysis revealed a first factor only 1.8 times larger than the second. This initial
plot suggested the existence of four distinct cultures of substance use and
abuse, but secondary analyses revealed two additional cultures (case labels
come from the cultures: S = Smoking; AS = Alcohol and Smoking; Asd
= Alcohol, Smoking, and [some illicit] drugs; ASD = Alcohol, Smoking,
and Drugs; D = Drugs; and O = No Substance Use). All of the men in
the culture marked by the combination of alcohol and cocaine not sur-
prisingly (e.g., Randall 1992) reported involvement in a violent altercation
($p<.001$). Forty-one percent of the men in the culture marked by the
heavy use of a variety of illicit drugs reported a current STD ($p=.002$).
Otherwise, the distinctions among these cultures solely reflected the consumption (or not) of alcohol, cigarettes, and varying quantities of different illicit substances. Even the proportion of problem drinkers varied
inconsequentially among the cultures characterized by alcohol consumption (p = .667).

A tiny number of informants (n = 6) represent a culture of No Substance Use. Analysis of this submatrix yielded a first factor 3.6 times larger
than the second, which accounted for 67.2 percent of matrix variance,
with 1 negative factor loading and an average loading of .62 (sd = .59—all

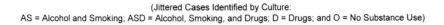

(Jittered Cases Identified by Culture:
AS = Alcohol and Smoking; ASD = Alcohol, Smoking, and Drugs; D = Drugs; and O = No Substance Use)

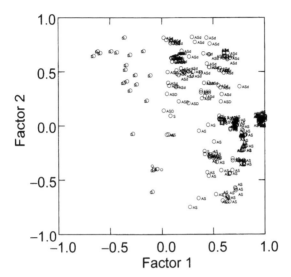

FIGURE 7.14
Scatterplot of Six Cultures of Substance Use and Abuse

but one of these elderly informants reported recent injuries; the one informant who didn't had a negative factor loading). Larger, but still small
numbers of informants represented cultures of Smoking ($n = 15$), Illicit
Drug Use ($n = 16$), and Alcohol, Smoking, and Drugs ($n = 9$). Analysis
of the submatrix of informants who only consumed cigarettes yielded a
first factor 8.5 times larger than the second, which accounted for 86.6 percent of matrix variance, with no negative loadings, and an average loading
of .91 ($sd = .19$). Analysis of the submatrix of informants who only consumed illicit drugs yielded a first factor 3.1 times larger than the second,
which accounted for 47.7 percent of matrix variance, with no negative
loadings, and an average loading of .68 ($sd = .15$). Analysis of the submatrix of informants who consumed alcohol, cigarettes, as well as significant
quantities of illicit drugs, yielded a first factor 3.2 times larger than the
second, which accounted for 61.2 percent of matrix variance, with no negative loadings and an average loading of .77 ($sd = .14$).

The numerically dominant cultures involved informants who con-

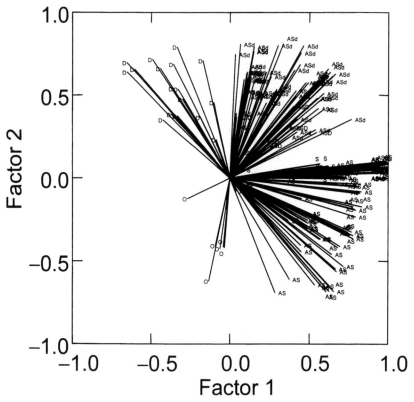

FIGURE 7.14 (Continued)

sumed both alcohol and cigarettes ($n = 102$), and informants who consumed both alcohol and cigarettes along with small quantities of illicit
drugs ($n = 62$). Analysis of the first submatrix yielded a first factor 5.3
times larger than the second, which accounted for 64.4 percent of matrix
variance, with no negative loadings, and an average loading of .79 ($sd =$
.15). Analysis of the second submatrix yielded a first factor 2.8 times larger
than the second, but a scree plot that showed clearly the presence of a
single factor in the matrix. This factor accounted for 50.1 percent of
matrix variance, contained no negative factor loadings and exhibited an
average loading of .69 ($sd = .69$).

Like the inter- and intracultural variation in the sources and balance of
violence and affection in Barbadian homes revealed in the previous analy-

sis, each culture of substance use and abuse implies distinctive behavioral dynamics. Construct validity analyses thus identify questions, issues, and topics to explore in greater depth through additional informal, semistructured, and structured interviews during the last phase of your field research.

How to Fine-Tune by Explaining Intra- and Intercultural Variation and Cultural Change

Complete your fine-tuning with two lines of data analysis and three lines of data collection:

- Use findings from your construct validity analyses to identify gaps in your text and structured interview data and fill them with new data.
- Use newly collected data to complete your construct validity analyses.
- Explore the sources of intracultural and intercultural variation and cultural change.
- Use findings from this analysis to identify gaps in your text data and fill them with data collected during intensive, informal interviews.
- Collect pertinent case studies to illustrate key findings.

Explicit analysis of the construct validity of cultural data permits you to identify key sources of cultural variability—and its absence—and to focus your next set of interviews and analyses to understand differences in meaning in greater depth. If you find cultural differences, redesign your sampling frame, conduct additional focused informal interviews, and collect new sets of data in structured interviews and observations. Conduct a new round of construct validity tests.

Design informal and semistructured interviews to elicit information on the adequacy of the life experience distinctions you started with. Ask informants if they know people who think differently, and interview people who take different points of view. Actively search for sources of cultural difference and change how you select informants in ways to reflect knowledge you gain during the course of field research. For example, closely examine diagnostic plots for unusual cases—talk with them again, if possible. Submit output from these analyses for discussion and evaluation to individuals and to focus groups composed of people from each culturally distinct population. Reflect on data from these Fourth Order Gossip interviews to formulate explicit hypotheses about the structure of meaning in these domains.

Start writing articles and book chapters no later than midway through your period of semistructured and structured interviews. Writing will highlight unexplained observations. For example, you might have observed, without well-integrating or contextualizing the observation, that older, poor men you came to know were treated badly by their daughters. Is this a general phenomenon, or one limited to circumstances you haven't yet clearly identified? How do daughters and fathers think about the treatment that strikes you as "maltreatment." Writing about marriage, you may begin to wonder why, exactly, women want to marry when they are young and men don't, why men only want to marry after they reach middle-to-old age and, although women of that age often disparage marriage, they marry anyway. Do you have enough information on how gender relations change over the life course to explain these observations?

Writing your analysis thus will lead to new questions, which will suggest new lines of investigation. Pursue these questions during intensive interviews, as well as a phase of Fifth Order Gossip in which you take your initial findings to key informants. Present these findings to focus groups and ask the participants to help you find the errors, to help you see things you missed, and to answer questions that you didn't know enough to ask earlier. Findings from intensive interviews, focus group interviews, and Fifth Order Gossip will help you improve second drafts of your articles and book chapters.

Use your accumulated understanding to design, carry out, and interpret your final structured interviews. Put all of this into your second chapter drafts. As you write, identify the kind of case studies and life histories to collect—so you can both check your emerging explanation and make your understanding deeper. Assemble these case studies and life or event histories during intensive interview sessions with selected informants.

Give copies of article or chapter drafts that have gone into their second incarnation to members of your research team and to informants in the general community. Ask them to tell you where you go wrong. Then, during a final period of intensive interviews and Sixth Order Gossip, ask the questions and make the observations that let you get it right.

EXAMINE SOURCES OF INTRACULTURAL AND INTERCULTURAL VARIATION

Use multivariate regression methods to tease out explanations for intracultural and intercultural variation and cultural change. QE procedures (chapter 3) normally employ a Posttest Only Control Group research design that, in the absence of randomization, measures internal validity confounds explicitly. This means for you to explain cultural variation and change as a function of variation in experience and to search for concrete events and circumstances that shape those experiences. Remember that what people think and do must reflect not only their individual life histories but broader regional and global histories of people, events, and social interaction into which they were born and in which they grew up. Identify events, circumstances, and processes that provide one set of choices to some people and a different set of choices to others. Ask individuals to identify life experiences that were significant to them and to help you understand why those experiences were significant. Pay particular attention to discrepancies between the two and how and under what circumstances individuals iron out the discrepancies. Keep in mind that core mental processes, which occur consciously only after the fact, may work primarily to rationalize what people actually do. Plan to explain why people believe, feel, and act the way they do by reference to information you collect on their prior experience, on their current experiences, how those are perceived and conceptualized, and the inferred processes by which individuals integrate these to produce knowledge and behavior.

Similarity coefficients and statistical tests applied to data such as these will tell you what goes with what and how strongly and thus provide a warrant for believing that a given relationship between a specific life experience and intracultural or intercultural variation is *real,* not merely a figment of your imagination (McEwan 1963). Unfortunately, analysis of the relationship between only two variables (*zero-order analysis*) tells you next to nothing. Adding another variable to the analysis may produce dramatic changes—a zero-order similarity coefficient may disappear, grow stronger, or change from positive to negative. Warrant for inferring that a relationship is *determinant,* as well as *real* (McEwan 1963), requires you to isolate a suspected relationship so you can tell whether or not it exists, and its strength, even after you control for other variables. Of course, experimental designs do just that. In the absence of randomization, multiple regression operations with explicitly measured internal validity confounds accomplish the same goals.

Create standard informant-by-variable data matrices to conduct the analyses illustrated next. You SAVED the factor loadings from your construct validity tests to create measures of intracultural variation. To make use of these new variables:

- Open the factor loadings file;
- Transpose the matrix to make it an informant-by-variable matrix;
- Name the variables F1 and F2, or another appropriate label;
- Select both variables, and copy them;
- Paste them into the master data file that contains the internal validity confounds you measured.

If you identified multiple cultures, create an appropriate CULTURE variable in your master data file so that you can conduct appropriate analyses of intercultural variation or cultural change. For two cultures, code the cultures with 1s and 0s, as you would an ordinary binary variable. For three or more cultures, code the cultures 1, 2, . . . , k, for the k cultures you identified.

Think about Relationships with Regression Models

Answers to "Why?" questions consist of a claim that one phenomenon is linked to another. Multiple regression constitutes a way of thinking about these claims as general functions. General functions of the form Y

$= f(X_k)$ constitute claims about the existence of a set of rules that allows us to translate values of *independent* variables (X_k)—explanatory variables like childhood violence experiences, intervention training, and age or ethnicity—into values of one or more *dependent* variables (Y), like participation in a culture of drug use or not, participation in a culture of Serious Student Identity or not, or participation in a culture that defines *stress* and *social support* by reference to specific forms of experience. A simple additive (*linear*) model looks like this:

$$Y = \beta_0 + \beta_1 X_1 + \beta_2 X_2 + \ldots + \beta_k X_k + \epsilon$$

Each X represents an explanatory variable, and the Greek epsilon (ϵ) constitutes explicit recognition that we will make the best predictions possible, but that we anticipate prediction error. The Greek betas (β) represent the relationships that may exist between Y and each explanatory variable:

- The influence of childhood violence experiences (X) on later participation in a culture of drug use (Y);
- The influence of intervention training (X) on someone's self-identity as a student (Y);
- The influence of age (X_1) or ethnicity (X_2) on someone's understanding about the nature of stress and social support coming from daily social interaction (Y).

Model Intercultural Variation or Cultural Change Like This

Analyses of intercultural variation or cultural change commonly measures the independent variable as binary codes, yes/present (1) or no/absent/otherwise (0). In the outcomes-evaluation example, students constructed and participated in only one of two cultures of student identity. The intervention aimed to produce Serious Students, so that culture receives a code of 1. A model that tests for the effect of the intervention looks like this:

$$Y = \beta_0 + \beta_1 X_1 + \epsilon, \text{ where}$$

$Y = 1$ if a student constructed a Serious Student Culture, and 0 otherwise, and

$X_1 = 1$ if a student participated in the intervention program, and 0 otherwise.

If a student did not participate in the intervention program, $(X_1 = 0)$. Hence, the likelihood that the student constructed a Serious Student identity would be identified by (β_0):

$Y = \beta_0 + \beta_1{}^*0 + \epsilon$, or (β_0), plus or minus some degree of random error, ϵ.

By contrast, if a student did participate in the intervention program $(X_1 = 1)$, hence, the likelihood that the student constructed a Serious Student identity would be identified by $(\beta_0 + \beta_1)$:

$Y = \beta_0 + \beta_1{}^*1 + \epsilon$, or $(\beta_0 + \beta_1)$, plus or minus some degree of random error, ϵ.

The regression coefficient (β_1) thus measures the influence of the intervention program on the likelihood that a student participates in the Serious Student Culture.

Properly specified models include explicitly measured internal validity confounds, like number of semesters in college (*maturation*) and gender and high SAT scores (*history*). If you include a variable for gender (X_2), the beta for gender (β_2) will tell you the influence of gender on the likelihood that a student constructed a Serious Student identity, after you remove the influence of (control for) participation in the intervention program. If you include a variable for high SAT scores (X_3), in addition to gender, the beta for high SAT scores (β_3) will tell you the influence of high SAT scores on the likelihood that a student constructed a Serious Student identity, after you remove the influence of (control for) *both* gender *and* participation in the intervention program.

Model Intracultural Variation Like This

Analyses of intracultural variation use the loadings on factor 1 and factor 2 as dependent variables. In the culture of stress and social support example, working women exhibited different degrees of participation in the single culture, measured by their loadings on factor 1. A model that tests for the effect of Native American ethnicity on participation in the culture looks like this:

$Y = \beta_0 + \beta_1 X_1 + \epsilon$, where

Y = a working woman's loading on factor 1, and

X_1 = 1 if the woman identified herself as Native American, and 0 otherwise.

If a woman did not identify herself as Native American (X_1 = 0), hence, the degree to which she constructed a culture of stress and social support identical to the consensus would be identified by (β_0):

$Y = \beta_0 + \beta_1{}^*0 + \epsilon$, or ($\beta_0$), plus or minus some degree of random error, ϵ.

By contrast, if a woman did identify herself as Native American (X_1 = 1), hence, the degree to which she constructed a culture of stress and social support identical to the consensus would be identified by ($\beta_0 + \beta_1$):

$Y = \beta_0 + \beta_1{}^*1 + \epsilon$, or ($\beta_0 + \beta_1$) plus or minus some degree of random error, ϵ.

The regression coefficient (β_1) thus measures the influence of Native American ethnicity on the degree to which a woman constructed a culture of stress and social support identical to the consensus.

Properly specified models include explicitly measured internal validity confounds, like age (*maturation*) and growing up in poverty (*history*). If you include a variable for age (X_2), the beta for age (β_2) will tell you the influence of age on the degree to which a woman constructed a culture of stress and social support identical to the consensus, once you remove the influence of (control for) Native American ethnicity. If you include a variable for growing up in poverty (X_3), in addition to age, the beta for poverty (β_3) will tell you the influence of growing up in poverty on women's understandings of the meaning of stress and social support, once you remove the influence of (control for) *both* age *and* Native American ethnicity.

USE OLS REGRESSION FOR INTRACULTURAL VARIATION

Variables measured quantitatively elicit questions like, *How much* does a person's individually unique culture correspond to the shared culture (the dependent variable) under different sets of conditions (independent variables)? Variables measured qualitatively elicit questions like, What's the *likelihood* that a person will construct one culture or another (the dependent variable) under different sets of conditions (independent variables)? The question pertinent to analysis of intracultural variation thus differs significantly from the question pertinent to analysis of intercultural variation.

Ordinary Least Squares (OLS) regression operations tell you how much variance in cultural participation comes from a set of life experience variables (e.g., Schroeder, Sjoquist, and Stephan 1986; Gujarati 1995). The Sum of Squares for the loadings on factor 1, for example, tells you how much intracultural variation your informants show. OLS models estimate model parameters (β_k) with statistics (b_k). OLS regression makes these estimates using the same criteria applied to the calculation of means (see chapter 6). The result is a set of *regression coefficients* (b_k) that estimates values of the dependent variable (Y) in ways that guarantee that the sum of prediction errors (the absolute differences between the value of each case and the model estimate for the case, called *residuals*) equals 0.0. Each coefficient tells you the average change in Y for each change in one independent variable (X), once you remove the influence of (control for) the effects of other independent variables.

Table 8.2 shows SYSTAT output for an analysis of the intracultural variation exhibited among students who had constructed a Serious Student identity. The CONSTANT tells you that the average degree of cultural participation (loading on factor 1) among men (gender = 0) who had not participated in the intervention (intervention participant = 0) and who did not enter college with high SAT scores (high SAT scores = 0) was .932. This degree of participation rose by .008 for women (gender = 1), rose by .007 for intervention participants (intervention participant = 1), and fell by .012 for people who entered college with high SAT scores (high SAT scores = 1).

How well does the model work? OLS regression gives you two answers.

1. *Multiple R^2*: If you square the residuals and add them up (the *Error* Sum of Squares, .044), you find the intracultural variation you can't explain with your independent variables. If you subtract what you cannot explain from the total Sum of Squares, your find how much intracultural variation you can explain (the *Regression* Sum of Squares, .003). If you express what you can explain as a ratio of the total intracultural

variation, you find *Multiple R²*, the proportion of the total intracultural variation your independent variables explain (.059). A caution: Multiple R^2 grows with each independent variable you include in your model. Pay attention to the *adjusted* Multiple R^2, which controls for the number of independent variables (.000). In this example, gender, intervention participation, and admission with high SAT scores account for an inconsequential amount of intracultural variation in the Serious Student Culture.

2. *Standard Error of the Estimate:* The *average* degree to which individually unique cultural configurations do *not* correspond with the shared cultural configuration (.046).

T-statistics test the null hypothesis that individual independent variables produce no intracultural variation ($\beta_k = 0.00$). An F-ratio tests the null hypothesis that *no* independent variable produces intracultural variation (Multiple Rho² [ρ^2] = 0.00). In this instance, the probability that no independent variable produced intracultural variation is .730. This test is superfluous when one or more *t*-statistics are high. In the current instance, however, all *t*-statistics are low (.376 for Gender, .293 for Intervention Participant, and −.584 for high SAT scores), and the probability of finding the observed relationships just by chance is very high (.710 for Gender, .772 for Intervention Participant, and .565 for high SAT scores). However, when some *t*-statistics are high and others are low, use post-hoc tests of the null hypothesis that $\beta_k = 0.00$ for control variables to assess which independent variables may be usefully discarded.

Check Your Findings

Inferences such as these depend on the absence of selection bias and an ideal world of data collection, in which you:

- include all pertinent and no irrelevant or extraneous internal validity confound,
- correctly specify the functional form of all supposed relationships between dependent and independent variables,
- measure all variables perfectly,

TABLE 8.1 Sources of Intracultural Variation among Serious Students

Dep Var: F1   N: 25   Multiple R: 0.242   Squared Multiple R: 0.059
Adjusted Squared Multiple R: 0.000   Standard Error of Estimate: 0.046

Effect	Coefficient	Std Error	Std Coef	Tolerance	t	P(2 Tail)
CONSTANT	0.932	0.077	0.000	.	12.137	0.000
Gender	0.008	0.021	0.080	0.983	0.376	0.710
Intervention						
Participant	0.007	0.025	0.080	0.607	0.293	0.772
High SAT						
scores	−0.012	0.020	−0.159	0.603	−0.584	0.565

Analysis of Variance

Source	Sum of Squares	df	Mean-Square	F-ratio	P
Regression	0.003	3	0.001	0.436	0.730
Residual	0.044	21	0.002		

- predict dependent variables in such a way that errors exhibit a normal distribution,
- select cases in such a way that independent variables exhibit no correlation, and that
- findings of the model solution generate no correlated residuals.

Of course, the real world and the ideal world don't often correspond very closely. Sometimes, they match badly. Much data collection and analysis involves trying to determine which of these conditions you meet acceptably and which you don't, and correcting particularly bad matches between the ideal world and the real one. For example, the first assumption tells you to make your final evaluation of model variables by including only those independent variables for which you find evidence (low probabilities) that they belong. If you have grounds for believing that you've met the other assumptions, do an appropriate post-hoc test with all variables that otherwise appear extraneous, to test for otherwise hidden additional effects.

The second assumption (correct functional form) tells you to assess possible nonlinearities. If relationships between variables exhibit proportional changes rather than fixed unit changes, logarithm transformations will produce a model that fits the data better (see Bracewell 1990).

The third assumption (perfect measurement) cannot be fulfilled in the real world. However, this assumption bears more on the precision of model estimates than on their accuracy. Random measurement error makes it harder to see real-world relationships, and measurement imperfections in the dependent variable exhibit minor effects compared with measurement imperfections for independent variables. Because the *power* of your analysis goes down, judgments about the influence of an independent variable become conservative.

Violations of the fourth assumption (normally distributed residuals) rarely invalidate findings. However, violations of the fifth assumption (no correlation among independent variables) pose major dilemmas, and violations of the sixth (no correlation among model estimates) are deadly. These conditions mean that the F-ratio and *t*-tests don't yield valid probabilities. Sophisticated diagnostic techniques now allow us to evaluate whether or not our data violate these assumptions, and equally sophisticated techniques give us means to avoid the analytical confusion such violations create (e.g., Gujarati 1995).

Explicit randomization in true experimental designs meets the fifth assumption, since it guarantees that relationships among independent variables exist only by chance. All other data violate the assumption that no relationships exist among independent variables. For all practical purposes, all data sets contain *multicollinearity*. Nonetheless, multicollinearity doesn't always invalidate probabilities. The following conditions signal the presence of enough multicollinearity to distort model estimates:

- *Condition indices* greater than 30 (see Belsley, Kuh and Welsch 1980).
- Including a new variable increases rather than decreases the standard error of the estimate.
- A new variable exhibits a high probability and *also* raises the probability of a variable already in the model.
- The model exhibits a low F-ratio probability but exhibits no low *t*-statistic probabilities.
- Your software tells you that it can't solve for the coefficients.

Factor analysis provides one solution to multicollinearity problems. If the troublesome collinear variables load highly on a single factor, you can measure all simultaneously with *factor scores.* Factor scores measure the contribution of each variable to the underlying factor and thus integrate all variables into a single score. If you suspect that significant multicollinearity still gives you invalid probabilities, identify a promising model and enter additional (control) variables one by one. Report the *t*-tests. A factor analysis that reveals inconsequential structure among a set of independent variables (e.g., 1 factor for each independent variable) confirms the absence of collinearity.

Violations of the sixth assumption, that prediction errors associated with any one case remain uncorrelated with errors made for other cases, appear as patterned relationships among residuals called *heteroskedasticity.* For example, errors in estimation *(residuals)* may be small, when you estimate low values of the dependent variable, and grow increasingly larger as you estimate increasingly high values of the dependent variable. Estimation errors may exhibit high similarity for people who live close to each other and decreasing similarity for people who live increasingly far away, a pattern called *spatial autocorrelation.* Similarly, estimation errors may exhibit high similarity for cases that occur close to each other in time and decreasing similarity for cases increasingly far away, a pattern called *temporal autocorrelation.* Models that make the dependent variable in one equation an independent variable in the other frequently produce OLS solutions in which the errors for dependent variable estimates correlate with the same variable used as an independent variable. Figure 8.1 shows, in the current example, that errors in estimation *(residuals)* appear large when you estimate low values of intracultural variation-dependent variable and grow increasingly smaller (although, in this example, not by much) as you estimate increasingly high values of intracultural variation. The degree of heteroskedasticity in this example, however, is well within the range of variation one can expect by chance in small samples.

Methods for diagnosing and correcting spatial and temporal autocorrelation may be fruitfully applied when the unit of analysis corresponds to an explicitly identifiable regional or historical unit. *Measurement unit transforms* (e.g., logarithm transformations), *weighted least squares,* and *differencing* procedures may eliminate the correlated errors associated with cross-sectional heteroskedasticity and many forms of temporal and spatial autocorrelation. *Two-Stage Least Squares* (2SLS) procedures eliminate the

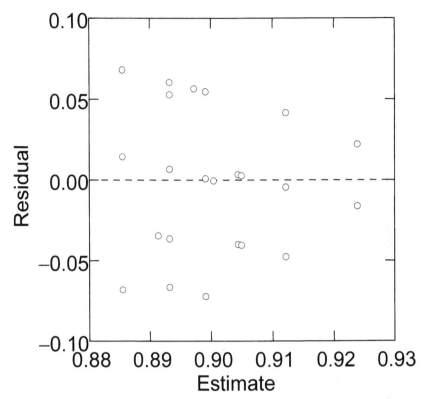

FIGURE 8.1
Plot of Residuals against Predicted Values

correlated errors produced by sets of equations in which independent variables in one equation appear as dependent variables in the other. To learn these procedures, consult standard econometric texts (e.g., Gujarati 1995; Johnston 1984).

Findings that survive exhaustive diagnostic evaluation warrant substantive interpretation.

USE LOGISTIC REGRESSION FOR INTERCULTURAL VARIATION

Logistic regression constitutes one of several (e.g., *Probit*) regression operations that constrain model estimates to the probability range (0, 1). Logistic regression identifies its regression coefficients iteratively using *maximum likelihood* criteria rather than OLS criteria. Solutions that use White's (1982) quasi-maximum likelihood method guard against erroneous standard errors arising from model misspecification. Regression textbooks like Gujarati's (1995) or Johnston's (1984) introduce the issues pertinent to the analysis of binary dependent variables. Steinberg and Colla's (1997) software documentation constitutes an excellent midlevel source. Hosmer and Lemeshow (1989) will help you develop advanced technical expertise.

Ordinary binary logistic regression models interpret multivariate general linear hypothesis models as:

$$\text{Probability } (Y = 1) = \exp (X) / 1 + \exp (X)$$

Thus, logit output is much like OLS regression output. It gives parameter estimates for each independent variable. Like OLS estimates, logit parameter estimates tell you how much the probability $(Y = 1)$ increases for each unit increase in an independent variable. Unlike OLS, however, this probability is a nonlinear function of the estimate. Logistic regression coefficients express units of change along the S-shaped logistic probability distribution (*logits*). The rate of change in probabilities changes, depending on where you are along the probability distribution. Unlike OLS regression coefficients, you can't directly interpret logistic regression coefficients. However, taking the exponent of the logit yields an odds-ratio, and an odds-ratio table provides coefficients that can be interpreted like ordinary regression estimates.

The odds that $Y = 1$ is given by $p/(1 - p)$. Thus, the odds ratio shows how much the odds that $Y = 1$ changes for each unit change in an independent variable. Two events equally likely (a 50/50 split), like drug use or its absence, produce an odds ratio of 1.00. One event more likely to occur than another (a 75/25 split) produces odds ratios over 1.00. One event less likely to occur than another (a 25/75 split) produces odds ratios under 1.00. Positive logistic regression coefficients produce odds ratios over 1.00; negative logistic regression coefficients produce odds ratios under 1.00.

Table 8.2 shows SYSTAT output of an analysis of sources of intercultural variation and cultural change in student identity. Intervention participants were 76 times (OR: 76.039) more likely than nonparticipants to construct a Serious Student identity, after we remove the influence of high SAT scores and gender. The informants who entered college with high SAT scores were 12 times (OR: 11.803) more likely than students who didn't to construct a Serious Student identity, after we remove the influence of intervention participation and gender. The likelihood that women constructed a Serious Student identity was 55 percent higher than for men (OR: 1.552), after we remove the influence of intervention participation and high SAT scores.

T-statistics test the null hypothesis that individual independent variables produce no intercultural variation or cultural change ($\beta_k = 0.00$), although LogExact software offers exact probabilities. In this instance, the t-statistics for Intervention Participants and High SAT scores are high (4.434 and 4.323, respectively) and the t-statistic for Gender is low (.680). The probability that intervention and high SAT scores produced no intercultural variation or cultural change is very, very low (less than .001 in both cases). The probability that gender produced no intercultural variation or cultural change is high (.478). With Logit models, a log-likelihood Chi-squared test substitutes for an F-test of the null hypothesis that no independent variable influences the dependent variable. Like the analysis of variance for all independent variables in OLS regression, this test is

TABLE 8.2 Sources of Intercultural Variation and Cultural Change

Dependent Var: Culture = Serious Student
Log Likelihood: − 43.248

Parameter	Estimate	S.E.	t-ratio	p-value
1 CONSTANT	− 10.232	2.014	− 5.081	0.000
2 Intervention Participant	4.331	0.977	4.434	0.000
3 High SAT scores	2.468	0.571	4.323	0.000
4 Gender	0.439	0.620	0.708	0.478

Parameter	Odds Ratio	95.0% bounds Upper	Lower
2 Intervention Participant	76.039	515.785	11.210
3 High SAT scores	11.803	36.144	3.855
4 Gender	1.552	5.228	0.461

Log Likelihood of constants only model = LL(0) = − 66.081
2*[LL(N) − LL(0)] = 45.666 with 3 df Chi-sq p-value = 0.000
McFadden's Rho-Squared = 0.346

superfluous when one or more t-statistics are high. However, post-hoc tests of the null hypothesis that ($\beta_k = 0.00$) for control variables, albeit using a log-likelihood test rather than an F-test, help assess which variables may be usefully discarded. The *Hosmer-Lemeshow statistic* (and others) tells you the probability that model estimates of the number of cases that exhibit given probabilities of adolescent drug use correspond with the number of cases actually found in the data. SYSTAT's logistic implementation computes a McFadden's Rho-Squared, which, in an attempt to approximate an OLS Multiple R^2, transforms the model log-likelihood into a value between 0 and 1. McFadden's Rho-Squared values tend to be much lower than OLS equivalents, however, and Rho-Squared values higher than .20 identify strong models (Steinberg and Colla 1997). Prediction tables tell you the model's capacity for correctly discriminating between someone who used illicit drugs in adolescence and someone who didn't. But Hosmer and Lemeshow (1989:146–47) emphasize that prediction tables don't address the question of model validity, as we'll discuss further on.

How well does the model work? With logistic regression, this question disaggregates, potentially, into two. The primary question bears on model validity: How well does the model fit the data? Models that fit the data well give us theoretical direction. Whether or not valid models provide practical tools hinges on answers to the second question: How well does the model discriminate between people who participate in one culture or another?

Check Your Findings

Valid models meet two criteria (Hosmer and Lemeshow 1989). First, observed values (1/0) should correspond well with predicted values (in the range 1, 0); summary measures of the correspondence between observed and predicted values (residuals) should exhibit differences best explained by chance. Second, no cases exist with a combination of high leverage and poor fit that distort model coefficients.

Information bearing on the first criterion comes from Hosmer-Lemeshow, Pearson, and Deviance statistics. These tests evaluate the null hypothesis that (observed-predicted) differences like those found in the following table exist only by chance. For the probability category of 0.004, for example, the model predicted .001 Serious Student (0 were observed) and .999 Basic Students (1 was observed). At the other extreme, the probability category of 1.00, the model predicted .988 Serious Students (1 was observed) and .012 Basic Students (0 were observed). The high probabilities tell us that the model fits the data very well.

Information bearing on the second criterion comes from graphical analyses that identify cases with high leverage and poor fit. High values of the diagnostic statistic DELBETA (1) identify cases with high leverage. For a specific case, DELBETA (1) measures the difference between the model estimates based on all cases and model estimates based on all cases *minus* the case in question. Large differences thus mean that including or excluding a specific case changes the model coefficients in significant ways. High

TABLE 8.3   Deciles of Risk Diagnostics

Records processed: 142
Sum of weight = 142.000

	Statistic	p-value	df
Hosmer-Lemeshow*	14.483	0.152	10.000
Pearson	145.553	0.313	138.000
Deviance	86.497	1.000	138.000

*Large influence of one or more deciles may affect statistic.

Category	0.004	0.007	0.025	0.055	0.083
Resp Obs	0.000	0.000	0.000	0.000	1.000
Exp	0.001	0.040	0.113	0.052	1.789
Ref Obs	1.000	8.000	11.000	2.000	31.000
Exp	0.999	7.960	10.887	1.948	30.211
Avg Prob	0.001	0.005	0.010	0.026	0.056
Category	0.168	0.239	0.410	0.510	0.817
Resp Obs	2.000	1.000	6.000	3.000	5.000
Exp	4.376	0.169	2.700	2.057	5.723
Ref Obs	50.000	0.000	4.000	2.000	6.000
Exp	47.624	0.831	7.300	2.943	5.277
Avg Prob	0.084	0.169	0.270	0.411	0.520
Category	0.987	1.000			
Resp Obs	6.000	1.000			
Exp	6.992	0.988			
Ref Obs	2.000	0.000			
Exp	1.008	0.012			
Avg Prob	0.874	0.988			

values of the diagnostic statistics DELPSTAT and DELDSTAT identify cases with poor fit. For a specific case, DELPSTAT measures the difference between the summary Pearson statistic based on all cases and the Pearson statistic based on all cases *minus* the case in question; DELDSTAT measures the difference between the summary Deviance statistic based on all cases and the Deviance statistic based on all cases *minus* the case in question. Large differences thus mean that including or excluding a specific case changes the fit between observed and predicted values in significant ways. Cases with high leverage and poor fit may represent important new findings or outliers that distort model estimates. In either case, they deserve special attention.

For example, depending on the research problem and theory, one might remove specific outlier cases, reestimate the model, and examine how removing the case changes the model coefficients. Figure 8.2 plots DELPSTAT by PROB (model estimated probabilities) and makes the size of cases proportional to DELBETA(1). This plot identifies one case with a combination of high leverage and poor fit as a significant bubble in the upper right-hand corner. This case warrants attention since removal of a case with high leverage and poor fit may change model estimates in significant ways.

Answers to the question of how well valid models discriminate Serious Students from Basic Students come from prediction success tables like the following table 8.4.

The terms *Sensitivity* and *Specificity* come from the biomedical literature. The Correct quantities are Sensitivity for the response group (Serious Students) and Specificity for the reference group (Basic Students). The model correctly identified about 50 percent (48.2 percent) of the Serious Students and nearly 90 percent (88.9 percent) of the Basic Students. Since few students constructed Serious Student identities and many students constructed Basic Student identities, by themselves these numbers can mislead. The 90 percent of Basic Students correctly identified represents a gain of only 6.5 percent over chance (the *success indicator*). The 50 percent of Serious Students correctly identified represents a gain of 30.6 percent over chance (the *success indicator*).

False Reference gives a false negative (falsely-predicted-as-reference) rate: around 50 percent of people predicted *not* to be Serious Students

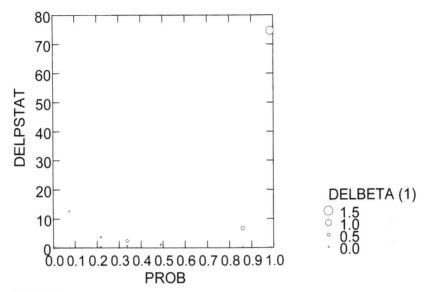

FIGURE 8.2

did construct such identities. False Response gives a false positive (falsely-predicted-as-response) rate: around 10 percent of the people predicted to be Serious Students actually did *not* construct such an identity.

BE PREPARED TO SEE CULTURES YOU DIDN'T ANTICIPATE

It has become commonplace to hear people ascribe differences in what people think and do (*cultural* differences) to labels for race, gender, class,

TABLE 8.4 Prediction Table

Actual Choice	Predicted Response	Choice Reference	Actual Total
Response	12.056	12.944	25.000
Reference	12.944	104.056	117.000
Pred. Tot.	25.000	117.000	142.000
Correct	0.482	0.899	
Success Ind.	0.306	0.065	
Tot. Correct	0.818		
Sensitivity:	0.482	Specificity:	0.889
False Reference:	0.518	False Response:	0.111

and ethnicity, in much the same way that we use to ascribe cultural differences to tribal identities. I have a very personal sense and understanding of a West Indian culture that emerged among people of Northwest European and West African origin brought together in a plantation economy. So I have no doubt that there exist distinctive cultures legitimately called African-American or Puerto Rican or broadly American. I feel equally sure that a women's culture and a men's culture exist. But I feel like the boy who looked for the Emperor's clothes when I look for evidence that validates their existence. Until we answer two simple questions, we shall never know whether or not, or the degree to which, *specific* cultural differences correspond with *any* difference in social labels. The questions are:

1. Do we have evidence of one or more than one culture?
2. If so, how well can we predict what people know/do (their *culture*) from one or more of their social labels?

The case studies reviewed in chapters 7 and 8 suggest that we shall find it easy to document the construct validity of cultures. They also suggest that, all too often, the answer to the second question will be: very, very poorly.

Data on similarities among the components that go into the construction of meals pointed to a cultural difference between people who identify themselves as members of distinctive ethnic communities and people who do not. But it made no difference whether or not the ethnic community was Puerto Rican, South Asian, or Ukrainian. Moreover, figure 7.11 suggested that some of the former were just as clueless about similarities among the meal components we asked about as the generic Euro-Americans were—they, too, constructed meals from items like "pizza," "hamburgers," and "salad," not items like "beans," "tomatoes," and "greens." A finding like this tells us that self-identification as a member of an ethnic community only partially captures variation in life experiences that explains variation in the knowledge that people bring to the problem of constructing meals. But self-identification as a member of an ethnic community *doesn't* tell us what specific patterns of experiences and social interaction of our informants cross-cut age, gender, and ethnicity differences to produce the observed shared understanding about the items from which one constructs meals.

We may find *no* cultural differences by race, gender, class, or ethnicity, depending on the specific domain of cognition, emotion, and behavior we look at. In a series of papers (e.g., 1996, 1997, Dressler et al. 1996, 1998, 2000), William Dressler has demonstrated the existence of broad community agreements cross-cutting differences by race, gender, class, or ethnicity about what constitutes a reasonable standard of living. By standards like these, working-class Barbadians live in poverty. Barbadians, like residents of North America, commonly ascribe violence to working-class homes. The second case study demonstrated the existence of two cultures of child rearing in Barbados—a dominant culture of affection and a minority culture of violence. However, logistic regression analysis reveals that people who grew up in working-class homes were no more likely to grow up in a culture of violence than people who grew up in middle- or upper-class homes ($t = 0.339$, $p = .734$; see Handwerker 1996).

Dressler used his measure of broad community agreements about what constitutes a reasonable standard of living to develop culturally specific measures of relative deprivation-induced stress. The meaning of stress coming from daily social interaction, similarly, shows no differences by race, class, or ethnicity. A multiple regression analysis of the data on the single culture of stressors and social supports that uses the loadings on factor 1 as the dependent variable yields a multiple R-squared of .081 and an F-ratio of 0.895 (1-tailed $p = .566$; probabilities based on 10,000 random permutations). Independent variables included appropriate internal validity confounds: the degree to which they had recently experienced stressful behavior (*history*), the degree to which they had recently experienced mood disorder symptoms (*history*), their age (*maturation*), their educational attainment (*history*), whether or not they grew up in poverty (*history*), and their ethnicity (as European, Hispanic, African, or Native Americans; *history*). This analysis thus reveals that informant agreements about what constitutes a stressor or a social support bear no relationship to the degree to which they had recently experienced stressful behavior, the degree to which they had recently experienced mood disorder symptoms, their age, their educational attainment, whether or not they grew up in poverty, or their ethnicity. These findings warrant the inference that there exists, independent of age, education, class, or historical origins, cultural agreement that words or acts that imply respect, equality, active assistance, or otherwise make one feel special and important are *always* acceptable and function as social supports. By contrast, words or acts that imply inferiority, impede achievement, or otherwise make one feel bad about oneself are *never* acceptable and function as stressors. Women with a recent history of high stress by these measures were 85 times more likely than women without such a history to exhibit symptoms of depression (Handwerker 1999b).

The six cultures of substance use and abuse in Alaska and the Russian Far East provide a case in which ethnicity captures important influences on one's participation in one or another culture. But other life experiences appear just as important. Keep in mind that, although behavioral data on a small number of variables provide the defining characteristics of these six cultures, the existence of qualitatively different behavioral configurations implies an equivalent, qualitatively different set of cognitive and emotional configurations embedded in distinctive social networks and patterns of interaction. Smoking and drinking means something fundamentally different for people who do neither than for people who do either or both. People who smoke and drink but avoid illicit substances ascribe a meaning to glue sniffing or the use of hash or crack cocaine very different from the meaning ascribed by people who use illicit substances. Illicit substances possess an importance in the lives of people who use more than one of them far greater than they possess in the lives of people who use only one. These implicit differences in cognition and emotion come out in differences in how often illicit substances are used and in whom one interacts with, how, and how often. The strikingly high incidence of STDs among men participating in the drug culture suggests fundamental differences between these men and others in the character and pattern of their interaction with women. We should thus anticipate that these qualitatively different cultures reflect qualitatively different sets of life experiences.

Two obvious sets of influences on these cultures include maturation and mortality effects and the historical and regional availability of illicit substances. Cigarette smoking and alcohol use constitute risk factors for mortality, so we might expect that men who both smoked and drank in their early adulthood might cease drinking and smoking with age, or they may die. In the present case, members of the No Substance Use culture average around 56 years of age, members of the Smoking only culture average around 46 years of age, and members of the cultures involving some combination of smoking, drinking, and illicit substance use average around 36 years of age. Similarly, at least up to 1993 when we collected the current data, illicit substances were very difficult to obtain in the Russian Far East. In Alaska, by contrast, illicit substances were available in the early 1980s and have become increasingly easy to obtain. Whether life experience differences captured by ethnic labels (natives/non-natives) show any influence remains an open question. Table 8.5 shows logistic regression findings for the influence of various life experience markers on the likelihood of an informant participating in one or another of the illicit drug-use cultures compared to others. Zero-order analysis (Models 1a and 1b) shows that natives are no more likely to participate in drug-use cultures than non-natives, but Alaskans are far more likely to do so than Russians. This finding holds when we look at the relationship between regional ethnicity and drug-use cultures, controlling for the relationship between the distinction between natives/non-natives and drug-use cultures (Model 2).

This finding also holds when we examine the influence of other precursors. We measured several variables that might bear on behavioral health morbidity, including: living in a cohesive family, affection and violence experienced as a child from family members, and affection and violence experienced as a child by nonfamily members. We measured current family bonds and cohesion with a 24-point scale constructed from self-reports of the extent to which family members asked each other for help, felt very close to one another, consulted each other on decisions, spent free time with one another, felt that family togetherness was very important, and felt closer to family members than to nonfamily members. Research participants reported current family cohesion scores that ranged from 3 to 24 (mean = 19.4, sd = 4.3). Natives reported slightly higher current family cohesion scores than non-natives (20 compared to 18, p = .011), and Russians reported slightly higher current family cohesion scores than Alaskans (20 compared to 18; p = .025). The affection and violence items and scales have been reported on elsewhere (e.g., Handwerker 1997; see chap-

TABLE 8.5   Logistic Regression Findings for Determinants of Participation in Illicit Drug-Use Cultures Compared to Participating in Other Cultures

	Odds Ratio	Upper 95% CL	Lower 95% CL	2-tailed p
Models 1a and 1b for Zero-Order Relationships				
Alaskan/Russian	17.6	37.0	8.4	<.000
Native/Non-Native	1.6	3.1	.8	.201
Model 2 for Relationships after Controlling for the Other				
Alaskan/Russian	17.8	37.9	8.3	<.000
Native/Non-Native	.9	2.2	.4	.908
Model 3				
Alaskan/Russian	29.2	77.7	11.0	<.000
Age	.95	.98	.92	.001
Balance of Interethnic Stress and Support (Factor Scores) Experienced by the Cohort of Young Native Men	2.2	4.0	1.2	.007

Logistic Diagnostics for Model 3

McFadden's Rho-Squared .36
Hosmer-Lemeshow test $p=.204$
Pearson test $p=.097$
Deviance test $p=.812$

Tests for Independent Effects from:

Educational attainment by age 18 ($t = .734, p = .463$),
Living as part of a cohesive family ($t = 1.217, p = .224$),
The balance of family violence & affection experienced during childhood
($t = .712, p = .477$),
The balance of interethnic childhood violence and affection for non-natives
($t = .474, p = .636$),
The balance of intraethnic childhood violence and affection for non-natives
($t = .069, p = .945$),
The balance of intraethnic childhood violence and affection for natives
($t = .679, p = .497$).

Classification Results Success Indices	Sensitivity .678	Specificity .757
	Response .248 Cultures	Reference .187 Cultures

ter 5) and consist of items identified by the culture of stressors and social support discussed earlier. Examples of ethnic violence experiences include overhearing or hearing directed at oneself comments about "ignorant," "dirty," or "drunken" natives and experiencing being denied employment or educational opportunities offered to non-natives. The measure of family violence used here consists of factor scores from the combined sources

of family affection and violence. This variable ranges from (1.1 to 4.6 but by construction exhibits a mean of 0.0 and a standard deviation of 1.0. The factor score "traumatic stress inflicted on children by non-natives" variable ranges from -1.5 to 3.0 but by construction exhibits a mean of 0.0 and a standard deviation of 1.0. Natives and non-natives reported equivalent intensities of "traumatic stress inflicted on children by non-natives" ($p = .884$), although Alaskans reported slightly higher-intensity rates than Russians ($p = .010$). We created an equivalent variable to measure childhood trauma inflicted by natives. This "traumatic stress inflicted on children by natives" variable ranges from -1.2 to 3.5 but by construction exhibits a mean of 0.0 and a standard deviation of 1.0. Natives reported slightly lower intensities of "traumatic stress inflicted on children by natives" than non-natives ($p = .007$), Alaskans reported higher intensities than Russians ($p < .000$), and Alaskan natives and non-natives reported slightly higher intensities than their Russian counterparts ($p = .031$).

Model 3 coefficients reveal that Alaskans are nearly 30 times ($OR = 29.2$) more likely than Russians to participate in one or another illicit drug-use culture. The coefficient for Age, which reveals that the likelihood of participating in an illicit drug-use culture falls by 5 percent ($OR = .95$) for each increase in age, points to the mortality and maturation effect mentioned earlier. Older men grew up when drugs weren't commonly available and did not take to them once they arrived. Younger men who grew up when drugs were commonly available may have taken to them, but they stopped as they grew older or died. However, the last coefficient identifies an effect from ethnic violence experienced in childhood. The coefficient for this factor score measure of the balance of interethnic violence and affection experienced by young native men ($OR = 2.2$) shows that the likelihood of participating in an illicit drug-use culture more than doubles for each increase in interethnic violence experiences. Other variables show no influence on cultural participation. Tests for independent effects from educational attainment ($p = .463$), living as part of a cohesive family ($p = .224$), family violence ($p = .477$), interethnic violence experienced by young men from the majority ethnic group ($p = .636$), or intraethnic violence experienced by either native (p = .497) or non-native ($p = .945$) men yield high probabilities.

Deciles of risk diagnostics exhibit the high probabilities (Hosmer-Lem-

eshow $p = .204$, Pearson $p = .097$, and Deviance $p = .812$) that show
that the model generates predictions that cannot be distinguished from
the observed data except by chance. Classification findings reveal that
Model 3 constitutes a reasonably specific (specificity $= .678$) and sensitive
(sensitivity $= .757$) predictor of participation in one or another drug culture. Overall, the model correctly classifies 72.3 percent of the cases. Success indices of .248 and .187 show that the model correctly predicts culture
much better than a random guess would. Model simulations reveal that a
36-year-old Alaskan who experiences the highest levels of interethnic supportive interaction (factor score of -1.5) has a probability of 49 percent of
participating in an illicit drug-use culture. This probability rises to 76 percent if interethnic supportive interaction balances stressful (violent) interaction (factor score of 0.0) and to 97 percent if interethnic violent interaction greatly exceeds supportive interaction (factor score of $+3.0$). By
virtue of differences in the accessibility of illicit substances, a comparable
36-year-old Russian who experiences the highest levels of interethnic supportive interaction (factor score of -1.5) has a probability of only 3 percent of participating in an illicit drug-use culture, which rises to only 10
percent if interethnic supportive interaction balances stressful (violent)
interaction (factor score of 0.0). But it grows to 55 percent if interethnic
violent interaction greatly exceeds supportive interaction (factor score of
$+3.0$). Regional ethnicity thus captures an important component (accessibility to illicit substances) that shapes participation in the drug-using
cultures. On both sides of the Bering Sea, however, so do hurtful words
and behavior that members of powerful ethnic groups direct at children
who belong to powerless ethnic groups.

QE PROCEDURES AUTOMATICALLY BUILD METHOD TRIANGULATION

The quality of your finished ethnography is a function of the validity of
the data you collect. The social and behavioral sciences have developed a
rich literature on diagnostic data analysis tools to address issues of validity
(e.g., Gujarati 1995, Belsley, Kuh and Welsh 1980). As a consequence, for
life experience data we conduct survey pretests to determine the questions
that "make sense" to people and whether or not people respond to the
questions for which we seek answers. We examine responses for character-

istic patterns or their absence—for example, unusually large numbers of people who report ages 20, 25, 30, and so forth, or unusually large gaps in fertility histories—and adjust our data accordingly. We look for outliers for possible measurement errors and we examine scatterplots for departures from randomness. We examine residuals to assess possible heteroskedasticity or autocorrelation and make appropriate corrections. We conduct explicit tests of the construct validity and reliability of scales created to measure multidimensional variables. Principal components analysis and diagnostics provide explicit tests of the construct validity and reliability of our claims about the character of the temporal and spatial autocorrelation embedded in the cultural phenomena we study. For some phenomena, social labels like Puerto Rican, Iñupiat, and Bajan may measure important precursor life experiences that contributed to the creation of cultural differences, although they will not pinpoint just what those life experiences consisted of. For other cultural phenomena, age, gender, and other precursor life experiences may contribute to the creation of cultural differences. For still other cultural phenomena, you may find a consensus that holds, irrespective of precursor life experiences.

QE procedures address more fundamental issues. Remember that research, like all other social activity, entails the construction of culture. We rely on mental constructions—labeled definitions of phenomena and the associations we attach to them, which we may distinguish from other cultural phenomena by the labels "theory" or "model"—to tell us

- what constitutes a "measurement,"
- the labels we give the variables we measure,
- the definitions of both those variables and what shall constitute a "relationship" between variables, and
- the means by which we "measure" variables and "relationships" between variables.

Indeed, we can measure phenomena as simple as "length" *only* by reference to arbitrarily chosen units like "inches" or "meters," the definitions of which can be proven neither true nor false, merely evaluated as more-or-less useful. You, like me and everyone else, *use* culture to interpret sensory input from the world of experience, and we use a variety of internal mental processes to alter both culture and behavior in ways that reflect variation in sensory input.

So, do so when you address the question of data and finding validity. The assumptions on which you base your understanding of the world, like everyone you will meet while you conduct research, contain biases that mirror everything you have experienced and everything you have not experienced over the course of your life. Hence, your mental constructions, like those of everyone you will meet while you conduct research, consist, at least partly and perhaps largely, of *fantasy*, figments of your imagination. To distinguish mental constructions that consist largely of fantasy from constructions that consist of less, aim to construct a matrix consisting of data collected on many variables measured in many different ways (Campbell 1970). Think of *validity* as a relationship between the definitions of specific mental constructions and your observations. Assess data and finding validity with reference to whether or not, or the degree to which, specific mental constructions correspond with specific observations, and discriminate those observations from others.

To help yourself distinguish constructions that exist nowhere outside your imagination from those that may exist in the world of experience, explicitly identify the variable(s) you want to explain and the variable(s) you suspect does the explaining, and explicitly identify means to make observations. QE procedures thus require that you explicitly *measure* each variable, explicitly assess *construct validity,* and explicitly measure the *effects* of your explanatory variable(s). This procedure helps you avoid covert tautologies, requires that you think out the implications of particular choices, and so helps you find your more obvious mistakes and at least some of the more subtle ones. This procedure also forces you to look for and take into account alternative points of view, key issues of internal validity that you might otherwise overlook.

Then, ask for help. You help the people who try to help you when you explicitly identify the variable(s) you want to explain and the variable(s) you suspect does the explaining, explicitly measure each variable, and explicitly measure the effects of your explanatory variable(s). QE procedures require you to build your findings from cultural data because those data provide the *only* means available to escape the limitations of your own past experience—they give you access to the experiences of other people. Draw on the expertise of people with very different life experiences, whom you will meet in the course of your research. Your initial cultural data will help you correct mistakes you made before you arrived in the field. As you proceed in data collection and analysis, you will begin to think about old subjects in new ways. New assumptions imply new variable definitions. New definitions improve your explanations because they point to dimensions of the world you did not see before. They tell you to measure variables differently and to look for connections you never before suspected.

By requiring you to integrate the collection and analysis of both text

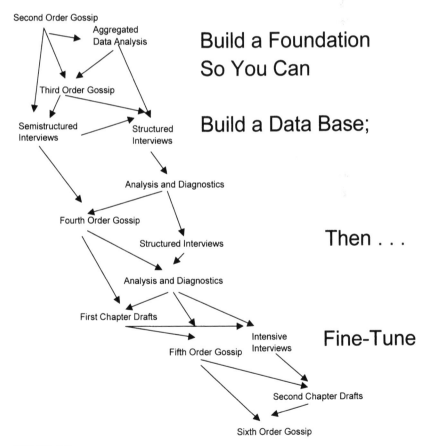

FIGURE 8.3
Selected Project Iterations

and numerical data, QE procedures automatically build method triangulation to assess data validity and reliability. Figure 8.3 illustrates by showing interdependencies between and among selected project iterations. Information from Second Order Gossip interviews provides a foundation for finding pertinent sets of aggregated data, as well as for understanding the findings of your analysis. It also raises new issues that can be pursued in Third Order Gossip interviews. Findings from your analysis of aggregated data will, too. In the Antiguan case mentioned earlier, it led me to select informants who grew up during strategically different historical periods to help me understand how life was different on the island at different times over the previous forty years and how it changed.

Both forms of foundational inquiry identify topics and sampling frames appropriate to collection of data through semistructured and structured interviews of various kinds. Analysis of text collected during semistructured interviews and principal components analyses of data collected during initial structured interviews or observations will raise questions that Fourth Order Gossip interviews can address. They also yield insights you can bring to those interviews for testing and refinement, as well as reflection. These provide the foundation for your first chapter or article drafts and more finely tuned data collection through structured interviews.

For example, in a study of foster mothers (Wozniak 2001), findings from a construct validity analysis of informants' assessments of family members and their permanency revealed a puzzling finding—foster mothers thought of foster sons as "very" permanent family members but thought of foster daughters as only "somewhat" permanent family members (see Handwerker and Wozniak 1997). She presented this and other findings to focus groups of foster mothers and asked if the women thought the findings were true and, if so, why. Focus group discussions revealed that foster mothers experienced a family dynamic common to biological mothers: Once foster daughters reached their teens, foster mothers and daughters often began to experience conflicts over the daughter's sexual and reproductive behavior. Characteristically, these conflicts escalated and culminated with the pregnant daughter leaving or being told she must leave. Foster mothers and daughters subsequently had little if any contact for several years. Once daughters established their own families, however, they usually re-established relationships with their foster mothers. Foster sons might well be the father of a foster daughter's child. But foster sons were "very" permanent family members: sons brought home the baby and the girlfriend, and foster mothers incorporated both into their families (see Wozniak 2001).

QE procedures automatically build method triangulation because they require you to collect different kinds of data with different tools and to use findings from specific data collection phases to set the stage for subsequent data collection. By helping you see things that you'd otherwise miss, they also identify questions that lead to a greater depth of understanding. Short projects require much more tightly focused questioning but the same degree of method triangulation. See how to triangulate in three-day projects in chapter 10.

III

WHILE YOU'RE THERE

Friends Provide the Best Assistance; They Also Make the Best Assistants

QE's Fieldwork Rule No. 1 states:

> Start collecting data the moment you arrive in the field; don't stop until you leave; and don't waste time studying variables not built from your focus variables.

But you cannot complete sophisticated research quickly without help. You can't even complete it well.

First, ethnography achieves enviable levels of validity only when Principal Investigators build the personal relationships that provide access to information that otherwise remains hidden or unnoted. Ethnography achieves much quickly only when Principal Investigators effectively coordinate research tasks. Both activities require time. Research assistants free you to use time to your greatest advantage.

Second, research assistants can go places, ask questions, and have access to observations and knowledge that you can't. Every person brings a distinctive set of biases to the questions he or she asks and the observations he or she makes. That includes you. Without research assistance, you're stuck with your own biases. Having access to biases—points of view—different from your own allows you to find errors that would have remained hidden and to make corrections that otherwise you could never make.

Chapters 2, 3, and 4 showed how to correct three of the four sets of inefficiencies in ordinary ethnography. The fourth set comes from trying to do everything yourself. Create friendships. Draw on your friends and friends of your friends. Ask for help. Most important, reciprocate. This chapter explains how to do so in ways that effectively build and run a research team.

FIND RESEARCH ASSISTANTS EVERYWHERE
My best assistants initially came to me

- through formal contacts provided by colleagues,
- through Peace Corps Volunteer teachers,
- through a "women in development" job training and placement service,
- through the recommendation of a restaurant owner,
- as someone who came to my door to conduct a national census interview,
- by striking up a conversation in a bar, and
- by having heard from one of their friends of the research I planned to do.

Look for potential research assistants everywhere. Don't neglect the obvious places—colleges and universities; clinic staff if you work in a medical setting; agricultural extension workers if you work with the Ministry of Agriculture. But don't neglect less obvious places, either. Anyone aged fifteen and over may prove to be an invaluable research assistant. People even younger may perform some tasks better than anyone else. So, talk to teachers in local secondary schools. Try the local employment bureau. Post notices in the newspaper or on public bulletin boards. Talk with neighbors, bartenders, taxi drivers, and shop keepers. Strike up conversations as you walk around. Explain what you want to do and that you want to hire research assistants. Employment information spreads quickly.

MATCH TEAM DIMENSIONS AND CHARACTERISTICS
TO RESEARCH GOALS
Don't skimp on assistants. Hire enough to do the job. Two or three assistants may suffice if you intend a limited study entailing only a small num-

ber of semistructured interviews and the collection of ratings, pile-sort, triads, or time-allocation data. Hire 4–10 assistants if you intend more extensive interviews. Aim for the higher number if you want to conduct 200–400 interviews. Hire 20–30 assistants if you aim for a sample of 1,000–1,500 cases. Don't ask any assistant to conduct more than 100 standardized interviews. Standardized interviews begin to be a bore after about 50, as you know if you have ever done them yourself. Interview quality begins to decline soon afterward. After 100, interview quality deteriorates rapidly. Make allowance for pretest interviews within this limit of 100 total interviews.

Hire men, women, or both men and women, depending on the kind of data and the kind of data collection circumstances you anticipate. Don't make the mistake of supposing that people who have been trained in research methods or who make their living conducting interviews can perform well or even adequately. Conversely, don't make the mistake of supposing that people with little formal education—or no prior experience—will not perform well. Women generally make better observers than men. Women also usually make better interviewers, except for gathering information accessible only by men. This does not mean to avoid male research assistants. Just anticipate that male assistants will need more intensive and thorough training.

Look for assistants whose identities (gender, age, color, status) correspond with the issues you want to study. More important, look for skills you can't teach: intelligence, reliability, imagination, curiosity, and sensitivity. No research assistant must have all these qualities—or even much of just one—to perform excellently. However, excellent interview and observation performance generally presupposes some or most of these qualities.

LIKE YOUR RESEARCH ASSISTANTS, OR LEARN TO

You can work around problems that arise from having too few assistants or assistants who don't shine in the areas of social identity, intelligence, reliability, imagination, curiosity, or sensitivity. But *don't* violate the following rules:

1. *Hire* people who have a personal interest in your study subject; *don't* hire people if they don't.
2. *Hire* people you like or can learn to like; *don't* hire people you don't like and don't feel comfortable with.

People with a significant personal interest in the findings of *your* specific project regularly overcome fundamental shortcomings merely by being determined to collect good information. You can't effectively build a research *team* with people you don't like and don't feel comfortable with.

THE OPERATIONAL WORD IS *TEAM*

Send no assistant into the field without a clear understanding of the information that he or she needs to collect. Send no interviewer into the field unless you have good reason to believe that the person not only has that understanding but also can conduct sensitive interviews. Assume that you need a minimum of one week of intensive training to create this understanding. Two weeks often create better results. Anticipate a significant trainee drop-out rate. Begin training sessions with twice the number of assistants you want to hire. Use training sessions for multiple purposes—to impart data collection skills, to select the people who will comprise your research team, and to begin building a team, not a collection of assistants.

Explain your project and your goals as "our" project and goals and in terms that make it clear to your assistants how the project goals will provide information in which they are interested. Make research team training a part of your First Order Gossip interviews. Explain your goals. Solicit the assistants' views. Suggest a list of questions that you think you will need to answer. Do the questions make sense to your research assistants? If not, why not? If so, why? What additional questions can they suggest? What different ways might you collect the information? What ways might work; what ways probably won't? How do you have to change your project? Help the team reach a consensus on which questions to ask.

Ask research team trainees to conduct limited semistructured interviews with each other. Observe and suggest improvements. Send trainees out to conduct such interviews on their own. Meet jointly. Have everyone describe what they experienced, what they learned, and what they think might be the best next step to take.

Collect initial ratings, triads, and pile sorts from your trainees. They should know from experience what they'll be asking other informants to do. Plus, it will both provide preliminary data for analysis and reflection and give you some insight into your prospective team members. Have all of the assistants describe what they experienced, what they learned, what they liked and what they didn't, and what they think might be the best way to collect structured interviews.

If you anticipate collecting extensive life experience data, provide a preliminary interview schedule that you can eventually cut down into an interview that takes no more than thirty minutes (on average) to complete. Go over each question, one-by-one, to identify potential problems (the question may be obscure, biased, offensive, difficult to answer, or otherwise). Ask for suggestions as to how questions might be best phrased. Ask for new questions. Once you pare the original question schedule to a manageable size, direct practice interviews within the research team. Use pretests to select the final set of questions and the actual members of the interview team.

PAY TEAM MEMBERS WELL
Don't forget that hiring people creates a commercial relationship. Pay your research assistants well. This means money. Pay them *more* than they usually receive for equivalent work. Distinguish pay during the training period, which merely compensates for their time, from pay for carrying out interviews. Pay for specific work produced. Allow for incentive payments for exceptional work.

Even more important, build personal relationships with intensive, open, honest, and clear interaction. Prepare yourself to be clear with your assistants about who you are and what you want to accomplish. Be just as clear about how you respond to what they say and do. Tell your assistants when you feel anger, joy, frustration, or exhilaration. Be clear about what's OK and what's not. If they act inappropriately, tell them, and explain. If they perform excellently, make sure they know that you treasure great performance. If they ask you for something you can't give, tell them and explain. Give whenever you can. Better, anticipate their needs.

You have to be hard-nosed about work quality. But you also have to be sensitive to their strengths and weaknesses, their likes and dislikes, and the things that make them comfortable and uncomfortable. You have to create circumstances in which they can carry out the necessary work satisfactorily—do they need transportation, official permissions, letters of introduction? What else can you do to make their lives easier?

When research assistant trainees begin collecting data, spend a day or half a day with each one. Observe how he or she conducts interviews, and use this as a further field training period. See the problems that your assistants encounter from *their* perspective, and solve them. Let each research assistant know that you are personally concerned both with the quality of his or her work and with the difficulties that he or she encounters.

Make sure that your assistants know when they perform well; when they don't, don't accept their work. But *don't* blame when someone makes a mistake. *Solve the problem in ways that teach new skills.*

The importance of personally accompanying individual assistants declines after the first week or so, but the importance of your personal relationship with each assistant does not. Don't make the mistake of thinking that the commercial dimension of relationships with field assistants takes priority over personal dimensions. Top performance does not come merely because you pay high salaries to people interested in your subject matter. Pay your field assistants well with your time, attention, and trust. Anticipate that some of your field assistants will become life-long friends. Build personal relationships with each.

See your assistants regularly and not always during "working hours." Invite them to your home for talk and afternoon tea. Go out for a drink. Have team dinners. Celebrate birthdays. Do everything you can to show your field assistants how valuable they are. Go out of your way to show your assistants how they contribute to the success of your joint project. Show them what you are doing with the information they collect. Tell them your findings. Ask for their critique. Pursue leads they suggest. Show them chapter or article drafts you write. Make arrangements to get them copies of your publication(s) when they become available. With a data collection task as intensive as a survey, you probably will not have time for anything else. If you do, you probably are not paying sufficient attention to your research assistants, or you are falling behind in data entry and analysis.

Expect your research assistants to reciprocate with equally open, honest, and clear communication. *Make it possible*—listen, encourage, and don't blame. Remove assistants from the team if they don't.

10

Pulling It All Together

QE's Fieldwork Rule No. 2 states:

> Develop a high tolerance for ambiguity.

This may constitute QE's single most important rule. No matter how well you plan or how hard you work, you will confront ambiguity from the beginning of your fieldwork until its end. You won't know for sure if you can get appropriate data—or even permissions to carry out the work you intended—until you get them. For every hour of data collection, expect to spend at least two wondering what, if anything, you learned. Don't let your pre-fieldwork Gantt charts and PERT charts deceive you. Anticipate that pre-fieldwork plans describe a world that you won't recognize once you arrive in the field.

BE REALISTIC ABOUT REACHING YOUR FIELDWORK GOALS

Reaching fieldwork goals comes agonizingly slowly. You won't achieve some goals—or won't realize that you did until long after you leave the field. You'll achieve others only by fundamentally reshaping a portion of your project. You will see new goals to aim at, far more important than your original set. Much of your time in the field must go into managing the exigencies of real life and adapting pre-fieldwork plans to field reality.

Real disasters strike occasionally. You may not receive necessary permissions. You may not like the people in the fieldsite. They may not like you. You can never be sure you measured key variables in the best possible way (assume you messed up). You can never be sure you collected all the data you need (assume you didn't).

THIS IS WHERE QE PROCEDURES PAY OFF

Use QE procedures imaginatively to survive the collapse of your research plans. Build a project that improves on the one that collapsed. You will carry out an important piece of work if you have learned to think in terms of variables and if you can effectively coordinate the collection of different kinds of data with different kinds of research tools. You probably will produce hash if you haven't.

Review the basics you worked through before you arrived. Inefficiencies and ineffectiveness in ordinary ethnography come from

- not creating a clear vision of where you want to go,
- not creating a clear vision of how to get there,
- getting lost along the way, and
- wasting time and generating bias trying to do everything yourself.

To create a clear vision of where you want to go, think about your research topic as a variable. Identify no more than five *focus variables* that embody the essentials of your research goals. Identify your field tasks by building on your focus variables. Imagine what each focus variable may consist of. Ask yourself why each dimension of each focus variable may exhibit one value rather than another. Keep asking "Why?" Link one variable to another (or others) until you're exhausted. Don't worry about being wrong. You will be. Correct your mistakes in the field, where you'll have access to corrective information. Do research to create a *better* way to think about the world.

Make part of your consciousness QE's Field Preparation Rule No. 2, "Murphy's Law understates the facts; it *will* go wrong even when it can't." Management will make all the difference. Confusion inheres in doing good fieldwork. It requires you to select and complete an extraordinary number of tasks—and to coordinate each task with all the others. One set of inefficiencies in ordinary ethnography comes from the lack of a clear vision of where you are going. Focus variables provide you with that vision.

A second set of inefficiencies comes from the lack of a clear vision of how you might best get there. To create a clear vision of how to get to where you need to go, identify the ends you need to reach to complete your project. Then select the appropriate research tools for each end. Integrating the two creates a research design that addresses the two questions at the heart of all research:

- Did I get it right? (internal validity)
- To whom, if anyone, can I generalize? (external validity)

A third set of inefficiencies comes from getting lost along the way. *Iterative* data collection distinguishes good ethnography from bad. Design each observation and question to test at least one part of your theoretical understanding. Note errors. Ask for clarification. Rethink the theory. Link microlevel observations and interviews with historical records and macrolevel trends that only time-series data can reveal. Try again. As you do so, your fieldwork tasks will acquire complex linkages. Minimize your chances of getting lost by using detailed Gantt charts and PERT (Program Evaluation Review Technique) charts to coordinate the necessary iterations efficiently.

Plan to accomplish three management goals: (1) build a foundation, on which you can (2) build your data base, analysis of which and further data collection will allow you to (3) fine-tune your findings. Look again at the Gantt chart in figure 1.1, which outlines the basic components of a 12-week (90-day, summer) and a 4-week (30-day, contract) research project. The actual time involved in meeting these goals will vary with your project's duration, of course. Management goal overlap will not. Begin building your database about midway through the tasks involved in building the foundation for your project. Begin to fine-tune your findings about midway through the tasks involved in building your data base.

Employ a variant of a Posttest Only Control Group design and make it your job to accurately identify, describe, and characterize:

- variables (Xs and Ys, the labels that identify the components of cultures, the criteria that distinguish one from another, and the intellectual and emotional associations that give specific components their meaning), and

- relationships between and among variables (the intersections among individually unique cultural sets and the life experiences that create, maintain, and change them).

Make your first priority the collection of text data from informal and semistructured observations and interviews of cultural experts. Then introduce rigor so you can identify and control the various forms of internal validity confounds embedded in your fieldnotes and can see nuanced intercultural and intracultural variation. Select a random sample of informants if you need to estimate the prevalence of cultural phenomena. Otherwise, employ nested sampling frames for intentionally selected comparisons. Use findings from your analysis of text to formulate structured interviews to nail down key comparisons. Use these comparisons to establish the construct validity of key multidimensional variables, like the culture or cultures you study. Then examine and try to explain intracultural and intercultural variation. Anticipate these analyses by conducting a power analysis of the tests you build into your new project. Use this analysis to guide your decisions about numbers of informants, and your interpretation of findings completed later.

Build the foundation for your project by completing three major tasks quickly: (1) beginning tasks, (2) aggregated data collection, and (3) research team assembly. Some of your beginning tasks entail official meetings, but turn all beginning tasks into data collection opportunities. Focus on informal interviews. Use them to introduce yourself and your project, to explore the assumptions that your informants use to understand and respond to the world of experience, the components of that world, and how those components are organized to form social and behavioral ecosystems and to begin the process of confirming your findings.

Make a map, take a census, and collect genealogies. At least consider adding these tools to those discussed in earlier chapters. When we practiced ethnography primarily in community settings, standard field methods entailed walking around a community, mapping the territory, and going door-to-door to collect census data and genealogies. These tasks continue to provide a convenient means of introducing yourself and the research you hope to do in face-to-face interaction with community members. Aside from information on the size of the community, its age and sex composition, and how people organize themselves into residential units (households) and wider kinship units, a census and genealogies also yield key informants and research assistants.

The map also yields information to guide interviews and observations. Like an MDS plot (chapter 8), a map provides a tangible thing that can engage your informants. Once you have a sketch of the physical spaces, places, and things that provide the physical context for the lives of community members, have an informant walk with you and tell you what he or she sees. Who and what kinds of people carry on what kinds of activities and interactions in which space, place, and with what things? Make informal as well as structured observations of locations, activities, and actors. Narrow your initial general observations to focus on key locations, activities, and actors. With the help of key informants, dissect the most important locations, activities, and social actors into their constituent parts and relationships. Where appropriate, join the activities!

Collect aggregated data, create timelines, and use Lexis Diagrams, along with historical scatterplots and icon analyses, to integrate key historical events and trends with your fieldnote data. Use your selection of a research site and a research team to make a transition into the second phase of your project. Use semistructured interviews carried out one-on-one and in focus groups to find the limits of cultural variation. Use them, too, to fill out your understanding of the variables that compose cultures—how informants construct things like "families," "gender," and "age"; how they identify these things and discriminate one kind of thing from another; and how they identify, discriminate, and experience things like "power," "competition," and "cooperation." Incorporate focus group interviews into the training of your team of research assistants.

Build your data base with structured interviews. Data from these interviews will allow you to make explicit comparisons among informants and so address the analytical tasks of identifying cultures, cultural variation, and cultural change, controlling for measured internal validity confounds. Keep your structured interviews short and sweet and ask questions for which you already have preliminary answers from informal and semistructured interviews. Use questions that ask for binary responses to identify the properties of people and the world you investigate. Use rating scales to assess relative importance and pile sorts to assess relative similarity. Use Likert Scales for multidimensional variables. Use scales developed in earlier studies to contribute to a comparative data base, but make sure they fit your fieldsite and make sense to your informants. Don't hesitate to create your own scale to suit your specific research goals. Assess the construct validity and reliability of all scales you use. Collect time-series (historical) data. Draw on aggregated data collected by governmental and nongovernmental organizations. If necessary, incorporate design features into your survey to create your own time-series data. Plan to make basic comparisons early on. Employ norming and standardizing operations to facilitate comparison, and use pictures to assess the distribution of your variables. Look for relationships between variables and informants. In the process, beware of the effects of random error. Test hypotheses, and use the regularity of sampling distributions to assess plausible effects of random error.

Begin to fine-tune your findings by documenting the construct validity of the culture or cultures in your data. *Cultures* consist of configurations of cognition and emotion and an isomorphic configuration of behavior shared by a specific set of people. *A* culture thus constitutes a multidimensional variable, much like variables such as "violence" and "affection." You cannot see variables like these and cannot measure them directly. Validate that construct by demonstrating that people in a specific set do share that configuration of cognition, emotion, and/or behavior. To pinpoint cultural boundaries, if they exist, use principal components to establish the construct validity of the culture or cultures in your data. Findings from such an analysis will tell you whether or not, or the extent to which, cultural boundaries correspond with social labels like Eskimo or West Indian, men or women, or old and young.

Use multiple-regression models to focus your thinking about the sources of intracultural and intercultural variation and cultural change. Use OLS regression to explore sources of intracultural variation. Use logistic regression to explore sources of intercultural variation and cultural change. Be prepared to find cultures you didn't anticipate.

REMEMBER THE BASICS

Carefully distinguish between culture, cultures, and the life experiences that may have shaped both. *Culture* consists of the systems of mental constructions people use to interpret and respond to themselves and the world around them. *Cultures* consist of systems of mental constructions and behavior isomorphic with those systems of meaning *at the intersection of individually unique sets* and, so, shared among sets of people. *Cultural* data thus consist of measurements of the systems of mental constructions people use to interpret themselves and the world around them and of the behavior isomorphic with those systems of meaning. *Life experience* data, by contrast, consist of measurements of characteristics (like age, gender, class, or ethnicity) and events or processes that mark the prior life experience of particular people (like how many years people spent in school, if they grew up in poor or wealthy households, or the degree to which they experienced one or another form of violence as children). To produce ethnography, focus on similarities and differences among your informants, not your variables. The socially constructed nature of cultural phenomena means that any one person who knows about a particular culture participates with other experts in its construction. Aim to accurately characterize the autocorrelation embedded in the cultural phenomena you study.

To do this, focus on the three phenomena that comprise cultural phenomena:

- Labels, names, which identify the existence of distinct configurations of phenomenal experience;
- Definitions, which, however ambiguous in specific cases, differentiate one thing from another; and
- Intellectual and emotional associations, which give mental constructions distinctive meaning.

And pursue the implications of two key observations:

- Cultural differences reflect variation in personal experiences.
- Culture evolves.

First, what we know and how we organize what we know into different cultural domains come from where we live and the web of social relations through which we have lived our lives. This means:

- Where we were born and raised;
- When we were born; and
- With whom we have interacted, in what ways, and what we experienced at specific points in our lives over the course of our lives.

Remember: *no one possesses a single culture.* Cultural phenomena consist of multilayered meanings that we share variously with other people, having shared equivalent experiences or having negotiated a common understanding in more direct social interaction. Each of us, consequently, belongs to or takes place in multiple cultures, at different levels. When you first meet someone, you can't tell very well by that person's age, gender, dress, or skin color which cultures you share and which you don't. Knowledge about the visual signals of pertinent cultural differences comes only from listening for the right cues. Thus, interact intensively and create personal relationships with the people you want to understand. Spending time getting to know someone opens the only door available for you to learn what that person sees and what it means when he or she looks out at the world. Ethnography thus calls for the personal sensitivity and creativity to allow people to feel comfortable with you; it requires that you communicate clearly to your informants and that you pose no danger to them. Being a good listener helps. Sharing yourself helps even more.

Second, over the course of our lives and through various means—listening to news reports, reading, traveling, talking with friends or family members, taking courses or attending workshops, or engaging in explicit and rigorous research—we come to think differently about the components of a given cultural domain. We think of new ways to organize activities and new ways to think about the domain of knowledge itself. We tend to incorporate into our lives the new ways of thinking about the world that we infer yield better results. By interacting with other people—acting and responding to what we experience of other people's words and acts—we thus actively participate in an unceasing process that leads to the evolution of what we know and how we act. Because culture evolves, it makes a moving target. Ethnographers who have many years of experience working with a specific population may miss cues that signal important new cultural differences if they don't keep up with the cultural evolution that goes on around them all the time. Effective and efficient ethnographic research thus requires a conscious awareness of culture and means for identifying cultural differences. To successfully see the world through another person's eyes, you need (1) detailed descriptions of people, places, and things that make up this other person's world; (2) an awareness of features of the environment that shape the consequences of making one choice rather than another and, so, lead one to act and think about the world one way rather than another; and (3) a specific awareness that the recurrent patterns of behavior we call culture constitute a key feature of our environment and that we experience this influence in the form of concrete social interactions with specific other people. Document all three. In short, QE principles tell you to focus your study on who agrees with and acts like whom about what and to what degree and on how specific social relations contribute to the construction and change of culture. Treat everyone as a cultural expert in what he or she knows. Frame this starting point with the understanding that cultural differences reflect variation in internal processes of development and maturation, the time in human history when people live, the region(s) in which life stories take place, and the details of the gender, intergenerational, and intra- and intergroup relationships in which they take part. Search for concrete events and circumstances in people's lives that may shape the understanding they now work with. What people think and do must reflect not only their individual life histories but broader regional and global histories of people, events, and social interaction into which they were born and in which they grew up.

PAY ATTENTION TO HISTORICAL ORIGINS, MIGRATION, AND ETHNICITY

Key features of the contemporary world include cultural and racial diversity in all local communities (e.g., see Cohen 1995). Historical origins, migration, and ethnicity thus constitute primary criteria by which historically and regionally situated events, circumstances, and processes provide one set of choices to some people and a different set of choices to others. Cultures, in the form of shared assumptions and the expectations and behavioral patterns to which they lead, constitute the primary environment in which people live their lives. Cultures of childhood function and disability, for example, consist of the assumptions about the nature of children, child development, and child–caregiver interaction that generate parental expectations of children in the areas of self-care, mobility, and social function and parental responses to the specific developmental trajectory of specific children. Two broad sets of these assumptions appear to exist, one commonly called egocentric or individualistic, the other commonly called sociocentric (e.g., Shweder and Bourne 1984, Markus and Kitayama 1991, Kitayama, Markus, and Matsumoto 1995, Rogoff, Mistry, Göncü, and Mosier 1993, Harwood, Miller, and Irizarry 1995). Although we know in broad outline the components of these cultures, we do not yet know the answers to questions most pertinent to clinical settings:

1. What is the content of these cultures as they bear on specific forms of childhood function and disability?
2. How are these cultures changing in an increasingly diverse U.S. population?
3. Does variation in these cultures generate specific alternative developmental trajectories?

Integrate recognition that culture evolves into the methods you choose to address questions like these. Both native Anglo Americans and Puerto Rican migrants, for example, bring to parenthood assumptions acquired from their experiences with family members, teachers, friends, and other socially significant people, which may vary by birth cohort, gender, and specific social origins. The culture that Puerto Rican migrants bring with them evolves in light of specific personal experiences in new cultural environments. The acculturation construct, which erroneously assumes that (1) a fixed target culture exists and (2) only one culture undergoes change (e.g., Bee 1974), fails to accurately characterize the process of cultural change, however. Migrants don't merely become like host country natives. Migrants add to the cultural pool in those new environments and thus contribute to ongoing cultural evolution in their host regions, depending on age, gender, education, travel patterns, and the patterns, networks, and character of social networks, including experience with people from different ethnic and social class backgrounds, experience with health and education professionals, and household composition and caregiving responsibilities. This may explain why individualistic and sociocentric cultures map very poorly onto Anglo and Puerto Rican ethnic differences (e.g., Harwood, Handwerker, Schoelmerich, and Leyendecker in press). A project with significant theoretical, as well as policy and program, implications would aim to sort out the cultural differences that map well onto ethnic differences and those that do not.

We now know little about the specific forms of culture that migrants bring with them. We know less about the experiences that lead to specific cultural changes in host countries and the contributions that migrants make to the regional cultures they help evolve. What, exactly, do migrants from specific regions contribute to an evolving cultural pool in a specific neighborhood, town, or region? How and why, exactly, do specific cultural imports become part of that pool, and others not? A project with significant theoretical as well as policy and program implications would test the hypothesis that cultures of specific immigrants are functions of three sets of independent variables: (1) regionally specific cultures of childhood function, health care, or education in the sending countries; (2) regionally specific (e.g., country urban, suburban, and rural; Northeast, South, Southwest, Northwest) cultures of childhood function, health care, or education, as well as the regionally specific culture by which host-country populations interact with immigrant populations; and (3) life experiences influenced by variables like age, gender, travel patterns since birth, and size and character of pertinent social networks.

I emphasize *regionally* specific cultures because we should expect a socially constructed phenomenon to exhibit variation that corresponds with the density of communication networks. For many cultural phenomena, the density of communication networks is a function of distance. In West Africa, for example, people who live in Cape Palmas and people who live 100 kilometers up the coast in Sasstown speak in ways that the other cannot understand. Mutual unintelligibility identifies different languages—the people in Cape Palmas speak Grebo, the people in Sasstown speak Kru. People who live inland from Sasstown speak Kru. People who live inland from Cape Palmas speak Grebo.

But Grebo spoken inland is mutually intelligible with Kru spoken inland. Inland, Grebo and Kru constitute different names for the same language. Europe exhibits particularly dramatic and very well documented clinal variation in language (dialect chains, after Swadesh 1959). In a dialect chain that runs from Portugal to Italy through Spain, France, and Belgium, people in neighboring villages speak mutually intelligible languages. As distance grows, however, intelligibility shrinks. What was the same (mutually intelligible) language becomes different (mutually unintelligible) languages. Swedes in the south of Sweden speak more easily to Danes across the border than they can to Swedes in the north.

Although studies of clinal variation in language provide the most well-documented cases, we should expect other cultural phenomena to exhibit similar qualities. Indeed, cultures may rarely, if ever, correspond with bounded regional or social units. As Boas's (1894) study suggested and a large number of studies since by Kroeber, Driver, and others (e.g., Driver 1962, 1970) explored in greater detail, cultural variation may characteristically exhibit spatially continuous cultural variation, or clines. For a study like that suggested here, identify and document the cultures in different locations, measure their similarity, and map them. Caulkins (2001) uses tools equivalent to those discussed in chapter 7 and data on Celtic culture to show you how. Spatial analysis, Caulkins shows, creates new and more subtle ways to think about ethnicity and ethnic boundaries. In the case at hand, clinal maps of regions, cities, or even neighborhoods should help us better understand how processes of cultural synthesis work and suggest the circumstances that generate diversity in the process. Sharp clinal differences over short distances (across the street?) identify barriers to social interaction, for example. Multidimensional scaling (MDS) of cultural similarities produces maps (see Black 1976, Caulkins 2001). To what extent do maps produced by conventional cartographic procedures and MDS correspond? Dissimilarities between maps of the same cultural variation produced through different means may point to barriers to social interaction that you otherwise might miss. Determining what those barriers may consist of, how they came into being, and what circumstances maintain them should help us better understand how and why, possibly, cultural differences correspond well or poorly with ethnic labels at different times and places.

To effectively understand cultural variation, ask individuals to identify life experiences that were significant to them and to help you understand why those experiences were significant. Pay *particularly* close attention to people's emotional response(s) to specific events, processes, and circumstances. Culture may possess a cognitive core consistent with a specific behavioral pattern. But to understand why and how the configurations of cognition and behavior that comprise culture and cultures evolve, and the details of their social construction, look to how people emotionally experience and respond to specific events, processes, and circumstances. Identify, incorporate into your fieldnotes, and analyze your own feelings, as well.

In the process, keep track of life experience markers that people identify as important, as well as those that might be important. Design sampling frames for cultural phenomena in ways that encompass regionally and historically situated life experiences that may influence the patterns of social interaction through which people construct culture. This strategy implements the explicit measurement of internal validity confounds that must accompany a Posttest Only Control Group design without randomization.

Maturation confounds include age and the duration of any social event or process—like marriage, business, or ceremonial participation. *History* confounds include variables like gender, class, and ethnicity. Design informal and semistructured interviews to elicit information on the adequacy of the distinctions that you start with. Ask informants if they know people who think differently and interview people who take different points of view. Actively search for sources of cultural difference. Change the criteria by which you select informants and the life experiences you measure, to reflect knowledge you gain during the course of field research.

Internal validity confounds other than *maturation* and *history* don't make useful sampling criteria. They may produce intracultural and intercultural variation nonetheless. Posttest Only Control Group designs ordinarily eliminate *regression* and *mortality* confounds. They may exist nonetheless. Test for *instrumentation* effects by looking for the influence of different sources of data (e.g., interviews by different research assistants). Test for *diffusion* by looking for the influence of growing up in the same family, the same village, or the same region. Maps of cultural clines provide an explicit and more subtle means to evaluate the influence of location (diffusion) on intracultural or intercultural variation.

The problem of external validity resolves into this—you *observe* samples, arrive at findings (e.g., analytical descriptions, or computed statistics), and *estimate* population parameters. Generalize to the population defined by the geographically and historically bounded set of life experiences you studied. Your sampling criteria and the internal validity confounds you measure determine to whom you can validly generalize. Ask yourself how your chosen sampling method might unintentionally exclude an important subset of informants and how that exclusion may affect your findings. Select your informants randomly when you to need to know not only what cultures exist but also their relative prevalence. Select a sample large enough to detect the relationships you suspect might exist, and measure your variables reliably. The small amounts of random error (small standard errors) embedded in large samples with highly reliable measurements let you see small differences that you'd miss with smaller samples or less reliable measurements. Take advantage of the case-dependence built into cultural phenomena. Case-dependence produces small standard errors that classical tests overestimate. This means that ethnography requires fewer cases than other research, for the same precision. To make the most of this advantage, test hypotheses with bootstrap, jackknife, or permutation tests.

BUT I HAVE TO COMPLETE *THIS* PROJECT IN *THREE DAYS!*

Great! QE *really* pays off with project design needs assessment. Why? Because QE flows out of a theory of culture. QE procedures assume mastery of a wide variety of tools for data collection, data analysis, and the design and management of both. But the efficient collection and analysis of data with high reliability and construct validity come from how you integrate these tools. A theory of culture tells you how to do that quickly and well.

When you have three days to complete your project, you must prioritize extremely tightly. The theory of culture outlined in this book rests on the premise that culture consists of labels and names that identify the existence of distinct configurations of phenomenal experience; definitions that, however ambiguous in specific cases, differentiate one thing from another; and intellectual and emotional associations, which give mental constructions distinctive meaning. Hence, start by identifying the labels and definitions that tell you the kinds of people, social relations, events, processes, and artifacts that comprise the business challenge for the people who hire you. Make it your first priority, for example, to understand the current state of fisheries management if a State Department of Fish and Game (DFG) hired you to help it find ways to generate more tourist spending from freshwater fishermen and their families. What fish and inland waters does the DFG now manage, in what ways, for what purpose, and why? Elicit the specific intellectual and emotional associations that give meaning to this system of mental constructions, and listen for cues to these associations embedded in the language people use to talk about them. This information tells you the set of assumptions that rationalizes DFG's current operations. Complete this step in a three-hour review of the literature pertinent to the current product design and discussion with other design team members. Existing fisheries management may focus on providing lots of catchable fish, particularly trout, given an assumption that fishermen want to catch lots of fish and mostly want to catch trout. A look at fisheries population data may reveal healthy populations of black bass, northern pike, and bluegills, which reproduce effectively and grow to significant sizes. The same data may also reveal that the trout population depends almost solely on restocking programs. Fisheries management people use this observation as evidence of a market for lots of catchable trout.

Repeat these steps for your target population of consumers. Start by identifying the labels and definitions that tell you the kinds of people, social relations, events, processes, and artifacts that comprise the pertinent cultural domain. Elicit the specific intellectual and emotional associations that give meaning to this system or systems of mental constructions, listen for cues to these associations embedded in the language people use to talk about them, and watch for cues to these associations in the behavior you see. Begin with simple free-lists (e.g., What different kinds of freshwater fish can someone catch while fishing for sport? What different kinds of fishermen are there?). Ask questions that elicit similarities and differences (e.g., How is this fish different from that fish?) and preferences bearing on similarities and differences (e.g., What kind of fish do you most like to catch? Why? What kind of fish do you least like to catch? Why?). Ask

Grand Tour questions. For example, ask fishermen informants to tell you about a typical day, from beginning to end. Make a list of the events, activities, locations, and participants. Elicit contrasts with questions about wonderful fishing days and disastrous days. Ask about particularly memorable fish caught and about fish that your informant would like to forget catching. Make sure you record specific details, including words, behavior, and social actors. Clearly identify the criteria people use to discriminate wonderful from disastrous. You won't have time to fill in the gradations between the two for a nuanced analysis, but you're not there to produce one. Aim to paint a picture of one person's view of the highs and lows of fish and fishing. Then, actively search for variation so that your picture includes, at least in broad outlines, the complexity found in your study population. While you paint your word picture, add details from your observations of specific events, activities, locations, and participants. Ask how what you see compares to what you hear. Where are the discrepancies? What do *those* discrepancies tell you?

This information will tell you the set or sets of assumptions that consumers use to rationalize the cultural domain you want to learn about. Analysis will yield assumptions that your informants don't know about or don't think about. Pay particular attention to discrepancies between what you see informants do and what they tell you (see Squires 2001), although a three-day project may make it impossible to conduct effective observations. Compare the assumptions that consumer informants use to think about and act in the domain, and ask yourself "What evidence warrants each assumption?" and "What evidence points to missing assumptions?" Delete existing-but-unwarranted assumptions and add missing assumptions that are warranted by evidence to construct a new set of assumptions. Change in any assumption or the addition of a new one will produce a line of reasoning that generates your three to five recommendations for a new market, a new product, or ways to improve the current one.

Allow a day for data collection and analysis and another day to prepare your report. Lower your anxiety level with the following reminders:

- your data collection and analysis task is very tightly focused and equivalent to what would constitute only a *tiny* portion of one of the other projects described in this book;

- the social construction of culture means that
  - you don't need to select and should avoid selecting informants randomly; and
  - you don't need to talk to many people.

Pay close attention to your sampling frame, however. Select highly dissimilar informants, given the constraints of your target population of consumers. What did your informants tell you about different kinds of fishermen? Do they distinguish adults-and-children, men-and-women, serious-and-casual as different *kinds* of fishermen? Use criteria like these to construct your initial sampling frame.

Prepare a list of the assumptions that rationalizes the current product and a list of questions that will help you find evidence bearing on their validity. Approach the task of question construction by identifying forms of evidence that would invalidate existing assumptions or would point to alternative (and currently missing) assumptions. Can you find evidence that fishermen most want to catch lots of fish, mainly trout? Can you find contrary evidence? What do fishermen *really* want? Play a mind game with yourself, in which you question the validity of all existing assumptions and imagine alternatives. What evidence would invalidate your alternative assumptions? Make a list.

Take the remaining five hours of your first day's work to find informants and prepare questions. At first, make informal, exploratory interviews. This lets you treat interview construction as a form of product design research. Look for ways to reframe your questions and produce better ones, rather than remain bound to your initial (flawed) set. Make informal judgments about agreements among your informants. Try hard to locate disagreements (ask your informants to help you find them:) and pin down the basis of disagreement. By the end of the day, data collection and informal analysis should give you a sense of the degree of cultural variation in the domain you study. If your first three informants, who show marked differences in life experiences, tell you the same thing, try even harder to locate disagreements. If you can't, interview and observe other informants only to increase the material you might use for stories that will clearly convey your findings to the business persons, designers, and engineers who come from other cultures. If you find disagreements,

modify your sampling frame to search for informants from other potentially distinctive cultures.

Use the morning of your second day to explore agreements and to look
at disagreements in greater depth. Continually monitor relationships
between evidence and assumptions. By late morning, you should know
which assumptions are valid and which are not, as well as which alternative assumptions are missing from the set that rationalizes current thinking about the business challenge. If you don't, you're looking at evidence
that, as cultures evolve, markets change or disappear and new markets
come into being. Report back to your design team that you've uncovered
a significant amount of cultural variation. A large amount of cultural variation points to the need to redefine the target population of consumers.
You'll need longer than three days to determine the cultural boundaries
that validly redefine the cultures in the target population, perhaps a 30-
day project organized along lines outlined earlier in this book.

If you can distinguish valid from invalid current assumptions and can
identify one or two new assumptions, use the remaining day to nail down
your findings with explicit comparisons. You might find, for example, that
everyone (adults, children, men, women, and serious, as well as casual,
fishermen) likes (or would like) to catch very large fish. Everyone also likes
to catch a lot of fish. Casual fishermen tend to fish for trout. Serious fishermen tend to fish for black bass or northern pike. Because trout are so
small and so easily caught, serious fishermen don't take trout fishing seri-
ously. Stories told of trips to catch very large trout suggest that fisheries
management personnel have misunderstood the observation that the trout
population depends almost solely on restocking programs. You've found
a market for lots of trout. You've also found evidence of a potential market
for trophy trout that does not now exist in the state. Your observations
that serious fishermen tend to use more equipment and higher-quality
equipment suggest the potential dollar value of this market.

During late morning, while you complete informal interviews, formulate a structured interview that will take no more than five to ten minutes
of an informant's time. Binary codes and 4-point rating scales work well
for items bearing on assumptions for product design; include measures of
informant diversity that plausibly contribute to cultural variability. Locate
a new set of informants (will your assistant make the phone calls while

you type up the interview schedule or questionnaire?). Use the first part of the afternoon to collect and the second part to analyze the construct validity of these data. Use your third day to write and give your report.

A for-profit firm, of course, might hire you to apply the same ethnographic methods to discover new markets and opportunities for new products or services related to fishing boats, reels, rods, or lines.

Here's a final word of advice from Bryan Byrne (personal communication), who makes a living doing ethnography like this:

> Bear in mind that you, as the team's ethnographer, are supposed to help other professionals do their own work. You can't simply bring back findings and recommendations that start and end with social relationships or meaning. You must also work closely with the designers, engineers, and business administrators to make sure they understand how your findings affect their own search for materials, product shapes, features, functions, brands, market channels, price models, and business partners. To do that, you have to be very sensitive to the kinds of things that people are using and their perceptions of them. If you cannot take the designers and engineers into the field with you, then make sure you learn as much as you can about the kind of information members of both professions need to begin working. In particular, find out where people shop, how they make decisions, and what kinds of things attract and repel them about existing products.
>
> This vast laundry list of things to do may seem overwhelming but you *can* do it—especially if these kinds of questions become second nature to you.

FOCUS ON WHAT'S IMPORTANT

No matter the topic of your research or whether you have ninety days or three to complete it, focus your efforts on building relationships. Talk with your informants openly, honestly, and clearly, as you would with any potential lifelong friend. Expect and accept the obligations of reciprocity—the giving and acceptance of gifts—which characterize human relationships. Expect to experience profound emotions—some traumatic. Don't expect anyone to talk with you about subjects you won't talk about yourself. Make it clear that you want to accomplish particular data collection goals but that you don't ask questions you aren't willing to answer yourself. Invite questions. Answer them, even if only to say that you don't know or that you don't want to talk about the question. Thus, make it clear, too, that you will say so if you don't want to answer a question and that you expect others to do likewise. In short, become an active participant in the processes through which we all create meaning. Your finest work will come from integrating QE procedures with a capacity to share yourself.

References

Aberle, David F. 1966. *The Peyote Religion among the Navaho.* Chicago: Aldine.

Archambeault, B. 1991. Writing across the Curriculum: Mathematics. Paper presented at the Annual Meeting of the National Council of Teachers of English, Seattle.

Bargh, John A., and Tanya L. Chartrand. 1999. The Unbearable Automaticity of Being. *American Psychologist* 462–79.

Barkow, Jerome H., Leda Cosmides, and John Tooby, eds. 1992. *The Adapted Mind.* New York: Oxford University Press.

Barnett, H. G. 1953. *Innovation.* New York: McGraw-Hill.

Bebout, H. C. 1993. Using Children's Word-Problem Compositions for Problem-Solving Instruction: A Way to Reach All Children with Mathematics. In G. Cuevas and M. Driscoll, eds., *Reaching All Students with Mathematics.* Pp. 219–32. Reston, VA: National Council of Teachers of Mathematics.

Bee, Robert. 1974. *Patterns and Processes: An Introduction to Anthropological Strategies for the Study of Sociocultural Change.* New York: Free Press.

Beebe, James. 2001. *Rapid Assessment Process.* Walnut Creek, CA: AltaMira.

Belsley, D. A., E. Kuh, and R. E. Welsch. 1980. *Regression Diagnostics.* New York: John Wiley & Sons.

Berk, Richard A. 1983. An Introduction to Sample Selection Bias in Sociological Data. *American Sociological Review* 48:386–98.

Bernard, H. R. 2001. *Research Methods in Anthropology.* 3rd edition. Walnut Creek, CA: AltaMira.

———. 2000. *Social Research Methods: Qualitative and Quantitative Approaches.* Newbury Park, CA: Sage.

Bernard, H. R., and Gery W. Ryan. 1998. Text Analysis: Qualitative and Quantitative Methods. Pp. 595–646. In Bernard, H. R., ed. *Handbook of Methods in Cultural Anthropology.* Walnut Creek, CA: AltaMira.

Bersani, Carl A., and Huey-Tsuh Chen. 1988. Sociological Perspectives in Family Violence. In *Handbook of Family Violence*, Vincent B. Van Hasselt, Randall L. Morrison, Alan S. Bellack, and Michel Hersen, eds. Pp. 57–87. New York: Plenum.

Berwick, Donald M., et al. 1991. Performance of a Five-Item Mental Health Screening Test. *Medical Care* 29:169–76.

Bidney, David 1944. The Concept of Culture and Some Cultural Fallacies. *American Anthropologist* 46:30–44.

Black, Paul. 1976. Multidimensional Scaling Applied to Linguistic Relationships. *Cahiers de l'Institut de Linguistique de Louvain* 3:43–92.

Boas, Franz 1894. *Indianische Sagen von der Nord-Pacifischen Kuste Amerikas.* Berlin: Asher.

Boster, James S. 1994. The Successive Pile Sort. *Cultural Anthropology Methods CAM.* 6:11–12.

Bowker, Lee H., Michelle Arbitell, and J. Richard McFerron. 1988. On the Relationship between Wife Beating and Child Abuse. Pp. 158–74. In *Feminist Perspectives on Wife Abuse*, K. Ylló and M. Bogrod, eds. Newbury Park, CA: Sage.

Bracewell, R. N. 1990. Numerical Transforms. *Science* 248:697–704.

Broderick, P. A., and W. H. Bridger. 1984. A Comparative Study of the Effect of L-tryptophan and Its Acetylated Derivative N-acetyl-L-tryptophan on Rat Muricidal Behavior. *Biological Psychiatry* 19:89–94.

Brown, Robert. 1963. *Explanation in Social Science.* Chicago: Aldine.

Brunner, H. G., M. Nelen, X. O. Breakefield, H. H. Ropers, and B. A. van Oost. 1993. Abnormal Behavior Associated with a Point Mutation in the Structural Gene for Monoamine Oxidase A. *Science* 262:578–80.

Burns, M. 1995. Writing in the Math Class? Absolutely. *Instructor* 104:40–47.

Campbell, D. T. 1970. Natural Selection as an Epistemological Model. In *A Handbook of Methods in Cultural Anthropology.* Raoul Naroll and Ronald Cohen, eds. Pp. 51–85. Garden City, NJ: Natural History Press.

Campbell, D. T., and D. W. Fiske. 1959. Convergent and Discriminant Validity by the Multi-Trait, Multimethod Matrix. *Psychological Bulletin* 56:81–105.

Campbell, D. T., and J. C. Stanley. 1963. *Experimental and Quasi-Experimental Designs for Research.* Chicago: Rand-McNally.

Cannon, W. B. 1929. *Bodily Changes in Pain, Hunger, Fear, and Rage.* 2nd edition. New York: D. Appleton.

———. 1942. "Voodoo" Death. *American Anthropologist* 44:169–81.

Caulkins, Douglas. 2001. Consensus, Clines, and Edges in Celtic Cultures. *Cross-Cultural Research* 35.

Caulkins, Douglas, and Susan B. Hyatt. 1999. Using Consensus Analysis to Measure Cultural Diversity in Organizations and Social Movements. *Field Methods* 11:5–26.

Chambers, John M., W. S. Cleveland, B. Kleiner, and P. A. Tukey. 1983. *Graphical Methods for Data Analysis.* New York: Chapman & Hall.

Cheltenham, H. M. 1992. The Utilization of Primary Health Care Services among the Elderly in Barbados. Seminar paper presented at the University of the West Indies Cave Hill.

Cleveland, W. S. 1979. Robust Locally Weighted Regression and Smoothing Scatterplots. *Journal of the American Statistical Association* 74:829–36.

———. 1981. LOWESS: A Program for Smoothing Scatterplots by Robust Locally Weighted Regression. *The American Statistician* 35:54.

Cleveland, William S., and Robert McGill. 1985. Graphical Perception and Graphical Methods for Analyzing Scientific Data. *Science* 229:828–33.

Cohen, Robin, ed. 1995. *The Cambridge History of World Migration.* Cambridge, UK: Cambridge University Press.

Cohen, S., R. C. Kessler, and L. U. Gordon. 1997. *Measuring Stress.* New York: Oxford University Press.

Cook, T. D., and D. T. Campbell. 1979. *Quasi-Experimentation.* Chicago: Rand-McNally.

Council on Scientific Affairs, AMA. 1992. Violence against Women. *JAMA* 267:3184–89.

Cronbach, L. J., and P. E. Meehl. 1955. Construct Validity in Psychological Tests. *Psychological Bulletin* 52:281–302.

Cummins, J. 1981. The Role of Primary Language Development in Promoting Educational Success for Language Minority Students. *Schooling and Language Minority Students: A Theoretical Framework.* Los Angeles: Evaluation, Dissemination and Assessment Center.

———. 1994. The Socioacademic Achievement Model in the Context of Coercive and Collaborative Relations of Power. In R. A. DeVillar, C. J. Faltis, and J. P. Cummins, eds., *Cultural Diversity in Schools. From Rhetoric to Practice.* Pp. 363–90. Albany: State University of New York Press.

Desjarlais, R., L. Eisenberg, B. Good, and Kleinman. 1995. *A World Mental Health.* London: Oxford.

DeWalt, Kathleen M., and Billie R. DeWalt. 1998. Participant Observation. Pp. 259–300. In Bernard, H. R., ed. *Handbook of Methods in Cultural Anthropology.* Walnut Creek, CA: AltaMira.

Dressler, W. W. 1996. Culture and Blood Pressure: Using Consensus Analysis to Create a Measurement. *Cultural Anthropology Methods CAM.* 8, 3:6–8.

―――. 1997. Culture and Patterns of Poverty. Paper delivered to the annual meeting of the Society for Applied Anthropology, Seattle.

Dressler, W. W., J. R. Bindon. 2000. The Health Consequences of Cultural Consonance: Cultural Dimensions of Lifestyle, Social Support, and Arterial Blood Pressure in an African American Community. *American Anthropologist* 102:244–60.

Dressler, W. W., J. R. Bindon, Y. H. Neggers. 1998. Culture, Socioeconomic Status, and Coronary Heart Disease Risk Factors in an African American Community. *Journal of Behavioral Medicine* 21:527–44.

Dressler, William W., Jose Ernesto Dos Santos, and Mauro Campos Balierio. 1996. Studying Diversity and Sharing in Culture: An Example of Lifestyle in Brazil. *Journal of Anthropological Research* 52:331–53.

Driver, Harold E. 1962. The Contribution of A. L. Kroeber to Culture Area Theory and Practice. *International Journal of American Linguistics* 28, no. 2, memoir 18.

―――. 1970. Statistical Studies of Continuous Geographical Distributions. In *Handbook on Methods in Anthropology,* Raoull Naroll and Ronald Cohen, eds. Garden City, NJ: Natural History Press.

Elliott, F. A. 1988. Neurological Factors. In Van Hasselt, V. B., R. L. Morrison, A. S. Bellack, and M. Hersen, eds., *Handbook of Family Violence.* Pp. 359–81. New York: Plenum, 1988.

Edginton, E. S. 1980. *Randomization Tests.* New York: Marcel Dekker.

Efrom, Bradley, and Robert Tibshirani. 1991. Statistical Data Analysis in the Computer Age. *Science* 253:390–95.

Emerson, R. M., R. I. Fretz, and L. L. Shaw 1995. *Writing Ethnographic Fieldnotes.* Chicago: University of Chicago Press.

Essman, W. B., and E. J. Essman. 1986. Drug Effects and Receptor Changes in Aggressive Behavior. In Shagass, C., R. C. Josiassen, W. H. Bridger, K. J. Weiss, D. Stoff, and G. M. Simpson, eds., *Biological Psychiatry 1985.* Pp. 663–65. New York: Elsevier.

Ford, M. I. 1990. The Writing Process: A Strategy for Problem Solvers. *Arithmetic Teacher* 38:35–38.

Gazzaniga, Michael S. 1998. *The Mind's Past.* Berkeley: University of California Press.

Gluckman, Max. 1963. Gossip and Scandal. *Current Anthropology* 4:307–16.

Gelles, Richard J. 1987. *Family Violence.* Newbury Park, CA: Sage.

Goode, W. J. 1971. Force and Violence in the Family. *Journal of Marriage and the Family* 33:624–36.

Geertz, C. 1973. *The Interpretation of Cultures.* New York: Free Press.

Gray, Jeffrey A. 1995. The Contents of Consciousness: A Neuropsychological Conjecture. *Behavioral and Brain Sciences* 18:659–722.

Green, Edward C. 1999. *Indigenous Theories of Contagious Disease.* Walnut Creek, CA: AltaMira.

Greenacre, M. J. 1984. *Theory and Applications of Correspondence Analysis.* New York: Academic Press.

Gujarati, D. N. 1995. *Basic Econometrics.* New York: McGraw-Hill.

Hakuta, K. 1987. Degree of Bilingualism and Cognitive Ability in Mainland Puerto Rican Children. *Child Development* 58:1372–88.

Hammel, E. A. 1990. A Theory of Culture for Demography. *Population and Development Review* 16:455–85.

———. 1994. Meeting the Minotaur. *Anthropology Newsletter* 35 (4):48.

Handwerker, W. P. 1987. Fiscal Corruption and the Moral Economy of Resource Acquisition. *Research in Economic Anthropology* 9:307–53.

———. 1988. Sampling Variability in Microdemographic Estimation of Fertility Parameters. *Human Biology* 60:305–18.

———. 1989a. *Women's Power and Social Revolution.* Newbury Park, CA: Sage.

———. 1989b. The Origins and Evolution of Culture. *American Anthropologist* 91:313–26.

———. 1990. *Social Dimensions of Entrepreneurship in Africa.* With general bibliography and selected annotations compiled by Marion Pratt. Binghamton, NY: Institute for Development Anthropology.

———. 1992. *Epidemiological Transition in Barbados: Findings from the National Epidemiological Survey.* A technical report delivered to the Ministry of Health, Barbados, W.I.

———. 1993a. Empowerment and Fertility Transition on Antigua, W.I.: Education, Employment, and the Moral Economy of Childbearing. *Human Organization* 52, 1:41–52.

———. 1993b. Gender Power Differences between Parents and High Risk Sexual Behavior by Their Children: AIDS/STD Risk Factors Extend to a Prior Generation. *Journal of Women's Health* 2:301–16.

———. 1996a. Violence and Affection Directed at Children in Barbados, W.I. *Medical Anthropology* 17:101–28.

———. 1996b. Constructing Likert Scales: Testing the Validity and Reliability of Single Measures of Multidimensional Variables. *Cultural Anthropology Methods CAM.* 8:1–7.

———. 1997. Universal Human Rights and the Problem of Unbounded Cultural Meanings. *American Anthropologist* 99:799–809.

———. 1998. Why Violence? A Test of Hypotheses Representing Three Discourses on the Roots of Domestic Violence. *Human Organization* 57:200–8.

———. 1999a. Childhood Origins of Depression: Evidence from Native and Nonnative Women in Alaska and the Russian Far East. *Journal of Women's Health* 8:87–94.

———. 1999b. Cultural Diversity, Stress, and Depression: A Study of Working Women in the Americas. *Journal of Women's Health & Gender-Based Medicine* 8:1303–11.

Handwerker, W. P., and P. V. Crosbie. 1982. Sex and Dominance. *American Anthropologist* 84:97–104.

Handwerker, W. P., and R. Jones. 1992. STDs: To Clap, Add Leak, Coolant, and Bore. *JAMA* 267:1611–12.

Handwerker, W. Penn, and Danielle F. Wozniak. 1997. Sampling Strategies for the Collection of Cultural Data. *Current Anthropology* 38:869–75.

Hammel, E. A. 1990. A Theory of Culture for Demography. *Population and Development Review.*

———. 1994. Meeting the Minotaur. Anthropology Newsletter.

Harman, H. H. 1976. *Modern Factor Analysis.* 3rd edition. Chicago: University of Chicago Press.

Harwood, R., J. Miller, and N. Irizarry. 1995. *Culture and Attachment: Perception of the Child in Context.* New York: Guilford.

Harwood, R. L., W. P. Handwerker, A. Schoelmerich, and Birgit Leyendecker. Under review. What Do Ethnic Category Labels Tell Us about Shared Beliefs in Mothers' Childrearing Goals? An Exploration of the Individualism/Sociocentrism Debate. *Parenting: Science and Practice.* In Press.

Heise, L. 1995. Violence, Sexuality, and Women's Lives. Pp. 109–34. In *Conceiving Sexuality,* R. G. Parker and J. H. Gagnon, eds. New York: Routledge.

Hosmer, D. W., and S. Lemeshow. 1989. *Applied Logistic Regression.* New York: John Wiley.

Hubert, L., and J. Schultz. 1976. Quadratic Assignment as a General Data Analysis Strategy. *British Journal of Mathematical and Statistical Psychology* 29:190–241.

Johnson, Allen, and Orna R. Johnson. 1990. Quality into Quantity: On the Measurement Potential of Ethnographic Fieldnotes. In *Fieldnotes: The Making of Anthropology,* R. Sanjek, ed. Pp. 161–86. Ithaca, NY: Cornell University Press.

Johnson, Allen, and Ross Sackett. 1998. Direct Systematic Observation of Behavior. Pp. 301–32. In Bernard, H. R., ed., *Handbook of Methods in Cultural Anthropology.* Walnut Creek, CA: AltaMira.

Johnson, Jeffrey C. 1990. *Selecting Ethnographic Informants.* Qualitative Research Methods, Series 22. Newbury Park, CA: Sage.

Johnston, J. 1984. Econometric Methods. 3rd edition. New York: McGraw Hill.

Jones, Rose 1994. *Songs from the Village.* Unpublished Ph.D. dissertation, Southern Methodist University.

Jorgensen, Joseph G. 1971. On Ethics and Anthropology. *Current Anthropology* 12:321–34, 350–57.

———. 1974. *Comparative Studies by Harold E. Driver and Essays in His Honor.* New Haven: HRAF.

———. 1995. Ethnicity, Not Culture? Obfuscating Social Science in the *Exxon Valdez* Oil Spill Case. *American Indian Culture and Research Journal* 19:1–124.

Keesing, Roger. 1994. Theories of Culture Revisited. Pp. 301–12. In *Assessing Cultural Anthropology,* Robert Borofsky, ed. New York: McGraw-Hill.

Kilby, Peter. 1971. Hunting the Heffalump. In *Entrepreneurship and Economic Development,* Peter Kilby, ed. New York: Free Press.

Kish, Leslie. 1965. *Survey Sampling.* New York: John Wiley.

Kitayama, S., H. R. Markus, and H. Matsumoto. 1995. Culture, Self, and Emotion: A Cultural Perspective on Self-Conscious Emotions. In J. P. Tangney and K. W. Fischer, eds., *Self-Conscious Emotions: The Psychology of Shame, Guilt, Embarrassment, and Pride.* Pp. 439–64. New York: Guilford.

Krashen, S. D. 1985. *The Input Hypothesis: Issues and Implications.* New York: Longman.

———. 1994. *Fundamentals of Language Education.* Torrance, CA: Laredo.

Kruskal, J. B., and M. Wish. 1978. *Multidimensional Scaling.* Newbury Park, CA: Sage.

Lessow-Hurley, J. 1990. *The Foundations of Dual Language Instruction.* New York: Longman.

Levy, Robert I., and Douglas W. Hollan. 1998. Person-Centered Interviewing and Observation. Pp. 333–64. In Bernard, H. R., ed. *Handbook of Methods in Cultural Anthropology.* Walnut Creek, CA: AltaMira.

Lowie, Robert L. 1921. A Note on Aesthetics. *American Anthropologist* 23:170–74.

McEvoy, F. 1977. Understanding Ethnic Realities among the Grebo and Kru of West Africa. *Africa* 47:62–78.

McEwan, Peter J. M. 1963. Forms and Problems of Validation in Social Anthropology. *Current Anthropology* 4:155–83.

McNabb, S. 1990a. Native Health Status and Native Health Policy. *Arctic Anthropology* 27:20–35.

———. 1990b. The Uses of "Inaccurate" Data. *American Anthropologist* 92:116–29.

Maier, S. F., M. E. P. Seligman, and R. L. Solomon. 1969. Pavlovian Fear Conditioning and Learned Helplessness. In B. A. Campbell and R. M. Church, eds., *Punishment and Aversive Behavior*. Pp. 299–342. New York: Appleton-Century-Crofts.

Malamuth, Neil M. 1993. Using the Confluence Model of Sexual Aggression to Predict Men's Conflict with Women: A 10-Year Follow-Up Study. *Journal of Personality and Social Psychology* 69:353–69.

Malamuth, Neil M., R. J. Sockloskie, M. P. Koss, and J. S. Tanaka 1991. Characteristics of Aggressors against Women: Testing a Model Using a National Sample of College Students. *Journal of Consulting and Clinical Psychology* 59:670–81.

Markus, G. B. 1979. *Analyzing Panel Data*. Newbury Park, CA: Sage.

Markus, H. R., and S. Kitayama. 1991. Culture and the Self: Implications for Cognition, Emotion, and Motivation. *Psychological Review* 98:224–53.

Mawson, A. R., and K. W. Jacobs. 1978. Corn, Tryptophan, and Homicide. *Journal of Orthomolecular Psychiatry* 7:227–30.

Mayfield, D., G. McLeod, and P. Hull. 1974. The CAGE Questionnaire: Validation of a New Alcoholism Screening Instrument. *American Journal of Psychiatry* 131:1121–23.

Mlot, C. 1998. Probing the Biology of Emotion. *Science* 280:1005–7.

Mooney, Christopher Z., and Robert D. Duval. 1993. Bootstrapping. Quantitative Applications in the Social Sciences, vol. 95. Newbury Park, CA: Sage.

Morgan, D. L., and R. Krueger. 1998. *The Focus Group Kit*. 2nd edition. Thousand Oaks, CA: Sage.

Murdock, G. P. 1971. Anthropology's Mythology. Proceedings of the Royal Anthropological Society of Great Britain and Ireland. Pp. 17–24.

National Council of Teachers of Mathematics. 1991. *Professional Standards for Teaching Mathematics*.

National Research Council (NRC). 1989. *Arctic Social Science: An Agenda for Action*. Washington, D.C.: National Academy Press.

Paul, Amy 1997. *It Isn't Love, It's Business: Prostitution as Entrepreneurship and the Implications for Barbados*. Unpublished Ph.D. dissertation, UCLA.

Pelto, P., and G. Pelto. 1975. Intracultural Diversity: Some Theoretical Issues. *American Ethnologist* 2:1–18.

Philips, E., and Crespo, S. 1995. Math Penpals! Developing Written Communication in Mathematics. Paper presented at the annual meeting of the American Educational Research Association, San Francisco.

Pokorny, A. D., B. A. Miller, and M. B. Kaplan 1972. The Brief MAST: A Shortened Version of the Michigan Alcoholic Screening Test. *American Journal of Psychiatry* 129:342–45.

Pynoos R. S., A. M. Steinberg, E. M. Ornitz, A. K. Goenjian. 1997. Issues in the Developmental Neurobiology of Traumatic Stress. *Annals of the New York Academy of Sciences* 821:176–93.

Randall, T. 1992. Cocaine, Alcohol Mix in Body to Form Even Longer Lasting, More Lethal Drug. *JAMA* 267:1043–44.

Rogoff, B., J. Mistry, A. Göncü, and C. Mosier. (1993). Guided Participation in Cultural Activity by Toddlers and Caregivers. *Monographs of the Society for Research in Child Development* 58, serial no. 236.

Romney, A. K., S. C. Weller, and W. H. Batchelder. 1986. Culture as Consensus. *American Anthropologist* 88:313–38.

Rose, B. J. 1992. Using Expressive Writing to Support Mathematics Instruction. In A. Sterret, ed., *Using Writing to Teach Mathematics.* Pp. 63–72. Washington, D.C.: Mathematical Association of America.

Rummel, R. J. 1970. *Applied Factor Analysis.* Evanston, IL: Northwestern University Press.

Ryan, Gery W., and H. R. Bernard. 2000. Data Management and Analysis Methods. In *Handbook of Qualitative Research,* 2nd edition. Norman Denzin and Y. Lincoln, eds. Pp. 769–802. Newbury Park, CA: Sage.

Searight, H. R., and D. C. Campbell. 1992. Ethnography and Family Medicine: Issues and Overview. *Family Practice Research Journal* 12:369–82.

Secada, W. 1992. Race, Ethnicity, Social Class, Language, and Achievement in Mathematics. In D. A. Grouws, ed., *Handbook of Research on Mathematics Teaching and Learning.* Pp. 623–60. New York: Macmillan.

Selye, Hans. 1956. *The Stress of Life.* New York: McGraw-Hill.

Schroeder, Larry D., Savid L. Sjoquist, and Paula E. Stephan. 1986. *Understanding Regression Analysis.* Quantitative Applications in the Social Sciences, vol. 57. Newbury Park, CA: Sage.

Shweder, Richard A. 1977. Likeness and Likelihood in Everyday Thought. *Current Anthropology* 18:637–58.

Shweder, R. A., and E. J. Bourne. (1984). Does the Concept of the Person Vary Cross-Culturally? In R. A. Shweder and R. A. LeVine, eds., *Culture Theory: Essays in Mind, Self, and Emotion.* Pp. 158–99. Cambridge, UK: Cambridge University Press.

Sneath, P. H. A., and R. R. Sokal. 1973. *Numerical Taxonomy.* San Francisco: W. H. Freeman.

Sosis, Richard. 1999. Religion and Intra-Group Cooperation: Preliminary Results of a Comparative Analysis of Utopian Communities. *Cross-Cultural Research* 34.

Spradley, James P. 1969. *The Ethnographic Interview*. San Francisco: Holt, Rine-hart, and Winston.

Squires, Susan. 2001. Doing the Work: Customer Research in the Product Development and Design Industry. In *Creating Breakthrough Ideas: Collaboration in Research and Design*. Susan Squires and Bryan Byrne, eds. Westport, CT: Greenwood.

Squires, Susan, and Bryan Byrne, eds. 2001. *Creating Breakthrough Ideas: Collaboration in Research and Design*. Westport, CT: Greenwood.

Steinberg, Dan, and Phillip Colla. 1997. *LOGIT: A Supplementary Module for SYSTAT*. Evanston, IL: SYSTAT, Inc.

Sternberg, Robert J. 1985. Human Intelligence. *Science* 230:1111–25.

Straus, Murray A., and Richard J. Gelles, eds. 1990. *Physical Violence in American Families*. New Brunswick, NJ: Transaction.

Swadesh, Morris. 1959. The Mesh Principle in Comparative Linguistics. *Anthropological Linguistics* 35:1–4, 38–45.

Teicher, M. H., et al. 1997. Preliminary Evidence for Abnormal Cortical Development in Physically and Sexually Abused Children Using EEG Coherence and MRI. *Annals of the New York Academy of Sciences* 821:160–75.

Tooby, John, and Leda Cosmides. 1992. The Psychological Foundations of Culture. Pp. 19–136. In *The Adapted Mind*, J. H. Barkow, L. Cosmides, and J. Toomy, eds. New York: Oxford University Press.

Tversky, Amos, and Daniel Kahneman. 1979. Belief in the Law of Small Numbers. *Psychological Bulletin* 76:105–10.

Tylor, Edward B. 1871. *Primitive Society*. London.

———. 1889. On a Method of Investigating the Development of Institutions; Applied to Laws of Marriage and Descent. *Journal of the Royal Anthropological Institution of Great Britain and Ireland* 18:245–72.

Valzelli, L., S. Bernasconi, and M. Dalessandro. 1983. Time-Courses of P-CPA-Induced Depletion of Brain Serotonin and Muricidal Aggression in the Rat. *Pharmacological Research Communications* 15 (1983):387–95.

van Willigen, John. 1993. Applied Anthropology. 3rd edition. Westport, CT: Bergin & Garvey.

Voegelin, C. F., and F. M. Voegelin. 1973. Recent Classifications of Genetic Relationships. *Annual Review of Anthropology* 2:139–51.

Wallace, A. F. C. 1961. *Culture and Personality*. New York: Random House.

Walls, George. 2001. A Corporate Client's Perspective. In *Creating Breakthrough Ideas: Collaboration in Research and Design*, Susan Squires and Bryan Byrne, eds. Westport, CT: Greenwood.

Weller, S. C. 1987. Shared Knowledge, Intracultural Variation, and Knowledge Aggregation. *American Behavioral Scientist* 31:178–93.

———. 1998. Structured Interviewing. In Bernard, H. R., ed., *Handbook of Methods in Cultural Anthropology.* Pp. 365–410. Walnut Creek, CA: AltaMira.

Weller, S. C., and A. K. Romney. 1988. *Systematic Data Collection.* Qualitative Research Methods, Series 10. Newbury Park, CA: Sage.

Weller, S. C., and N. C. Mann. 1997. Assessing Rater Performance without a "Gold Standard" Using Consensus Theory. *Medical Decision Making* 17:71–9.

White, H. 1982. Maximum Likelihood Estimation of Misspecified Models. *Econometrica* 50:1–25.

Widom, C. S. 1989a. Child Abuse, Neglect, and Adult Behavior: Research Design and Findings on Criminality, Violence, and Child Abuse. *American Journal of Orthopsychiatry* 59:355–67.

———. 1989b. The Cycle of Violence. *Science* 244:160–66.

Widom, C. S., and J. B. Kuhns. 1996. Childhood Victimization and Subsequent Risk for Promiscuity, Prostitution, and Teenage Pregnancy: A Prospective Study. *American Journal of Public Health* 86:1607–12.

Wilcox, Rand R. 1998. How Many Discoveries Have Been Lost by Ignoring Modern Statistical Methods? *American Psychologist* 53:300–14.

Wilkinson, Leland, and Task Force on Statistical Inference APA Board of Scientific Affairs. 1999. Statistical Methods in Psychology Journals: Guidelines and Explanations. *American Psychologist* 54:594–604.

Winograd, K. 1990. Writing, Solving, and Sharing Original Math Story Problems: Case Studies of Fifth Grade Children's Cognitive Behavior. Paper presented at the annual meeting of the American Educational Research Association, Chicago.

Wolf, Eric R. 1982. *Europe and the People without History.* Berkeley: University of California Press.

Wozniak, Danielle F. 2001. *They're All My Children: Foster Mothering in America.* New York: New York University Press.

Wright, J. P., and D. C. Wright. 1986. Personalized Verbal Problems: An Application of the Language Experience Approach. *Journal of Educational Research* 79:358–62.

Young, T. Kue. 1994. *The Health of Native Americans.* New York: Oxford University Press.

Index

acculturation, 270

age cohort, 146–48

aggregated time series. *See* data

Alaska, 121, 148–49, 187, 213–17, 240–44

Americans, 65–66, 238; African, 24–25, 196–98, 238; Anglo, 270–71; Euro, 196–98; Hispanic, 196–98; Japanese, 24; Latina, 24; Native, Alaskan Natives, 42–44, 66, 72, 85, 111–12, 196–98; Puerto Rican, 238, 270–71

Antigua, 115–20, 150–51, 158, 248

Arctic, 65–66

autocorrelation (spatial and temporal), 19, 230

Barbados, 41, 114–15, 207–12

box-and-whisker plots. *See* plots

cluster analysis, 16, 192

confidence interval (CI), 98, 178. *See also* hypothesis; samples

confounds, 84, 86, 222; controlling for, 96, 224–26, 239–43, 273; diffusion, 85, 96, 273; history, 84, 93, 96, 273; instrumentation, 83, 96, 273; maturation, 84, 93, 96, 273; mortality, 84,

96, 273; regression, 83–84, 96, 273; selection bias, 84, 96–99, 273–74; testing, 83, 96, 273; in text data, 83–85. *See also* errors; experimental designs; relationships

consensus analysis. *See* ethnography

construct validity. *See* validity

control group. *See* experimental designs

correlation coefficients: Pearson's r, 16, 162–65, 168–69, 174, 179, 186; Phi, 165; Spearman's Rho, 165. *See also* similarity coefficients

correspondence analysis, 16, 192

culture: case dependence, 18–19, 274; clines, 271–72; components of, 17–21, 77, 266–67; and consciousness, 8, 67; cultural boundaries, 7, 21–22, 86, 119, 190; cultural diversity/variability, 7–8, 20–21, 23–25, 86, 268, 273; cultural experts, 22, 90–91, 269; definition of, 6, 10, 17, 21, 267; differences between cultural data and life experience data, 17; and ethnology, 10, 25–26; evidence of multiple cultures, 198–217, 240; evidence of a single culture, 195–98,

239–40; evolution of, 10, 268, 270–71; generalizability of, 23, 274; intercultural variation, 201–17, 221–22, 225–31, 266, 273; intracultural variation, 195, 210–12, 221–22, 231–37, 266, 273; and life experiences or histories, 8–9, 91, 93, 114–19, 221, 240–44, 267–69, 271–73; mistaken conceptions of, 6–11, 21–26; reliability and validity, 23; samples of, 19, 97–98; and social identities or groups, 21–26, 237–44, 272; as socially constructed, 10, 18–20. *See also* theory

data: analysis, 16, 113, 153–54; case-studies, 80, 221; census, 264; documents, 12, 80; event histories, 221; focus groups, 80, 121–22; genealogies, 264; informal interviews, 12, 80, 105–13, 220, 248, 264; Lexis Diagrams, 114–15, 265; life histories, 80, 221; maps, 264–65, 272–73; participant-observation, 80; semi-structured interviews, 12, 80, 120–24, 248, 264; text, 12–13, 79, 105, 107–14, 248, 264; time series, 114–16. *See also* measurement; structured interviews; triangulation; variables
dispersion. *See* frequency distributions
dot density plot. *See* plots

education. *See* outcomes evaluation research
errors, 37, 80–81; avoiding, 107, 119, 253; in constructs, 80–81, 86–87; correcting, 68–69, 81, 87, 107, 119,

221, 246–48, 253; in measurements, 13, 81–82, 229; power analysis, 99, 179–81, 229, 264; probability *p*, 177–79; random sampling error, 81, 169–76, 187–88, 224; sampling bias, 81; Type I (alpha), 177–79; Type II (beta), 177–81. *See also* confounds; hypothesis; samples; triangulation
ethics, 7, 92–93
ethnography: 3-day projects, 3, 6, 274–79; 30-day projects, 28, 100–101, 263; 90-day projects, 29, 100–101, 105, 263; applied, contract research, 6, 37–39, 51–58, 274–79; basic goals, 12; central problem, 10, 77; consensus analysis, 22; contextualizing with regional and global histories, 63–66, 112–19, 269; correcting your biases, 66–69; and culture theory, 5–11; definition of, 7; discrepancies between ideas and behavior, 20, 108; distinctive methods, 22; distinctive research questions, 4–5, 10–11, 22–23; and ethnology, 7, 25–26; and experimental designs, 21; formulating research questions, 37–66; frustrations and disasters, 33, 68–69, 261–62; generalizability of, 23, 274; Grand Tour questions, 108; inefficiencies in, 5, 26–27, 71, 262–63; informant biases, 60–61; informant selection, 90–91; informants, not subjects, 4, 126; iterative data collection, 71–72, 99–101; language, 53, 83, 107, 271–72; listening, 107; mistaken conceptions of, 11–21; organizing field tasks, 101–3; organizing

About the Author

W. Penn Handwerker (Ph.D., Oregon, 1971) is professor of anthropology and public health at the University of Connecticut, where he directs the graduate program in applied medical anthropology and currently serves as head of the anthropology department. Background for this book comes from field research in West Africa (Liberia), the West Indies (Barbados, Antigua, and St. Lucia), Russia (Moscow and Provideniya), and various portions of the contemporary United States (Oregon, California's North Coast, Connecticut, and Alaska). His research experiences encompass projects carried out over one or two days, four weeks, twelve weeks, six months, and periods ranging from one to four years. He has served as principal investigator, co-investigator, team member, and team leader. He has managed research teams consisting of as few as two people and as many as thirty. He has published in all five fields (applied, archaeology, biological, cultural, and linguistics) of anthropology.

21390760R00179

Made in the USA
Middletown, DE
27 June 2015